THE RISE AND FALL
OF EARLY AMERICAN
MAGAZINE CULTURE

THE HISTORY OF COMMUNICATION

Robert W. McChesney
and John C. Nerone, editors

*A list of books in the series appears
at the end of this book.*

THE RISE AND FALL
OF EARLY AMERICAN
MAGAZINE CULTURE

JARED GARDNER

UNIVERSITY OF ILLINOIS PRESS

Urbana, Chicago, and Springfield

Library of Congress Cataloging-in-Publication Data
Gardner, Jared.
The rise and fall of early American magazine culture / Jared Gardner.
p. cm. — (The history of communication)
Includes bibliographical references and index.
ISBN 978-0-252-03670-5 (cloth : alk. paper)
1. American literature—Revolutionary period, 1775–1783—History and criticism.
2. American literature—1783–1850—History and criticism.
3. Periodicals—Publishing—United States—History—18th century.
4. Literature publishing—United States—History—18th century.
5. American periodicals—History—18th century.
6. Authors and publishers—United States—History—18th century.
I. Title.
PS193.G37   2012
070.5'72097309033—dc23   2011034714

For Beth

CONTENTS

PREFACE

When one thinks of the magazine form today, certain formal characteristics tend to come to mind: photographs and other images, stories gathered around a particular topic or directed to a specific audience, advertisements, and letters to the editor. We also tend to think of the magazine as a largely ephemeral form, as something to be read in waiting rooms, on elliptical trainers, during the morning commute—and often left behind or discarded after reading.

None of these features describe the magazines that are the subject of this book. The American magazine of the colonial and the early national period was in many ways a form both materially and culturally as distinct from the modern magazine that would emerge in the nineteenth century as can be imagined. That early magazines contained very few images is understandable when considering the high cost of producing and printing engravings. But the early magazine differed from its modern successor in every other respect as well. Instead of being organized around specific topics and audiences, the magazine of the time was dedicated to a principle of miscellany and variety, rarely delimiting its intended audience even along gender lines—and almost never along any more specific demographic (regional, professional, and political). Unlike many newspapers of the period (particularly in the later years of the eighteenth century), the early magazine featured no advertisements, despite the fact that few of these ventures were able to survive even a year on subscriptions alone. And few of these magazines featured letters to the editor (although remarks *from* the editor acknowledging contributions were a regular feature of many early magazines).

This last point especially is worth pausing over. The lack of a department dedicated to letters from readers in the early magazine is not, as might first appear, a sign of the lack of interest these periodicals placed in the input of readers. Quite the contrary; there was no space set apart for readers' correspondence precisely because the whole of the early magazine was ideally to be constituted *by* contributions from readers. Even in cases where the editors ended up forced to contribute much of the material themselves (and such cases were far too common), the notion was preserved throughout that the magazine was itself the natural outgrowth of readers who had been summoned by the periodical to become contributors themselves.

Finally, these magazines were far from ephemeral. Unlike newspapers—which, then as now, were rarely preserved once the day's news had been consumed—the individual periodicals were often carefully saved, collected so that they might be bound at year's end into a handsome volume. These were items to preserve for posterity as well, and we can trace in the signatures that grace the title pages of bound volumes the generations through which many of these magazines passed.

The Rise and Fall of Early American Magazine Culture seeks to understand the investment readers made in these relatively expensive volumes and that publishers made in these inevitably money-losing periodical ventures. And in recovering the nature of those investments and the ideals of a literary culture that gathered for a time around the magazine form in the eighteenth century, this book seeks to recover an alternative model to the literary culture that would take solid shape in the early decades of the nineteenth century. Indeed, there might well be lessons and ideals of value for us today as the literary culture of the twenty-first century is once again transformed.

I begin, perhaps counterintuitively, by turning to the early American novel—or to books we have been trained to consider as "novels"—to examine how the "editorial function" manifests itself in these texts in ways that help us understand why so many of the nation's pioneering novelists turned away from the novel form and dedicated themselves to magazine writing and editing. After this first chapter, we turn to the origins of the English-language magazine in the periodical sheets of Addison and Steele in London and the century-long attempt to rekindle those founding energies on the other side of the Atlantic. The next two chapters consider in detail the magazine of the early national period, focusing on the editors, readers, and contributors who sought to establish a very different literary culture in its pages, while the last chapter examines the final experiments with early American magazine culture in the late writings of Susanna Rowson and Charles Brockden Brown and the early writing of Washington Irving. A short coda offers some thoughts on some parallels between eighteenth-century magazine culture and twenty-first-century Internet culture, and lessons to be learned as we look ahead to what comes next.

Before beginning, however, I must pause to express my deep gratitude to a range of institutions and individuals who supported the writing of this book over the course of a decade spent studying early American periodicals. The project first took shape in an invitation from Michael Moon and Sharon Cameron to contribute an essay to *ELH* in honor of my former graduate professor Larzer Ziff. An American Antiquarian Society—American Society for Eighteenth-Century Studies fellowship provided me with support for a vital early research visit, and the staff members at the Antiquarian Society were invaluable in guiding me toward everything I needed to read before I could begin this project in earnest.

It is hard for me to imagine this book without the input at conferences and over email from friends and colleagues who are fellow members of the Society of Early Americanists, the Research Society for American Periodicals, and the Charles Brockden Brown Society. At Ohio State University, I have been blessed by three chairs who patiently supported me during the long gestation of this book—Jim Phelan, Valerie Lee, and Richard Dutton—and by an exceptional group of colleagues who share my love of these strange periodical forms, including David Brewer, Steven Fink, Harvey Graff, Elizabeth Renker, and Susan Williams. With Steve and Susan, I edited *American Periodicals* from 2003 to 2010, and that experience shaped this book in countless ways I could never have anticipated.

Thanks as always to my parents, Susan Gardner, Bruce Brooks, Andrew Gardner, Trebbe Johnson, Myrna Hewitt, and John Hewitt; to Michael Trask, Stephen Trask, Aman Garcha, and Danielle Demko for being always more and always there; and to my remarkable young men, Eli Gardner and Gideon Hewitt, who never cease to astound me, not least for their remarkable capacity to humor their father when he is blathering on about magazines that ceased publication two centuries before they were born.

And finally, to Beth Hewitt, to whom this book is dedicated—my partner in everything mentioned above and so much more. She has read everything I have ever tried to write about these magazines, and to her enthusiasm and maddeningly brilliant questions I owe anything I got right about these magazines.

THE RISE AND FALL
OF EARLY AMERICAN
MAGAZINE CULTURE

THE LITERARY MUSEUM
AND THE UNSETTLING
OF THE EARLY AMERICAN NOVEL

I

In 1799 the *Monthly Magazine* published a sketch entitled "Portrait of an Emigrant" that recounts a conversation between the author and a Mrs. K, introduced as a woman who "never reads, not even a newspaper." The description continues, "She is equally a stranger to the events that are passing in distant nations, and to those which ingross the attention and shake the passions of the . . . politicians of her own country; but her mind . . . is far from torpid or inactive. She speculates curiously and even justly on objects that occur within her narrow sphere."[1] Evidence of this mental agility is demonstrated by her account of her new neighbors, a Frenchman and his wife: "he is a man of fair complexion, well formed, and of genteel appearance; and the woman is half negro." Mrs. K gives surprisingly precise descriptions, revealing that though she doesn't read books or newspapers she is indeed a close reader of her foreign neighbors. The man works in a compting-house for a French merchant, and the woman is employed as an actress in "Lailson's pantomimes"—a popular circus of the day.[2] The couple has also taken in a "negro orphan" who is forever begging food and favors from Mrs. K. Prompted by the correspondent, Mrs. K investigates and learns that the lady was formerly heiress of a large estate in Santo Domingo, and that her fortune was destroyed in the recent revolution. They "have since subsisted in various modes and places, frequently pinched by extreme poverty . . . ; but retaining, in every fortune . . . their propensity to talk, laugh and sing—their flute and their guitar." "Let you and I grow wise," the sketch concludes, "by the contemplation of their example."[3]

But what exactly is the lesson to be learned from this story? The most obvious moral would seem to reside in the fact that these people have maintained a song in their hearts despite the revolution in Haiti that has turned their world upside down. But this moral is undercut by the fact that this ambiguous family of immigrants would necessarily invoke in 1799 an array of hysterical alternative lessons. The identification of the couple as *French* immigrants, the invocation of the black revolution on Santo Domingo, and the ambiguous racial origins of the woman (as well as the fact of the adopted African American child) explicitly references the paranoid fantasies of federalist America.[4]

These racialist fantasies are found in the novels of Charles Brockden Brown, especially *Edgar Huntly*.[5] "Portrait of an Emigrant" was published in the same magazine in which Brown, then serving as the editor of the *Monthly Magazine*, published a long excerpt from *Edgar Huntly*, advertising the novel that he hoped would finally secure his prominence as America's first professional novelist. Juxtaposed with the excerpt advertising Brown's novel of Indians, immigrants, and the making of Americans, the sketch at first glance seems to invoke, like the pages from *Huntly*, specters of racial and alien enemies preying on vulnerable American women. But its lessons are quite different.

If Brown had come to understand that the national function of the novel lay in scripting the resolution whereby alien and racial others are imaginatively collapsed into one another so that an "American" identity might be defined, he has done so at great cost to his earlier ambitions for both novel and nation, as his letters after the failed reception of *Edgar Huntly* would seem to suggest.[6] It is this cost that the *Monthly Magazine* sketch seems to recoup. The "Portrait of an Emigrant" asks us to take seriously the possibility that *Huntly* could not admit: that the true meaning of the scene resides precisely in the *virtue* of this unconventional family, in their exemplification of perseverance, racial harmony, and generosity.[7] To read the fragmentary sketch this way is to produce a very different vision of the coming together of alien and racial others than that scripted by the novel *Edgar Huntly*. This might explain why Mrs. K is defined explicitly as a *non*-reader: By reading the world around her not through the plots scripted by her factional age but through active and close investigation, she is able to read more "justly" than those whose reading has been schooled by newspaper—or by novels such as *Edgar Huntly*.[8]

The fact that Brown himself almost certainly wrote this "Portrait of an Emigrant" only makes the piece—and the difficulties in trying to reconcile it with *Huntly*—more interesting.[9] But it is an anonymous "extract" in a literary magazine that, like so many others, was defined by miscellany, unattributed borrowings, fragmentary sketches, correspondences, transcripts, and opinions on everything from the French Revolution to the ethics of snuff. And it is the motley and cacophonous quality of these magazines that authorized my own privileging in *Master Plots* of the novel over the contradictory evidence and ambiguous conclusions offered by the anonymous periodical sketch. In doing so, I was risking little. Few critics in the past two centuries have devoted much energy to studying the vast and disparate array of anonymous texts that define periodical production in colonial America and the early national periods—an output many times greater (both in terms of quantity and quality) than that produced by all the novelists of the period.

Magazine and novel "rose" together in eighteenth-century America. By the 1820s, the novel would triumph, becoming increasingly central not only to the literary marketplace but also to the national imagination and to the fundamental definition of what it meant to *be* an American. But in the previous generations, the outcome was by no means certain, and many saw reasons for serious concern in the novel form and the stories it told. It was within the pages of the early American magazine that alternative models would be crafted and to which a different kind of literary citizen would be drafted. Indeed, all the reasons why we have dismissed the difficulties raised by a periodical sketch such as "Portrait of an Emigrant"—because it is anonymous, fragmentary, and willfully obscure as to its larger meanings or narrative or generic principles—are precisely the terms through which Brown and others sought out alternative models to the political and literary choices that were being narrated and naturalized at this time.

The unanswered challenge of early American literature lies in finding ways of reading its ambivalence and contradictions beyond the critical dichotomies insisted on by the logic of national identity and reinscribed by so many of its readers: Either a text speaks for dominant ideology or it "subverts" it by speaking for and from the margins. This Hobson's choice is nowhere more prevalent than in the critical study of the early American novel, which so often seeks to explain away the contradictory positions occupied by many of its central texts. The contradictions that abound in this literature had historically been understood as symptomatic of the insufficiency of the nascent literary culture or of the instability of the individual author. More recently, of course, as this literature has been restored to its rightful place *within* (and not merely as antiquarian footnote to) the literary culture of the United States, these contradictions have been interpreted somewhat differently: Operating always under the threat of censure, we have been taught to see how these texts mimic the dominant rhetoric of the day while speaking their "true" subversive logic at the margins or in meaningful interstices.

Having effected the rescue of this subversive potential, we can now step back more fully to consider the ways in which some of these texts worked to reject the notion of the "true" voice that would reduce the complex weave of contradictory voices and positions to a monologic discourse.[10] By reading the multivocal argument of these texts more fully in terms of magazine culture, and by recalling, as Jay Fliegelman has suggested, that the colonial and early national period had not yet fully articulated the shift from the belief that the author and editor were essentially synonymous to the notion of literary production as the product of the solitary original genius, we might now consider what remains in *excess* of the conventional explanation of the contradictory positions these early texts articulate.[11]

How could the same man who wrote *Edgar Huntly* also be responsible for editing and probably authoring the other fragment? In a sense, this book is my long answer to this question—or better put, it is my attempt to listen carefully to Brown and so many others who devoted much of their careers to this cacophonous, largely anonymous form. Like the majority of my colleagues, I had long used the defining features of periodical culture as an excuse to either ignore it or mine it for useful data to support my arguments about the texts I had been trained *really* mattered: the novels, the *books*. That Brown's "Portrait of an Emigrant" was a fragment, was possibly not even *by* Brown, and was contained within a text defined by miscellaneous and often contradictory ideas and arguments made it easy to push it aside when working on my chapter on *Edgar Huntly*. Like most of my colleagues in early American literary history, I have privileged the novel because ultimately I can read its arguments, and thereby form my own, more clearly. The magazine, by contrast, offers few clear or consistent arguments, plots, or conventions. But being forced finally to listen to the voices and ideals articulated in these texts, I have come to rethink many things I thought I knew about early American literary culture and history. Now, after a decade spent with such anonymous, fragmentary, and discordant voices, I am increasingly convinced it is perhaps time to start marginalizing *Edgar Huntly*—and the novel form in general—instead. After all, that is what so many of the figures we have identified as our "pioneering" novelists themselves chose to do at the time.

Of the novels of the early national period, those of Charles Brockden Brown have been especially privileged because they provide a vibrant predecessor for the psychological realism of the nineteenth-century novel. Brown's

novels, for all their excesses, are recognizable in relation to a more deliberately articulated national literary culture of two generations later. Thus it is
not surprising that Brown's last two novels, *Clara Howard* and *Jane Talbot*,
which privilege moral "lessons" over psychological ambiguities, have been
met largely with disdain or dismissal from readers who see in them a retreat
from the author's earlier accomplishments.[12] That this turn in Brown's career
coincides both with his rejection of his youthful radical republicanism and
his disavowal of his earlier literary ambitions has long been used as evidence
to support narratives of apostasy or martyrdom. Deeply disappointed by
the failure of his country to embrace him, Brown retreats into conservative
morality, making one last attempt at success through formulaic sentimental
novels. When these too are rejected, he abandons "literature" altogether,
save for some tinkering with editorial projects.[13]

Shortly after the failure of his last two novels, Brown writes, "I should
enjoy a larger share of my own respect, at the present moment, if nothing
had ever flowed from my pen, the production of which could be traced to
me."[14] This statement, coupled with the abrupt change in direction of his
post-novel-writing career, has provided potent evidence for the narrative of
Brown's retreat, a narrative that has remained largely intact from the earliest
biographies to the most recent.[15] His "failure" has been read variously as
telling of the inhospitable climate the early republic provided for original
genius or of the inimicability of Brown's newly articulated federalist politics
and mercantile career to the imaginative work of the novel. But whether
Brown is seen as martyr to the cultural wasteland of his day or traitor to
the cause of the novel, his "major" novels are preserved as ore to be mined
by the gifted writers of the nineteenth century and the knowing critics of
our own, while his nineteenth-century career is marginalized as footnote,
coda, or moral lesson.

But a different narrative emerges when we reconsider this apparent renunciation of his novelistic career in light of its site of publication. After
all, this quote is part of an editorial manifesto inaugurating Brown's new
venture, the *Literary Magazine*, in which Brown stakes out the editorial
position that will guide his stewardship of this new magazine and his literary career until his death in 1810: "I cannot expatiate on the variety of my
knowledge, the brilliancy of my wit, the versatility of my talents. To none
of these do I lay any claim. . . . I trust merely to the zeal and liberality of my
friends to supply me with them. I have them not myself, but doubt not of
the good offices of those who possess them, and shall think myself entitled
to no small praise, if I am able to collect into one focal spot the rays of a
great number of luminaries."[16] Here he defines the position of anonymous

editor: His job is to collect and reflect the productions of his nation, to give space and voice to the important ideas and productions of his time, to create what Brown terms a "repository" for the wisdom and genius of his nation. Brown goes on to imagine the reader's demand for the anonymous editor's identity: "'This is somewhat more than a point of idle curiosity,' my reader will say, 'for, from my knowledge of the man must I infer how far he will be able and willing to fulfill his promises. Besides, it is great importance to know, whether his sentiments on certain subjects, be agreeable or not to my own.'" This imagined reader will not submit himself to any publication without knowing fully the political, moral, and religious views of the editor: "'I must know your character. By that knowledge, I shall regulate myself with more certainty than by any anonymous declaration you may think proper to make.'" [17]

But Brown pointedly refuses to append his name to his declaration of principles, instead expressing regret that his name and his earlier productions might have the effect of giving precisely the "character" the imagined reader is mistakenly looking for. In the context of this editorial manifesto, his previous works, which had brought to their author a certain degree of celebrity (if not fortune), stand as the primary obstacle to his new project of defining a different kind of literary position—not as genius author of a novel but as anonymous editor of a text that is predicated on the disruptions and fragmentation of all the novel would make whole: plotting, characterization, and the authorial function.

Thus we might see the trajectory of Brown's later career in a very different light from that in which it is traditionally painted. Instead of a two-year novel-writing career followed by abandonment and betrayal of the novel, after Brown's last "major" novels of *Edgar Huntly* and *Arthur Mervyn*, we see instead a consistent and radical attempt to revise and reimagine the function of literature and the role of the editor in the new republic. This was not an experiment born out of isolation or retreat from a larger scene of literary production. It emerges out of Brown's own fierce engagement with the literature of his time and his deep firsthand experience with the politics of authorship, genre, and reception, a politics that Larzer Ziff has demonstrated was an object of Brown's critique from the very beginnings of his career. [18] Implicit in Brown's late work is an extensive critique of the novel he himself had helped bring to life: the novel of the autonomous individual, the story told through one voice, one psychology, and bound by the expectations of chronology, unity, and the totalizing conclusion. Although Brown's critique of the politics of the American novel emerges out of a commitment to a "literary federalism," to borrow William C. Dowling's useful term, it resonates as well with a contemporary critique of the liberal subject and the role of literature in defining and romanticizing individual desire and ambition.[19] And it resonates strongly and more immediately with the similar experiments articulated in other early texts we have insisted on reading in relationship to the history of the "rise of the novel," texts like Hannah Webster Foster's *The Coquette*, William Hill Brown's *The Power of Sympathy*, and Susanna Rowson's *Reuben and Rachel*—novels whose strange features look less anomalous and "primitive" when read in relation to the periodical culture of the period.

The common point at which to identify the turn in Brown's career is the publication in 1801 of his two epistolary novels, *Clara Howard* and *Jane Talbot*. As sentimental tales, focused not on spontaneous combustion and Indian wars but on the niceties of courtship and the ethics of filial obedience, these novels certainly were not likely to appeal to those readers drawn to the excesses and recesses of Brown's earlier gothic tales. If anything, these novels seem deliberately designed to displease, and his readers have historically responded in kind, seeing these novels as a last desperate attempt to play to the crowd by borrowing the moral absolutism of Samuel Richardson and his American imitators.[20] Yet the more relevant and immediate model for Brown's version of the epistolary novel is not *Clarissa* but *The Coquette*, a popular novel first published in 1797, and one that Brown, arguably the most devoted student of American literature of his day, most certainly read. In this novel Brown would have found a model not only for his last two novels but also for the editorial function he was working to define in his last fictions and in his periodical work of his final years.

II

The Coquette offers in its broad outlines a traditional seduction plot: The heroine, Eliza Wharton, recently redeemed from an arranged marriage by the death of the clergyman to whom she had been affianced, is courted by two men. The first, Boyer, is a respectable clergyman who bears an unfortunate similarity to his passionless and conservative predecessor; the second, Sanford, is a libertine with social standing who (as we know from the opening pages) will ultimately play the role of Eliza's "seducer." The charge continually leveled at Eliza is that she is a "coquette": She refuses to submit to the prescribed role of "wife," preferring instead to circulate her only capital—her eligibility as bride—on the open market. As she explains her refusal to choose between her suitors: "What a pity . . . that the graces and virtues [in men] are not oftner united! They must, however, meet in the man of my choice; and till I find such a one, I shall continue to subscribe my name ELIZA WHARTON."[21] This refusal to choose yields the seemingly inevitable tragedy of Eliza and her illegitimate child dying alone in a tavern away from friends and family.

The dominant trend in the recent criticism of the novel has been to recover the resistance embodied by Eliza's correspondence, a resistance that is silenced, subdued, and ultimately co-opted by the forces of conformity arrayed against her. Following Cathy Davidson's seminal work, critics have considered how a text that is dominated by the moralizing dictums of the ministers and friends who condemn Eliza works to subvert the logic of the seduction plot: seduced, abandoned, dies.[22]

On one level, the novel makes such readings difficult. Written in pure epistolary form, it offers no narrative voice that might easily be identified as speaking with or for the author. The novel fluently condemns Eliza's refusal to choose between the moralizing Boyer and the seductive rake Sanford, and it seemingly endorses the final moral lesson delivered by Eliza's friend and principle correspondent, Lucy Sumner: "that virtue alone . . . can secure lasting felicity" (167–68). On the other hand, however, the novel makes explicit use of the rhetoric and politics of the "founding fathers" themselves to offer what simultaneously reads as an explicit critique of the limits of republican freedom and self-fashioning as it extends—or fails to extend—to women.

It is Eliza's voice that has garnered the vast majority of critical attention in recent years. And rightly so. Situated within the federalist society of Boston and New Haven, Eliza reads as the lone republican—or more accurately as a proto-liberal individualist—seeking to define a model of citizenship that does not depend at every turn on prescripted hierarchy and rigid social structure. And in her explicit enunciation of the central cost of marriage for the community of female friends—"marriage is the tomb of friendship" (24)—this text registers the consequences of marriage for female friendship and women's writing, perhaps more powerfully than any other before Emily Dickinson's "wife" poems. However, in our justifiable desire to rescue Eliza from the prison house of the conduct manual to which the many forces within the fictional and historical society of the novel would relegate her, we risk reinscribing the very dualisms that the novel challenges.

One way to reconsider the meaning of the ambivalences of *The Coquette* is to shift our critical focus somewhat away from Eliza, the author of the majority of the letters until she drifts into fatal silence, to the *recipient* of the majority of the letters: Lucy. My interest in Lucy does not lie in redeeming her from the critical censure of her prominent role, especially in the first half of the novel, in castigating Eliza's behavior and exerting great pressure on

Eliza to make the "right" choice. As Julia Stern persuasively argues, Lucy functions throughout much of the novel as the "head of the chorus" that seeks to discipline, punish, and later monumentalize Eliza's career as a moral lesson for other young women.[23] But I would suggest that if we redirect our attention from the novel's critique of the role of women in the young republic to questions of literary production and the relationship between writer and the community for which she writes, then Lucy comes to speak, especially in her final letters to Eliza, some of the ambivalences that Foster herself brings to the subject. Lucy in the second half of the novel, specifically in her two long letters to Eliza in which she offers rigorous criticism not of her character but of the decline in her literary style, is in many ways a different character than the Lucy of the first. If the novel ends in profound melancholy over the loss of Eliza's unique presence in the community, it is Lucy who registers that loss in terms of epistolary voice, who understands Eliza's crisis to be a literary crisis, and who seeks to identify a way in which Eliza might recover herself by recovering her role as writer.

Specifically, we consider the epistolary structure of the novel not as simply convention (by 1797, after all, the epistolary form was far from a given) or as a privileged space for women writers, but as a mode by which Foster can orchestrate a complex nexus of voices and sources from a position that perhaps more closely resembles that of *editor* than autonomous *author*. By the time Foster writes her novel, almost a decade after the historical Elizabeth Whitman on whom the story is based has met her tragic end, her subject had become one of the essential object lessons of the young republic, cited as a shorthand in sermons, newspapers, and moral treatises.[24] Transforming these discourses into the stuff of a novel, Foster seeks not to privilege Eliza's version but to suggest the possibility of multiple interpretations cohabiting the literary–political space of the seduction plot and the nation.[25]

In an address of 1798, President Adams declared that "the distinction of aristocrat and democrat . . . is grounded on unalterable nature."[26] In the overwrought climate of the day in which political positions were essentialized as grounded in "nature," every choice—from candidates to newspapers to style of dress—seemed to determine the fate of the nation itself. In such a climate, perhaps the most radical position would be one in which *choice* itself is refused, and it is this position that Foster seeks to stake out for her novel.[27]

After all, Eliza doesn't like her choices, and the novel goes to great lengths to suggest what poor options they are. Representing the political choices of the day—the soulless conformity of "federalist" Boyer and the seductive savagery of "republican" Sanford—these options present for Eliza no choice at all. In much the same way, Alcuin presses Mrs. Carter, in Brown's early work, to answer his repeated question, "Are you a federalist?" As readers of the early novel, we often demand that these texts find meaning within an equally constricted set of choices.[28] The heroine of *Alcuin*, published the same year as *The Coquette*, refuses to consider the question, insisting that the only benefit she derives from her systematic disenfranchisement is the right to reject such choices, demanding instead a politics that would allow her to occupy both positions simultaneously. Foster's novel, like Eliza and Mrs. Carter, works to resist the either/or poverty of these choices, trying to have it both ways. But the challenge lies in distinguishing the desire not to choose from bland neutrality on one hand and the duplicity of the con man on the other. It is not being disinterested or neutral from positions but occupying multiple positions with complete interest that is the goal here. The work of the editorial function in the early republic is to refuse the dichotomies of the factionalist 1790s and to imagine a new public sphere in which individuals are able to rise above these choices.

It is Boyer who most explicitly insists that Eliza *must* make a choice: "Between his society and mine, there is a great contrast. Such opposite pursuits and inclinations cannot be equally pleasing to the same taste. It is therefore necessary, that you renounce the one, to enjoy the other" (79). That Boyer (and not the rake) is the true "villain" of the piece is made clear most spectacularly by the fact that Eliza utters the conventional cry of the fallen woman—"I am undone!" (105)—*not* when she surrenders her "virtue," which takes place some time later, but when Boyer rejects her proposal of marriage. We can trace Eliza's fall not to the machinations of Sanford, who exercises little agency in her final "fall," but to the gross misreadings by Boyer. In the fatal scene midway through the novel, Boyer comes upon Eliza and Sanford in the garden, and predictably he assumes that they have met for an assignation. Eliza is instantly transformed in Boyer's eyes into a fallen woman, one whose motives are "too apparent" (81) to require explanation, revealing Boyer to be a bad reader (or a compulsive reader of seduction novels), unable to penetrate to the complex motives that often underlie appearances.

But whereas Boyer will not hear Eliza out, Lucy will and does. And Lucy, far from condemning Eliza, works to restore Eliza to her powers. In the first half of the novel, Eliza is a gifted storyteller, confident in her own abilities and gathering a community of fellow women writers and male readers about her. After the initial scene of misreading in the garden, Eliza risks all to assume her ultimate role as writer, scripting a proposal to the man who had precipitously passed judgment on her. Eliza's response to the inevitable failure of her writing, which up to this point has remained relatively immune from the exigencies of the literary/marriage marketplace, is to turn into a bad writer, uttering for the first time the conventional rhetoric of the seduction plot, shifting her position from writer to subject in a plot scripted by someone else. Thus one lesson of the novel is that men are bad readers, and that women, who are the writers in this novel (when men write, their prose is either turgid or psychotic), must take into account the inadequacies of their audience. In these terms, Eliza's mistake is in assuming that she could script the responses of her readers. Eliza's attempt to write directly to her male audience, Boyer, in his preferred rational and reasonable style results in dismal failure, leaving her, in her next letter to Lucy, far from the rational tones she had assumed in her letter to Boyer: "I am shipwrecked on the shoals of despair!" (105).

Lucy responds by needling Eliza for her "truly romantic letter," containing "all the *et ceteras* of romance" needed to "make a very pretty figure in a novel" (107). Lucy does not simply voice here the chorus of societal judgment on Eliza's wayward character; instead, at this moment she engages in an act of fairly savvy literary criticism: "Where is that fund of sense, and sentiment which once animated your engaging form? Where that strength of mind, that independence of soul, that alacrity and sprightliness of deportment, which formerly raised you superior to every adverse occurrence? Why have you resigned these valuable endowments, and suffered yourself to become the sport of contending passions?" (107). Lucy does not here ask, as Boyer does, that Eliza be governed entirely by decorum and utility. Quite the contrary; Lucy now calls for a return to the independence and ironic distance that once defined Eliza's written style and shielded her from the responses of her male readers. As Eliza increasingly withdraws from society, it is Lucy who works to restore her by rallying Eliza to recover her rapidly crumbling powers as a writer.

Lucy continues her criticism of Eliza's declining epistolary style, describing Eliza's next missive as failing to "afford me those lively sensations of pleasure, which I usually feel at the perusal of your letters" (112). As in the previous letter, Lucy urges Eliza to "rise . . . above it; and prove yourself superior to the adverse occurrences which have befallen you" (112). Lucy's letter here is accompanied by a package of novels, "of the lighter kind of reading; yet perfectly chaste; and if I mistake not, well adapted to your taste." Knowing that the historical Elizabeth Whitman's fate had been considered a testament to the dangers of novel reading, this celebration of the "right" kind of novel is perhaps surprising. Still more surprising is what follows: a long and seemingly irrelevant editorial, at the moment of her friend's great crisis, on the theater and the circus, both of which meet with Lucy's moralizing judgment. On the one hand, Lucy's castigation of the theater, and particularly the circus, is part and parcel with her role as "head of the chorus."[29] But we must also understand the novel's digression as a central disquisition on competing cultural forms, working to defend productions like *The Coquette*, subtly but crucially, as a valorized form for the new republic. In these terms, Lucy's critique of theater and the circus has everything to do with Eliza's crisis and fate at this moment, because it has everything to do with the kinds of stories Lucy is calling on her friend to write.

The theater proves for Lucy an unsuitable model because of its predilection for tragedy. That the play in question is *Romeo and Juliet* might be understood as a nascent move of patriotic literary nationalism, a critique of "imported" forms in favor of native productions. Further, by focusing on a drama of factional war and the devastating human costs of this battle, Lucy offers a denunciation of the factionalism that surrounds her own scene, and particularly its cost for women. Ultimately, however, the theater is condemned because it demands too much emotionally of its *audience* ("How can that be a diversion, which racks the soul with grief"?); while the circus is condemned because it asks too much of its *authors*, the riders who put at risk both safety and virtue: "I cannot conceive it to be a pleasure to sit a whole evening, trembling with apprehension, lest the poor wight of a horseman . . . should break his neck contributing to our entertainment" (113).[30]

But Bowen's museum, which was famous in its day for its waxworks of historical and picturesque subjects, *does* meet with Lucy's approval. This form of entertainment, we are told, is one that Lucy and Eliza have enjoyed together, and it is celebrated here as "a source of rational and refined amusement. Here the eye is gratified, the imagination charmed, and the understanding improved" (113). This celebration of the museum, far from a random digression, suggests an attempt by Foster to realign the novel with the work of the museum. The word "novel" as it is used in the 1790s is shorthand for "dangerous reading"; imagining her book instead as a "museum," the author is set up as something like a curator—like Bowen, featuring "principal figures, large as life," "historical, theatrical, and fancy subjects," and "universally allowed to merit the patronage . . . of the publick."[31] In referencing Bowen's museum, Foster surely also has in mind the most famous curator of the day, Charles Willson Peale, who sought to present the "world in miniature." Peale had great ambitions for his museum, long seeking to transform it from private to national institution. At the time in which Foster writes, his "Temple of Wisdom" of natural and human history was extremely popular. Peale believed in the power of the world's bounty, properly ordered and displayed, to effect remarkable transformations. He especially cherished and popularized the story of a 1796 meeting in his museum between two hostile tribes—traditional enemies—who were so overcome by the natural harmony of the museum that they signed a peace treaty on the spot.[32]

The heyday of Peale's museum from the late 1780s through the end of the 1790s was also that of the early literary magazine in the United States, which repeatedly celebrated museums like those of Bowen and Peale. And much like Bowen's and Peale's museums, these magazines worked to "preserve for posterity" the genius and varied productions of the new nation. Many of the most prominent magazines of the early national period featured little original work, and instead sought to provide anthologies of a range of excerpted pamphlets, books, reviews, and letters. The early magazine explicitly figured itself as a museum; two of the most important magazines of the period identified themselves as such (the *American Museum* and the *Massachusetts Magazine and Monthly Museum*), with many others including the term in their titles.[33] Mathew Carey's *American Museum* proudly listed in its inaugural issue subscribers who included men who would in other contexts have little to do with one another, such as Thomas Jefferson, Alexander Hamilton, and Rufus King, and it prominently displayed the name of Peale among its readers.

It is important that it is Bowen's museum of waxworks that Foster explicitly celebrates. A predecessor to the dime museum of the mid-nineteenth century, Bowen's was an itinerant and eclectic museum that stood somewhere between the highbrow cabinet of curiosities of Peale or the American Philosophical Society and the decidedly lowbrow entertainments of the circus.[34] It is the ephemeral nature of traveling museums such as Bowen's that most explicitly links it to the literary magazine, which, like the dime museum, sought to balance Peale's drive for a fixed Linnaean order with the popular demand for eclecticism and variety. As Brown defined his own policies in the *Literary Magazine*: "Useful information and rational amusement being his objects, he will not scruple to collect materials from all quarters. . . . He will not forget that a work, which solicits the attention of many readers, must build its claim on the variety as well as copiousness of its contents."[35]

In thus implicitly aligning *The Coquette* with the museum (literary and otherwise), Lucy's late letters privilege her own editorial function as curator of miscellaneous correspondences. The early American novel often positioned its author as editor, telling a tale based on "fact," citing "documents" as source for the tale that is about to be told. This is in part convention, seeking to secure the novelist against the traditional critique of novel writing, promising—in the place of dangerous flights of fancy—fact, history, and moral stricture. But the celebration of the role of editor/curator is more than posture. The early novel often earnestly seeks out a mode of presentation in which the author governs the events and source material as adjudicator and compiler. *The Coquette* works not to present a totalizing understanding of the facts; that is the work of the sermons and conduct manuals that had by this time long mined the story, silencing Whitman and letting the "facts" speak for themselves. But neither is it simply the autobiography of Eliza Wharton, the would-be heroine of her own tale who would speak for herself at every turn. Where the sermonized version of Eliza's tale goes wrong is easy to see, as epitomized in the novel by Boyer's misreading and silencing of Eliza. Where Eliza's version goes wrong is perhaps harder to identify. But clearly it inheres in large measure in Eliza's fantastical belief that she can refuse *all* choices and connections and still control reception at every turn. The novel suggests that this refusal of connection to society is as equally suspect as the iron rules of the conduct book.

There is one central question that Lucy and Eliza's mother both raise that serves as a tenable challenge to Eliza's declarations of radical independence. As Mrs. Wharton asks the question: What position in this world is not a dependent position? "Are we not all links in the great chain of society . . . each upheld by others, throughout the confederated whole?" (41). The suggestion that "we are all links in the great chain of society"—that the individual cannot know herself without relation to others—points to the danger intrinsic in the model of radical individualism that underlies Eliza's politics. As Mrs. Carter chastises Alcuin, "Men are at liberty to annex to words what meaning they think proper. What should hinder you, if you so please, from saying that snow is of the deepest black? Words are arbitrary. The idea that others annex to the word black, you are at liberty to transfer to the word white. But in the use of this privilege you must make your account in not being understood."[36] To write from the position of authorial tyranny is to write the singular meanings of the conduct book, the "public papers" against which Foster explicitly positions her novel. But equally is there the danger, as spelled out here by Mrs. Carter, in taking radical revisions too far, so as to speak from a position in which meaning is anarchic, and language has ceased to communicate. For a writer, no fate can be more troubling. As Mrs. Carter makes clear, refusing the choices of the day does not mean refusing connection to society, and thus her concluding defense of marriage after her long and bitter denunciation of its conditions rescues her in the final instance from the anarchy—moral and linguistic—to which Alcuin had hoped to lead her.

What Lucy believes will redeem Eliza's talents from the anarchy to which they tend is *editorial* control, represented in Lucy's terms by the figure of the "good" husband. We see Lucy's own husband little in the novel, and his lack of agency is striking given the profound impact his arrival on the scene has on Eliza. But insofar as his presence does make itself felt, it does so in terms that explicitly challenge Eliza's model of literary autonomy: Mr. Sumner is explicitly defined as editor, looking over Lucy's shoulder as she reads Eliza's letters and interesting himself in the correspondence between the two women. When Eliza's proposal to Boyer is rejected, Lucy immediately understands this crisis to be a literary one and offers to supply the role of the would-be husband; that is, she plays editor for Eliza, challenging her decline in style and rallying her back to her earlier accomplishments as writer.

Although we are told that it is Eliza's heretofore unmentioned brother who gathers up her deathbed writings, none of *this* writing makes its way into the novel. Instead, the novel consists entirely of letters, and as Lucy has been by far the recipient of the most letters, it is Lucy who serves as stand-in for the editorial function mapped out by Foster. In an early letter in which she defends her decision to share her letters with her fiancé, Lucy writes, "I have pride enough to keep me above coquetry, or prudery; and discretion enough . . . to secure me from the errors of both" (31). Lucy is the only character who gets to have it both ways at once because she refuses the polar extremes of coquetry and prudery—the two choices epitomized by Sanford and Boyer and politicized as Republican and Federalist.

The Coquette accomplishes precisely what Lucy had advised Eliza to do: It "rises above it," refusing to choose between the two lessons its story would offer. Presenting both the radical individualism of Eliza and the moralizing stricture of the community, *The Coquette* ultimately privileges neither position but instead maps out the political work of the editorial function. Neither interested nor disinterested, the editor works to occupy multiple positions, to negotiate the complex relations between writer and audience, and to provide the "rational amusement" that was both Brown's and Foster's earnest goal. If the new nation required a new literature, then one important contribution the novel might offer as it sought out national legitimation was a space that spoke the spectacularly contradictory voices of that nation. Rising above the factionalism of the age that would define every question as an either/ or proposition, Foster's novel effaced the individual author in favor of an editorial position that gave voice, in the true spirit of the early national literary magazines, to the intricate weave of competing voices—working to make editorial interest a feasible mode of alternative citizenship to the poor choices that the nation had to offer citizens, whether in the Republican or Federalist parties or in the miserable choices of Boyer and Sanford.

III

Brown likely began work on *Clara Howard* in 1800, after his famous letter to his brother James in which he vowed to never again repeat "gloominess and out-of-nature incidents" of *Edgar Huntly*, promising in future writing to "substitut[e] moral causes and daily incidents in place of the prodigious or the singular."[37] For those readers drawn to the "prodigious" and "singular" in Brown's "major" novels, this substitution has long been understood as a poor bargain, and the novels that follow on the heels of this declaration have served as tombstones to the literary career. By turning to Brown's last two novels in light of the editorial model on display in *The Coquette*, we might reevaluate these texts and the turn in the career they mark as Brown's articulation of a complex and radical reimagination of the function of the author and the role of literature in the young republic.

For all the notable changes of subject matter and tone, what is most striking is the shift from consistent first-person narration to a pure epistolary form, in which the story is told entirely in the multivocal present tense of correspondence, with no narrative voice holding the fragments together. Where the earlier novels focused on a central consciousness (Clara Weiland, Arthur Mervyn, Edgar Huntly), in these last novels Brown refuses to privilege even his title characters.[38] Read in conjunction with the shift from the "prodigious and singular" to the "daily incidents" of life, these changes do not constitute a promising recipe for selling out. An essay Brown published in the *Literary Magazine* a few years later argues that it is precisely by providing an *escape* from the imagined "tameness and insipidity of common life and common events" that the novel secures its popularity.[39] A turn away from the "singular" characters and gothic plotting, which Brown understood, rightly, as essential ingredients in successful novels, is therefore not so easily read as a move designed to secure a *larger* audience. Instead the evidence points to Brown's serious reconsideration of both the value and the politics of the novelistic conventions he had helped pioneer.

Despite the avowed conventionality of *Clara Howard* in terms of its moral lesson, there is, as in the "Portrait of an Emigrant," profound difficulty in determining *what* exactly that lesson is, a difficulty that is amplified, as it was in *The Coquette*, by the use of the epistolary form. The novel begins in a moment of dislocation, with Edward Hartley writing a fragmented and almost incoherent letter to Clara in which he laments his fate and the failures of writing to resolve his current condition: "Why do I write? For whose use do I pass my time thus?" (5). This opening is all but conventional for Brown: the writer fully broken down, too close to the scene of trauma to go on. But here, unlike in *Wieland* and *Edgar Huntly*, the narrative begins not with the writer at the end of the experiences relating them to a silent audience, but with the writer in the *midst* of the experiences, narrating them to an audience who will not only respond but who will script his responses and actions as well.

For a short novel, the story is a fairly complex weave of love triangles, in which Edward, previously (though lovelessly) engaged to one Mary Wilmot, falls in love with Clara, stepdaughter of his benefactor (a plot device borrowed wholesale from *Edgar Huntly*). Mary, deprived of her lover and (not entirely unrelated to the first loss) her inheritance, disappears, at which time Edward informs Clara of his earlier commitments. Clara responds by breaking off their relationship, vowing that she will not marry him unless Mary is first married to another. She sends him off to do his duty by offering himself to the abandoned Mary. The problem is that Mary has disappeared without a trace, the letter in which she informs him of her decision having been mislaid (the first of several such misdirected letters in these novels). The first half of the novel describes the epistolary struggle between Edward and Clara, as Edward pleads his case while Clara reiterates her terms flatly—"my esteem can be secured only by a just and disinterested conduct" (20)—and demands that he recount his search of Mary in letters confined "to a mere narrative of your journey" (25).

The narrative Clara would script, in which she disinterestedly surrenders her love to the prior claims of the unfortunate Mary, is interrupted violently by a storm that overtakes Edward on his journey south. His next letter, written "by the hand of another" (28), tells of his near-drowning in a swollen river and of his current critical condition. This intrusion of accident into her narrative throws Clara into confusion, and she repents in her next letter all of her previous commands—"Good God! what horrible infatuation was it that made me write as I did!" (32)—taking all responsibility onto herself. But when Edward writes that he is recovering and will be with her shortly to claim his prize, she quickly reverses course as thoughts of Mary's plight return to the forefront. Edward is once again sent on his way.

Caught in these buffeting crosswinds, Edward continues on his journey, all the while sending to Clara reports, exhortations, pleadings, commands, rejections, and farewells, but never able to liberate himself from her narrative control. The ultimate effects on his constitution and sanity prove to be presaged by his early accident at the river, as he becomes ravaged in body and mind. His condition worsens when he finds the runaway Mary, only to have his attempts to follow the strict letter of Clara's law bring further rejection. The second half of the novel narrates Edward's rapid decline at the hands of the two women who compete for the title of disinterested virtue by rejecting his many offers of marriage.[40]

Although consistently read as a straight and unambiguous moral handbook, in the end, the novel turns out to be as hard on Clara's and Mary's selfless piety (their almost sensual pleasure in renunciation) as it is on Edward's material sensuality (his ambition for Clara's body and fortune). Both are held wanting, both revealed to be governed by ambition and desire. Indeed, the fatal flaw in Clara's "selfless" reasoning is that the only basis on which she can "contend with selfish regards" is "to judge the feelings of others by her own" (71). As Edward describes the situation, "she should derive more satisfaction from disinterested, than from selfish conduct" (72). As long as satisfaction, even pleasure, is the result of "disinterest," then the neat split between selfishness and disinterest—the very grounds on which republican virtue might be founded—are unsettled. Edward, who for the most of the novel is decidedly the weaker vessel in both reason and constitution, offers the novel's most insightful critique of Clara and the terms of her selfless renunciation: "You aspire to true happiness, the gift of self-approbation and of virtuous forbearance. You have adopted the means necessary to this end, and the end is gained. Why then should I pity you? You would not derive more happiness from a different decision. Another would, indeed, be more happy, but you would, perhaps, be less. . . . [F]or what gratification can be compared to that arising from the sense of doing as we ought" (110). By defining Clara's decision in terms of the "happiness" and "gratification" it brings her, he insists that her motivations are not so different from his own: While he covets her body and her fortune, she covets self-approbation in terms no less ravenous.

Edward's critique continues when, imagining himself as husband to Mary, he describes himself as "one who esteems her, indeed, but loves her not." In doing so, he all but quotes from the sentimental seduction tale she had a short time earlier narrated to explain the origins of Mary's family. Mary's mother, Clara had told him, was seduced by a man named Wilmot, who was betrothed to another; selflessly she had allowed him to marry his fiancée despite her rapidly advancing pregnancy, but her father, upon discovering his daughter's condition, at the last moment forced him to marry his daughter. The ceremony completed, the newlyweds were summarily exiled to the new world. Mary is the product and sole survivor of this sad union.

As Clara describes "Poor Wilmot," "he was compelled to pay the forfeit of past transgressions, by binding himself to one who had his esteem, but not his love" (102). In using almost the identical phrasing—"one who esteems her, indeed, but loves her not"—to that which Clara uses to describe Wilmot's relation to Mary's mother—"one who had his esteem, but not his love"—Edward makes manifest Clara's blindness to the parallels between the story she tells and the "exquisite justice" (72) she insists on.

Further, Edward complicates the easy solution Clara would find to her moral problem by calling to her attention the other "person affected by your decision" (113): Sedley. The early and rejected suitor of Mary has remained devoted and honorable, and has thus proved himself "more entitled to the affections of this woman than I, because he loves her." As Edward continues, "With regard to this man is she not exactly in the same relation as I am to her? Is it not her duty to consult his happiness . . . ? For him and for me, your benevolence sleeps" (113). Clara does not reply to these charges because there could be no reply; her attempts to claim a moral high ground from which to orchestrate the proceedings are complicated by the endless chain of attachments, ambitions, and accidents set in motion by the novel. Shifting his gaze from the "prodigious and singular" to "moral causes and daily incidents," Brown nonetheless describes challenges to right action that are no less dramatic than those in *Edgar Huntly* or *Wieland*, even if the consequences of failure are somewhat less spectacular than Indian war or spontaneous combustion.

Despite her ambitions, Clara ultimately cannot secure the necessary distance on her story, and therefore she has no ability to decide properly. In the end, Clara's impulses prove good ones, and she is rewarded for her ambitions by getting everything she wants. Mary finds happiness (although not in the terms originally intended) and Clara secures at the same time her own. Indeed, we can see many ways in which Clara, in her disinterest, her loyalty, and her writing and organizing of letters, functions similarly to Lucy Sumner in *The Coquette*. But even as this association is invited, it is complicated. As Clara is shown again and again unable to consistently occupy the editorial position, she is also made to figure as the "coquette"—as the one who imagines she can script responses without becoming invested herself. Desperately trying to do the right thing, Clara has Edward dangling dangerously over a pit into which he almost falls at the novel's end, when he is prepared to embrace a "savage" life in preference to the "civilized" treatment he has received at the hands of his two would-be brides.

What rescues the situation is the late arrival of a character seemingly so irrelevant to the "action" that summaries of the plot often fail to even mention her. Mrs. Valentine, along with her brother, Sedley, secures finally the editorial function that allows for the resolution to the vexed marriage plot, recalling Edward back from the savage frontier to the well-ordered hearth. It is Mrs. Valentine who chastises Mary (and by extension, Clara) for the mischief she has wrought in her failed attempts at selflessness (what Mrs. Valentine terms her "perverseness" [129]). As Mrs. Valentine rightly points out, by renouncing Edward as she did—disappearing melodramatically and without a trace—Mary's was ultimately not a selfless act but one designed to entangle Edward all the more fully in her fate. Mrs. Valentine then goes on to offer the example of her *truly* disinterested brother, Sedley, who, we now discover, had *anonymously* worked behind the scenes to provide the mysterious inheritance that was to have eliminated the last obstacle to his beloved Mary marrying Edward. To complete Mary's education, Mrs. Valentine bequeaths to her a packet of her brother's letters (which are presumably forwarded to Clara with her narrative); in reading them Mary submits finally to Sedley, without him ever having to make a direct command upon her.

For this reason it is important that the one silent corner of the overlapping triangles of the plot is occupied by Sedley. He speaks and writes always from a distance, which, along with his fortune and native good sense, allows him to secure the proper position to judge accurately the events surrounding him. Together he and his sister provide the model for the editorial position Clara and Mary wish to occupy; but the siblings also demonstrate, in the inadequacy of the young women's attempts, that this is not a position that *everyone* can occupy. Thus at the novel's end, we see a recasting of republican virtue in terms of editorial organization. Even as the novel undermines the idea of a universal code of virtue that could transparently govern individual action, it articulates the attendant risks of liberal relativism in Edward's descent into savagery. The editor emerges here as the idealized governor: he who organizes the private, conflicting, and self-contradictory voices that surround him, not by force or will, but by careful distance and display, allowing all the voices to be heard in their turn and in their own terms so that all will ultimately find their proper place and end.

Brown's supposed turn from Republicanism—a political party that he, like his friend and fellow editor Joseph Dennie, increasingly understood as bringing about the fatal "fall into self" of the liberal ego—to Federalism might usefully be recast in somewhat different terms than the biographies have conventionally told it.[41] For what is articulated here is less the straightforward "bourgeois moralism" that Steven Watts and others identify at the heart of these novels than it is a celebration of a new model of "natural aristocracy," in which it is the true editor alone who can serve as the proper governor for the nation. Even the most virtuous individuals, like Clara herself, are unable to achieve the proper judgment and necessary distance. Instead, it is Valentine and Sedley who occupy the role in this novel that Lucy Sumner and her husband do in Eliza's tale. Although Sedley and Valentine are the novel's two hereditary aristocrats, it is not the privileges of monetary aristocracy but the powers of the editorial function that the novel is finally interested in promoting.

If *Clara Howard* focuses on the duties and responsibilities of the proper editor, Brown's next and last novel, *Jane Talbot*, focuses on the reasons why such an editor is needed: because letters are continually misdirected and misread. Focusing on the unreliability of the letter brings this novel as well into a more serious consideration of the problems and responsibilities of *reading*. Here again we have the obstacle to romantic union that letters both describe and seek to overcome. The obstacle in this case proves to be Jane's wealthy and moralizing benefactress, Mrs. Fielder, whose strenuous objections to Jane's union with Henry Colden jeopardize Jane's tenuous claims on her "mother's" fortune. Mrs. Fielder's antipathy toward Henry proves to be founded on two misdirected correspondences. The first, a series of radical, atheistic effusions Henry had written as a young man, has been brought to Mrs. Fielder by his pious correspondent. More seriously damaging the reputations of the lovers and their prospects for union, however, is a stolen letter Jane had been writing to Henry while her late husband was still living, to which the town gossip forges a scandalous conclusion. This half-forged serial letter too makes its way to Mrs. Fielder, accompanied by a series of anonymous "reports" on Jane's relations with Henry. Mrs. Fielder proves the quintessential bad reader, victim of both the instability of the texts that provide her evidence and the rigidity of her moral and interpretive categories.

Without character or plot to drive this remarkably uneventful long and meditative novel, the drama comes to reside entirely in the letters themselves: how easily they are purloined, misread, displaced, or otherwise fail to arrive at their intended destinations. Characters are regularly finishing their letters abruptly for fear "of losing the post" (206). By the novel's end, the epistolary evidence that Mrs. Fielder had gathered seems to prove beyond doubt Henry and her daughter's "depravity" (221). The question we are left with is not why letters miscarry, but how to read and pass judgment in a world of necessarily unreliable representation.[42]

As we will see in chapter 4, it is toward a consideration of precisely these questions that Brown will devote himself in his final years, defining the periodical as the space in which unstable texts, fragments, and anonymous diatribes can be made stable, ordered, and organized without the totalizing narratives and central consciousness of the conventional novel. Ultimately *Jane Talbot* works to show how the rigid judge who practices "strict government" (223) is as vulnerable to bad reading as the woman Mrs. Fielder accuses Jane of being—defined by "an inattention to any thing but feeling: a proneness to romantic friendship and a pining after good not consistent with our nature" (223). Even as Mrs. Fielder works to "ke[ep] at a distance all such books and companions as tend to produce this phantastic character" (223), her own experience as bad reader proves the strict, antiromantic reader as vulnerable to dangerous texts as the novel-reading female quixote she believes Jane to be.

If the novel offers a resolution to this crisis, it is one similar to that presented by *The Coquette*: not in the privileging of any character's position but in the model of the novel itself. The long collection of letters adjudicates between our three principle characters neutrally. In the end, there is no clear villain, no strong hero, not even a strong plot. It is as if Brown is experimenting with a novel that would refuse *all* judgments, all loading up of the evidence one way or the other. Instead he presents the novel as a collection of fragments, a truly neutral history; here, in the face of inevitably unreliable correspondence, the best that can be hoped for is someone to organize writer and reader toward the necessarily collaborative work of making meaning.

"How does it fall out," Jane wonders, "that the same object is viewed by two observers with such opposite sensations" (301)? This becomes for Brown in his later writing one of his central questions. "Remarks on Reading," an essay by Isaac Disraeli published without attribution in Brown's *Literary Magazine* in 1806, argues that just as writing is an art, so too must reading be understood in commensurate terms. "Two persons of equal taste rise from the perusal of the same book with very different notions," he points out; the difference lies in the distinction between "the facile pleasures of perception in preference to the laborious task of forming ideas."[43] Disraeli goes on to describe the habits and skills that contribute to a *proper* model of reading, including, prominently, avoiding becoming "a prisoner chained to the triumphal car of an author of great celebrity," surrendering one's own judgments to the fame of an author.[44] Instead, readers and writers alike must remember that reading is a mutually creative act in which each party brings "something" to the table. Here Brown's *Literary Magazine* advises authors not to try to please and make themselves comprehensible to all readers; instead their texts should serve as a space in which collaborative creative acts might take place. As the essay concludes, in an original paragraph by

Brown appended to Disraeli's essay, "One ought not to see every thing distinctly, but only certain parts of it; the imagination properly supplies the intermediate links."[45]

This is not the manifesto of a man who has abandoned, as the story goes, "real ambiguity" for bourgeois moralism.[46] The periodicals Brown edited after 1800 provide the ground on which we must rethink the turn in his career. For example, the turn to "daily incidents" of life must be read in conjunction with meditations in the *Literary Magazine* on the dangers conventional historical narratives pose to our abilities to recognize and value the "obscure individuals" of our own time and place.[47] As this sentiment is picked up in other periodical writings, we see that Brown's turn from gothic spectacles to the "romance of real life" is part and parcel with a larger critique of the tendencies in narrative history and fiction to diminish the possibilities of the present. And Brown's rejection of literary celebrity for the mantle of anonymous editor must similarly be reconceived not as sour grapes or bitter retreat but as a bold attempt to define an authorial role to which readers will not risk being made "prisoner."

Finally and most importantly, we must rethink as well the turn from the central narrative point of view of his "major" novels to the epistolary fragments of his final two. Just as Brown has come to question "prodigious" events and individuals and the tyranny of the author, so too has he become suspicious of the tyranny of the central consciousness, through whose eyes the whole story is filtered.[48] Moving in the opposite direction, Brown, like Foster, works in his last novels and in his subsequent magazine work to create precisely the kinds of texts called for in "Reading," in which the reader would be called on to do the work of making ideas, "the imagination properly suppl[ying] the intermediate links": epistolary novels, periodical fragments, and sketches, and the anonymous editor as he who gathers the material and presents it to the reader so that all can engage in the "art of combination, and . . . exertion of the reasoning powers."[49]

In 1804, Brown's *Literary Magazine* described a tour of Peale's museum: "There is no institution of the kind, in North America," the *Literary Magazine* enthused, "which bears any comparison, in importance, value, and extent, to [this] museum." After concluding the tour, the writer, likely Brown himself, notes that "A considerable number of other subjects are now . . . waiting for such an arrangement in the museum as will enable them to be systematically displayed, without which they answer no other end than mere show, enough of which already exists; since the chief value of a museum depends upon an arrangement calculated as much to instruct as amuse."[50] Throughout his editorial writings in the first decade of the 1800s, this was to be Brown's model: to "collect materials from all quarters" and arrange them so as to build the most important and ambitious literary museum of his day.[51] As he promised in inaugurating his previous venture, the *American Review*, in 1801, the day of America's cultural coming-of-age was nigh at hand, "and no means seem better calculated to hasten so desirable an event, than those literary repositories, in which every original contribution is received, and the hints and discoveries of observation and ingenuity are preserved."[52]

The literary museum provides a very different model for a national literature than that which was ultimately monumentalized as the "American Renaissance." Yet if Brown's experiments at the end of his career moved him away from the main currents of the rising national literary culture, we might nonetheless identify the legacy of this late work in the periodical experiments of Poe, the literary political experiments of Melville, or the critique of the conventional novel and celebration of the "little magazine" at the heart of American modernism. Even if the future turned out to belong to the novel Brown had pioneered and then abandoned, we do a disservice to this work when we write the end of his career as a scene of literary silence and failure.

More important, Brown's late work and the consideration of the editorial function he, Foster, and others worked to define during this period provides us with an alternate model for the foundation of a national literature, one that does not center on the novel and its attendant national narratives. In Brown's late experiments with the epistolary form and editorial function, we see attempts to write a very different model of the relationship between writer and reader, book and nation—one that worked to rise above the poor choices the novel and the nation had to offer.

IV

Foster's career witnesses an even more abrupt turn away from the novel. Her second book following the success of *The Coquette* was *The Boarding School* (1798). Although classified as a novel by scholars eager for a "sequel" to *The Coquette*, it is clear that Foster herself did not consider the book to be anything of the kind. *The Boarding School* is written in the style of Sarah Fielding's *The Governess*: a compilation of lessons, anecdotes, letters, and reviews—in many ways itself a periodical production.[53] And it contains within its pages one of the period's more extensive critique of the novel; in the words of Mrs. Williams, the governess of the school: "Novels are the favourite, and the most dangerous kind of reading, now adopted by the generality of young ladies. . . . The style in which they are written is commonly captivating; and the luxuriance of the descriptions with which they abound, extremely agreeable to the sprightly fancy, and high expectations of the inexperienced and unreflecting."[54] In a pattern repeated throughout *The Boarding School*, Mrs. Williams illustrates her lesson for the day with a story—in this case, a familiar story about the tendency of compulsive novel reading to form unhealthy notions of romance and loyalty in the minds of young readers. Mrs. Williams admits that some novels might be worth reading, although the dangers inherent in so captivating a form make the process of coming to a "useful selection" especially important. "Those," Mrs. Williams suggests, "which are sanctioned by the general voice of delicacy and refinement, may be allowed a reading; yet none should engross your minds, to the neglect of more important objects; nor be suffered to monopolize too large a portion of your time."[55]

Throughout the early American novel one finds a consistent and occasionally even vitriolic critique *of* novels. Contemporary critics have largely read the critique of the novel as a recognition by those in power of the unique "subversive" power of the novel to liberate the self, crossing class and gender lines in opening up new freedoms of thought and desire. For the most part, when this critique is articulated in novels themselves, it has been interpreted as a canny strategy by early American novelists to dance around these cultural gatekeepers, sneaking forbidden fruits into the closed garden under the cover of virtuous native goods.

And yet, looking closely at the anxieties raised about the novel by these early American writers, we might find reason to take them a bit more seriously—to not dismiss them as either opportunistic pandering or conservative hysteria. After all, Mrs. Williams's concerns about the dangers of novels have much less to do with the subject matter than with the *style* of novels, their dangerous power to "captivate" the imagination, to enslave the passions. Such language, indeed, is everywhere in the early critique of the novel form, and the periodical was often the place where it was most clearly articulated. As late as 1810, for example, the *Weekly Visitor* published "Lines, Sent to a Lady, Addicted to Reading Novels," describing the progress of the disease:

> The soft contagion rends the tender breast;
> First, fond emotions enervates the heart,
> And imitation bids us act a part
>
> Then pains more tender seize the sick'ning mind
> With fever'd rapture of the novel kind:
> We burn with exstacy, to head the stage,
> And be the subjects of some future age.[56]

The "first American novel," so advertised by Isaiah Thomas when he published *The Power of Sympathy* (1789), is also the first American "novel" to contain a lengthy critique *of* novels. And this critique was reprinted by Thomas himself in the first issue of his new *Massachusetts Magazine* as one of the examples of the "Beauties of 'The Power of Sympathy.'" "Novels, not regulated on the chaste principles of true friendship, rational love, and connubial duty, appear to me totally unfit to form the minds of women, of friends, or of wives," the novel's sage Mr. Holmes declares in the middle of an extended discussion of one of early America's most pressing topics: how best to direct the reading of the young nation. As an advertisement for the first "novel," this is a strange excerpt for the *Massachusetts Magazine* to choose. And if we consider *The Power of Sympathy as* a novel, Mr. Holmes's critique of novels looks all the stranger: After all, *The Power of Sympathy*, whatever else might be said of it, is not a book "regulated on the chaste principles of true friendship." For one thing, it is a book about incestuous desire and about the adulterous sins of fathers being handed down to the children. But it is also a book that contains many other moments that don't even fit with this seemingly central story of star-crossed lovers (who happen also to be siblings): seduction tales, disquisitions on reading, poetry, even a meditation on the fate of Elizabeth Whitman, the real-life model for *The Coquette*. Although the ill-fated romance between Harrington and Harriot ends tragically, it is only one part of the book, and at times, much to Harrington's dismay, his correspondent, Worthy, seems to lose all interest in his melodramatic tale, preferring instead the rational conversation of Mrs. Holmes and her family at their country estate.

In fact, it is not the story of the star-crossed lovers Harrington and Harriot but "The Story of Ophelia" that is illustrated in the book's frontispiece. Ophelia's story is a conventional seduction tale with a conventional ending, one of several such short stories contained within the book, and it is the kind of tale readers were well familiar with from magazines.[57] For example, another claimant to the title of "first American novel" is in the periodical founded in Philadelphia in 1786, the *Columbian Magazine*. "Amelia: or, the Faithless Briton an Original Novel, Founded upon Recent Facts" is also a seduction tale, and the first to openly lay the claim to being a "novel." That it does so within the pages of a magazine (coupled with the relative brevity of the story) has made it very easy for critics to dismiss the claim. But we might equally question the claim Thomas makes on behalf of *The Power of Sympathy*, published the same year he launched his new magazine and copiously interpolated with the magazine itself. Further, while Isaiah Thomas might have sought to package *The Power of Sympathy* as the first

"American novel," it is by no means clear that William Hill Brown had any thought of writing one when he set out to put this book together. In fact, if anything, it is structurally much closer to the miscellaneous forms of the periodical than to the novel.

My goal here is not to overly worry such generic distinctions. After all, these categories were far less fixed at the time, and authors and editors delighted in exploring the boundaries for both literary and financial reasons (for example, in 1787, Isaiah Thomas had temporarily taken his long-running newspaper the *Massachusetts Spy* and turned it into the *Worcester Magazine*, to evade new postal fees directed at newspapers). But when we consider the "early novel" in relation to the periodical culture of the period, we begin to realize that much of what looks fragmented, discontinuous, and frankly "primitive" about the early novel looks far more familiar, of a piece with a broader literary culture and practices.

What if many of these authors did not imagine that they were writing novels at all, but instead saw themselves as seeking to do what so many of these "novels" call for: experimenting with a new form for a new nation of readers? After all, the ideal recipe for this new form is spelled out clearly in books such as *The Boarding School* and *The Power of Sympathy*. The reader must never be enslaved to the book; "even in the best books," Mr. Holmes insists, readers must retain skepticism. "In books written in an easy, flowing style, which excel in description and the luxuriance of fancy, the imagination is apt to get heated." Therefore, the reader must "discern with an eye of judgment, between the superficial and the penetrating—the elegant and the tawdry—what may be merely amusing, and what may be useful."[58] Further, reading too deeply or long in any one subject or the works of any one author can cause its own form of servitude: It is important to know when to "put down" a text and what to pick up in the first place. "By *immoderate reading* we hoard up opinions and become insensibly attached to them," Mr. Holmes insists. "*Conversation* only can remedy this dangerous evil; strengthen the judgment, and make reading really useful. They mutually depend upon, and assist each other."[59]

This model of disciplined, engaged, and varied reading is similarly promoted by Mrs. Williams in Foster's *The Boarding School*. Passive reading, Mrs. Williams argues, is wasted effort. Reading with too little or too much interest are both dangerous extremes; skimming tedious reading or being consumed by passionate novels both have the effect of dulling the intellect and making one passive in the face of others' arguments. As in *The Power of Sympathy*, the point is not that *all* novels are bad but that a diet of steady novel reading—and even the reading of one coherent and immersive novel—can only have bad effects. Unless chosen wisely, doled out selectively in combination with other texts, and allowed to share the reader's time with poetry, history, essays, and letters, novels will dull the mind. And as in *The Power of Sympathy*, *conversation* about reading and the ideas generated is the surest method to make ideas one's own. "If convenient," Mrs. Williams suggests, "always recapitulate what you have been perusing, and annex to it your own sentiments and remarks, to some friends."[60]

Even more explicitly than in *The Power of Sympathy*, *The Boarding School* seeks to realize formally the method of reading Mrs. Williams describes. The lectures, moral essays, and short stories that dominate the first half are put into circulation in the second half of the book in a series of letters between the former students of the boarding school, now out in the world, striving to put their lessons to work through epistolary conversation. We call this a "novel." But is it? Or is this book attempting to imagine into existence another form altogether, one that bears more in common with the magazine and its cultures of circulation and conversation than with the novel form? In fact most of the "pioneers" of the early American novel ended up largely abandoning the "novel" entirely for anonymous periodical work at the end of their careers. Although this turn away from the novel has often been read as evidence of the harsh reality of the literary marketplace in a new nation unprepared to support genius, such an explanation does not begin to account for why these writers would have turned from a marginally profitable enterprise to one from which it was understood in advance no profits could possibly be derived. Instead, we might recognize that there was something in the magazine form that attracted these men and women, something we need to comprehend to recover properly the literary culture of late-eighteenth-century America.

Or, from another angle: consider where we are after more than a generation of "recovery" of the early American novel. We have a canon that effloresces in the 1790s with a handful of novels that are now taught in most classes devoted to the literature of the period, and then, after 1800, silence—a long gap while literary history seems to wait for the next chapter in the story of the novel's rise. What is now clear is that the questions we asked a generation ago to recover the vitality and importance of the literature of the 1790s have done little to illuminate the work of the subsequent two decades. What if part of the problem we face when trying to account for what happens between the recently canonized novels of Brown, Rowson, and Foster and the novels of Cooper is due to our determination to see *only* novels—or to see "novels" when what is before us might be something else? After all, in 1789, at the time of the "first American novel," Anne Radcliffe had just published her first novel in England. Americans *knew* what novels were supposed to look like, and by almost any stretch of the imagination *Power of Sympathy* did not look the part.

For years, of course, this fact was taken either as a sign of the early American novelist's primitiveness or slavish imitation to out-of-date British conventions. But it is hard, even going back a generation, to find the British novel that would have been imitated here. While we have rightly dismissed the traditional explanation of a "primitive" literary culture in late-eighteenth-century America (as if the same culture capable of *Common Sense* and the Constitution could not figure out how to plot a coherent novel), in our desire to make the case might we have overly insisted that the case *must* be made on the basis of the form that would be most valued in American literary culture *after* 1820? Instead we need to begin to rethink our literary history as focused around goals not entirely consistent with those of the nineteenth-century novel. Differently and with varying degrees of success, these books seek to imagine another kind of form whose closest relatives might well be the miscellany forms of the day—schoolbook, almanac, and especially the periodical.

Thus it is that in turning to the beginnings of periodical culture in the early eighteenth century to recover alternate models to the story of the rise of the novel that has dominated our literary historiography for so many years, we must start with the men who became most explicitly associated with schoolbooks, almanacs, and periodicals—men like Addison and Steele, Noah Webster, and of course, Benjamin Franklin.

CHAPTER ONE

AMERICAN SPECTATORS, TATLERS, AND GUARDIANS

Transatlantic Periodical Culture in the Eighteenth Century

I

In its April issue for 1776, the *Pennsylvania Magazine*, which had been founded the previous year by Scottish-born printer Robert Aitken, published "A Reverie." Aitken's anonymous correspondent, after declaring himself a "great admirer of the Spectators, Tatlers, and Guardians," goes on to describe the effect of a recent encounter with issue no. 35 of Richard Steele's *Guardian* from 1713: "After having read the paper, I closed the book; and reflecting on the oddity of the thought, fell into one of those deep reveries, whereby the mind is entirely absorbed, and rendered, for a while, totally inattentive to the objects of sense; forming, as it were, a kind of waking dream."[1] The "reverie" had been a staple of the periodical essay ever since Joseph Addison first deployed it in *Spectator* no. 3 in 1711, describing a "Methodical Dream" of Lady Credit. Of the many innovations Addison and Steele brought to the periodical form in its infant years, the "Vision or Allegory" was to be one of the most lasting and most imitated throughout the next century. For Addison and Steele, the reverie or vision often emerges from deep contemplation of the busy world around them—in the case of *Spectator* no. 3, for example, from a visit to the fledgling Bank of England where Mr. Spectator is delighted "to see the Directors, Secretaries, and Clerks, with all the other Members of that wealthy Corporation, ranged in their several Stations, according to the Parts they act in that just and regular Oeconomy."[2]

In the case of Aitken's American correspondent, there are no such banks to visit, no busy city streets to stalk or smoky coffee-shops to observe. In the *Pennsylvania Magazine*, the vision results instead from *reading* an installment of the London-based *Guardian* from sixty years earlier, in which a "correspondent" wrote in to tell of how, "having determined the *pineal gland* to be the chief place of the soul's residence, he had procured from a great philosopher a box of snuff, having this remarkable property, that a pinch of it duly administered, so affected his pineal gland, as to enable his soul to leave her residence for a while, and enter that of any other person."[3] The *Guardian*'s correspondent, one "Ulysses Cosmopolita" (George Berkeley) had gone on to describe remarkable cosmopolitan voyages from pineal gland to pineal gland through the vehicle of this remarkable snuff. And so inspired was the *Guardian*'s editorial persona, Nestor Ironside, that he declared his *own* acquisition of the "Philosophical Snuff" "and gives Notice that he will make use of it, in order to distinguish the real from the professed Sentiments of all Persons of Eminence in Court, City, Town and Country."[4] Two generations later and an ocean away, in the pages of the *Pennsylvania Magazine* there is no "Philosophical Snuff" to be had; but imported copies of the *Tatler*, the *Spectator*, and the *Guardian* themselves serve to produce similar hallucinogenic effects.

As Mr. Cosmopolita wrote, "You may imagine it was no small Improvement and Diversion, to pass the time in the *Pineal Glands* of Philosophers, Poets, Beaux, Mathematicians, Ladies and Statesmen."[5] This was the guiding fantasy of the magazine form as it emerged in England over the course of the eighteenth century, expanding on the periodical sheets popularized by Addison and Steele and coming into its own with the *Gentleman's Magazine* in 1731, the first successful English-language miscellaneous periodical. In the opening issue of the *Pennsylvania Magazine* in 1775, Aitken's editor, Thomas Paine, celebrated the ideal of the magazine as a place where, even though "we are not all Philosophers, all Artists, nor all Poets," we can store and share the "sweets" in a common "bee-hive."[6] As Paine argued here, on the brink of the American Revolution, the new magazine could serve as the engine of genius and a necessary prophylactic against imported vice: "It has always been the opinion of the learned and curious that a magazine, when properly conducted, is the nursery of genius; and by constantly accumulating new matter, becomes a kind of market for wit and utility."[7] But it is not only the *collections* of the magazine (the *Pennsylvania Magazine* was subtitled "The American Monthly Museum") but its *serial* nature that made it so powerful a tool. Unlike the book or the newspaper, the periodical returns serially, picking up stories, ideas, and conversations from past issues and other magazines and carrying them forward. As Paine argues, the magazine—more than any other form—offers potential benefits but also dangers, for "of all publications none are more calculated to improve or infect than a periodical one. All others have their rise and their exit; but *this* renews the pursuit."[8]

Paine would himself ultimately exit the magazine to devote himself to writing and defending *Common Sense*, but the terms by which he celebrated the periodical form would continue to govern the ideals of Aitken's magazine after his departure, as they had the earlier colonial magazines of the previous generation. The story of the early American magazine is the story of men and women continually "renew[ing] the pursuit," picking up the arguments, agendas, and ambitions of their predecessors and contemporaries and attempting to carry forward that original ideal from Addison and Steele of universal "improvement"—an ideal that was suddenly becoming increasingly urgent as the colonies prepared to become a nation.

The author of "A Reverie" was Francis Hopkinson who had joined with Paine and Aitken in helping to launch the magazine the previous year. Hopkinson had an especial proclivity for the vision or reverie genre, and his first contribution to the *Pennsylvania Magazine* was "An Extraordinary Dream" about a visit to the "Garden of human Knowledge." There, his guide, the Lady Truth, leads him to different fertile plots—Law, Physic, Natural Philosophy, and Astronomy—and finally to a fountain "from which issued several streams of pure water. On a handsome pediment in the front of this fountain was written in large gold letters, The PENNSYLVANIA MAGAZINE."[9] The idea that the magazine could be the fountain that would nourish the diverse garden of human knowledge had been a long-standing conceit, and it was one that was taking on more significance as the colonies prepared to forge a new nation, potentially severing themselves from the springs that had long nourished cultural and intellectual life. This is not, that is, simply ornament on the part of the magazine's founders. The ideals invested in the periodical form are always hyperbolic and yet always deadly serious. Even for Paine, who ultimately did not have the patience or the purse to put up with the slow publication schedule and nonexistent financial returns of the monthly magazine, the ideal of the periodical he celebrated in the *Pennsylvania Magazine*'s first issue would continue to inform his fantasy of the kind of collaborative work he saw himself as engaged in throughout his political writings—especially the fantasy of the pamphlet as part of a larger conversation in which the people might participate to solve the unprecedented problem of crafting a modern republican government: "[A]s an opening into that business I offer the following hints; at the same time modestly affirming, that I have no other opinion of them myself, than that they may be the means of giving rise to something better. Could the straggling thoughts of individuals be collected, they would frequently form materials for wise and able men to improve into useful matter."[10] This is the premise of the magazine: a place where "straggling thoughts" could be collected and where new manners, thoughts, and even nations could arise as a result.

For all Paine's attraction to the magazine, however, he was always temperamentally more suited to the "public papers" and "pamphlet wars" so crucial to the revolutionary moment. For the most part, the men who edited and wrote for the early magazine were men more like Hopkinson: moderate patriots and later moderate federalists, committed, as David Paul Nord puts it, to an ideal of "participation, not social revolution."[11] As Hopkinson distinguished the magazine from other papers in 1775, the "public papers" were a cacophonous space dominated by "your *Citizens*, your *Philadelphians*, your *Lovers of liberty*, and your *Lovers of no liberty at all*," and as a result "there is no such thing as getting a word or two in edge-ways amongst them." The *Pennsylvania Magazine*, on the other hand, served "as a pleasant little path, where a man may take an agreeable walk with a few quiet friends, without the risk of being jostled to death in a crowd."[12]

And thus it is, as Paine's *Common Sense* is circulating in unprecedented numbers in the spring of 1776, that we find Hopkinson again playing anonymous dreamer, this time in a voyage through the pituitary glands of his countrymen, a voyage inspired not by the tumultuous political events on the city streets but by a reading of a British periodical essay from two generations earlier. Even as Paine in *Common Sense* and in his "Forester" essays in the *Philadelphia Ledger* is celebrating the youthful American "virtue" that makes it so urgent to found the ideal nation at this precise moment in time, Hopkinson, with a backwards glance to Addison and Steele, raises doubts. After all, when Hopkinson's narrator imaginatively partakes of the magic properties of the "Philosophical Snuff," not by ingesting the stuff but by reading the *Guardian* and allowing himself to be intoxicated vicariously, his glandular journey proves to be significantly less inspiring than was that of the *Guardian*'s correspondent two generations earlier. Instead of "Philosophers, Poets, Beaux, Mathematicians, Ladies and Statesmen" (or even "Coffee-House Politicians"), the *Pennsylvania Magazine*'s correspondent finds himself transported to the pineal glands of a miser, a libertine, and a sot, rescued finally from a potentially fatal "connection" to the latter by the sound of a "fife and drum, which just then passed my window, and by calling my attention, put an end to this strange *revery*."[13] And while the fife and drum ultimately saves Hopkinson's dreamer from being trapped forever in the glands of the drunkard, it is still a republic of sots, misers, and libertines to which he returns. As this example necessarily reminds us, the magazine was rarely a space for utopianists or wild-eyed reformers, and even a revolutionary like Hopkinson questions whether the republic was ever as virtuous or youthful as Paine's "public papers" would have it. The fife and drums save him from a gruesome fate, but the reality that he awakens to remains as far from the ideal nation Paine imagines as it does from the ideal coffeehouse republic Addison and Steele defined.

One reminder of how far from utopia was the America of 1776 can be found in a poem to Washington from "the famous Phillis Wheatley," published in that same issue of the *Pennsylvania Magazine*. Wheatley introduces the poem with a letter to Washington himself, apologizing for the "inaccuracies" of the utterance to follow but also insisting implicitly on her right to speak (through the medium of the magazine) to General Washington himself:

> In bright array they seek the work of war,
> Where high unfurl'd the ensign waves in air.
> Shall I to Washington their praise recite?
> Enough thou know'st them in the fields of fight.
> Thee, first in place and honours,—we demand
> The grace and glory of thy martial band.[14]

Wheatley addresses Washington directly, praising his soldiers and "demand[ing]" on his behalf the glories he deserves. And in addition to serving as a reminder of the ongoing fact of slavery in America (especially in Washington's home colony, whose 400,000 slaves are mentioned in the same issue in "Some Account of the Colony of Virginia"), the inclusion of this poem serves as a warning regarding the difficult work of democracy that lies ahead. Ultimately, the poem implicitly challenges the rhetoric of colonial "slavery" being regularly deployed by many of the revolutionaries, including Paine and John Witherspoon, whose "Dialogue on Civil Liberty" in the same issue of the *Pennsylvania Magazine* concludes by expressing a preference for "anarchy" and "even extermination itself" "to slavery rivetted on us and our posterity."[15] Even as the pamphleteers effectively deploy what Ruth Bloch has termed "apocalyptical Manichaeanism" to frame the choices facing Americans on the brink of revolution, the periodical form—including at the hands of some of the staunchest revolutionaries of the day—pulled in different, and often contradictory, directions.[16]

But I am getting a bit ahead of myself here, as well as perhaps giving a false impression of the form I consider over the course of the next several chapters. It is certainly true that leading revolutionary figures and a celebrated African American poet play a central role in this issue of the *Pennsylvania*

Magazine. And it is undeniably the case that, during the eighty-year period this book covers, nearly every major literary and political figure in America participated in some way—and often in central ways—in periodical culture. But the magazine is not a form devoted to Founding Fathers, great authors, or "Names" of any kind. Here the example of the *Pennsylvania Magazine* is illustrative of a larger tendency in this body of writing: With the exception of Wheatley's contribution, all the contributions are anonymous. We only know as much as we do about the contributors today because this magazine happened to be staffed by men who would go on to be labeled "Founding Fathers," their every word excavated and enshrined by subsequent generations of antiquarians. Further, much of the magazine, even in April 1776, is about decidedly unpolitical stuff. In fact, a large proportion of what was published in this issue (and every issue) of even this most revolutionary of magazines was remarkably pedantic ("Extraordinary Heroism of the ancient Scandinavians") or mundane (weather, marriages, intelligence, statistics).

This seemingly random juxtaposition of a "Reverie," a debate on civil liberties, a poem by Phillis Wheatley to General Washington, and tables describing the relative humidity in Philadelphia over the course of the previous month is the defining feature of the magazine as colonial Americans inherited the form from the *Gentleman's Magazine.* The image overseeing the table of contents of each issue of the *Pennsylvania Magazine* describes this arrangement (figure 1.1). Here the plough and the anchor frame a still life centered around an olive-entwined shield, a lyre, and a globe, all resting on a closed volume whose contents could equally pertain to any of these emblems: a ledger, a volume of poetry, an atlas? Of course, the magazine itself purports to be all of these at once. The motto—"*juvat in sylvis habitare*" ("it is pleasant to live in the woods")—refers simultaneously to Penn's woods and also to the pastoral isolation of America in general. Although many of the readers of the early magazine did not live in the woods but in the cities, almost universally they saw their remove from the cultural centers of Europe as effectively isolating them as completely as a hermit. It is the bound volume of the magazine that promises to serve as the connecting link, bringing together not only the many occupations and regions of the new nation (plow, anchor, ledger) but equally importantly forging vital connections between the soon-to-be independent nation and the network of culture and ideas in the Old World.

For many, and particularly after independence, the American magazine came to be imagined as an ideal form on which to erect a new literary culture, one at once revolutionary and conservative, "original and American" yet deeply English, radically inclusive yet rigorously organized, polyphonous

Figure 1.1. Header to the monthly table of contents, *Pennsylvania Magazine* (1775–76).

yet unified. Ultimately, of course, it is not a wholly utopian story. In the long history of the failures of so many magazines attempting to embody these ideals, we find the wreck of many intellectual and financial fortunes and ultimately the defeat of a model of literary culture whose possibilities would not be fully revisited again for almost two centuries.

Traditionally the early American magazine has been seen as a kind of "overture" to the "Golden Age" of the American magazine to follow.[17] And if we are to judge the success of magazines based entirely by their ledgers, then the early magazine indeed should remain relegated to a primitive past. Yet, if we instead consider the magazine in terms of the ambitions and energies with which it was invested, there are unique aspects and aspirations to periodical culture before the 1820s that mark it as discrete from the magazine to follow, in ways not dissimilar to the relationship between silent cinema and the sound cinema that emerges after 1927. Technological, bureaucratic, commercial, and cultural changes made possible the periodical form that emerged in the middle decades of the nineteenth century, and from the perspective of *that* magazine (a form that has strong continuities with the form in the present day) the early American magazine looks decidedly "primitive" (a term used frequently to describe early silent cinema as well). But understood in its own terms and in relationship to a broader transatlantic circulation of energies and texts, the early American magazine can be seen to represent something very different from the magazine that was to follow. This book attempts to recover the early American periodical culture in which many men and women invested much of their energies and ambitions (including some of the most important canonical figures of the period, from Ben Franklin to Washington Irving). On one hand, my goal here is modest: to understand why these brilliant and rational individuals remained devoted to a form that looks, to our eyes at least, marginal, ephemeral, and most decidedly unprofitable. But as suggested in the introduction, I harbor more quixotic ambitions of offering a different take on early American literary history and the foundations of an "American" literary culture, one in which the novel and its rise is no longer the central story we tell and the celebrity and careers of authors is no longer the primary vehicle by which we tell it.

But first there is much work to do in simply recovering for modern readers the forms, fantasies, and energies that gathered around the American magazine in the eighteenth century. To start with, since my focus is on U.S. periodicals, we must consider what is unique about the early American magazine. In many ways, when comparing the first magazines in what will become the United States to their predecessors in England, the answer is: very little. The early American magazine closely modeled itself on its counterparts in London, often brazenly so (even down to borrowing slogans and icons from well-known British magazines to adorn new publications on the other side of the Atlantic). Although many of the early magazines framed patriotic rationales in justifying their publications, these same magazines continued to circulate English news and source material, often without attribution. One of the primary reasons for the neglect of the early American magazine has been their tendency to circulate reprints from the robust periodical culture in England at this same time. Over and over again, American publishers called on the "native genius" of their fellow citizens to create an "original" magazine of their own, and over and over again, these same magazines found themselves forced to beg, borrow, and steal from others, especially from European periodicals.

But in truth, the borrowing was not solely or even predominantly the result of a paucity of original contributions. American periodicals participated enthusiastically from the start in what Meredith McGill, focusing on a later period, has influentially termed "reprint culture" and what David Brewer, focusing on literary culture in eighteenth-century Britain, has termed the "textual commons" of literary culture before the enclosures of modern legal and critical standards and practices.[18] Living at a great physical distance from London, the center of literary culture for all eighteenth-century Americans, heightened the need to stake claims to that textual commons. And colonial Americans maintained relatively generous access to the textual commons precisely through their participation in the exchanges and correspondences of periodical reprint culture. For colonial Americans especially, the periodical was a more potent medium for tapping the energies of this imaginative space than was the book. Both periodical and book made their way regularly across the Atlantic, to be sure, but it was the periodical—with its regularity of publication, its spaces for direct interaction, and the practice of anonymous contributions—that made it a favored form for provincial citizens seeking access to the textual commons of English letters.

The permutations, contradictions, and paradoxes inherent in this fantasy are discussed at length in the pages to follow, but from the start we must acknowledge what remains even today a concept hard to fully grasp: Literary culture, and especially that grounded in the periodical form of the eighteenth century, was not based on great authors or national boundaries, the two cornerstones of literary history in our modern university (despite a half century of theory militating against them). It was premised instead on a close, highly interactive relationship between writers, readers, publishers, and editors—an attempt to replicate in print the intimacies, conversations, politics, and aesthetics of the club and the coffeehouse. It saw borrowings and recyclings as neither theft nor as homage but as something closer to what we today would call "remix" culture—the means for participating in a perpetually replenishing commons on which a new literary culture might be founded.

My gesture to remix culture is more than a desperate attempt to make a dusty archive seem more hip and relevant. After all, precisely because of the living, interactive nature of this periodical culture, the early magazine will remain to some degree a hive of bees trapped in amber. We can imaginatively reconstruct the activity of that hive and its relationship to the larger ecosystems of its time, but we cannot ever fully set it in motion again. And yet, the changing nature of the text in the digital age—the ways in which, for instance, we see the increasing collapse between author and reader, or the mounting cultural and technological challenges to the inviolability of intellectual property or the authority of both author and critic—bring us today closer to the place where our story begins in the early years of the eighteenth century. It serves as a reminder, perhaps most importantly for the literary history that must be now rewritten in the twenty-first century, of how very short the reign of the novel, the author, and the critic has been—and as a reminder that, for all the treasures the reign of this literary culture has brought us, it was from the start a selection that served those (such as publishers, authors, and scholars) who sought to shore up their own profits, titles, and cultural authority. As profits, titles, and cultural authority are increasingly encroached upon once again in the reemerging textual commons of the digital age, we might return to the periodical culture of the eighteenth century as a kind of road-not-taken to see what lessons we might usefully and productively translate into the metamorphosing literary culture of our own time.

II

In order to begin telling this story, we must go back a couple of decades before the first modern magazines of the 1730s, to a space that has been extensively excavated and even somewhat idealized in recent decades: the coffeehouse of the late seventeenth and early eighteenth centuries. The coffee-house, associated most explicitly with the Whigs and rising urban economies and socialities, emerged in England in the late 1600s in part as an alterna-tive to the increasing paralyzing codes of the court. Outside of the watchful eye of the courts and its baroque rituals and etiquette, the coffeehouse was a space where the social border-crossings necessary for the transaction of new commercial, political, and cultural exchanges could take place. It was a place where intellectuals and wits could forge their own mock "courts" and "little senates" distinct from the corridors of official power; and it was a space where old money and new business could find common cause free from the roadblocks of traditional class structures.

The coffeehouse and the rise of the periodical form are famously inter-twined, most explicitly in Addison and Steele's periodical productions, the *Tatler* and the *Spectator*, both written from, about, and for the denizens of these establishments. But it should be remembered that when Steele and Addison set out in the early eighteenth century to publish their periodical sheets, they were seeking as much to reform the coffeehouse society as to celebrate it. During the height of the plots and conspiracies that dominated the previous generation, Roger L'Estrange, a devout Tory, had satirized the coffeehouse Whigs as responsible for fomenting turmoil: "We are come to govern our selves by Dreams and Imaginations; We make every *Coffeehouse Tale* an Article of our Faith; and from Incredible Fables we raise Invincible Arguments."[19] By the late seventeenth century, the coffeehouse had become firmly associated with the "coffee-house politician": "He is one whose Brains having been once over-heated, retain something of the Fire in 'em ever after. He mistakes his Passion for Zeal, and his Noise and Bustling, for Services. He is always full of Doubts, Fears, and Jealousies, and is never without some notable Discovery of a deep laid Design, or a dangerous Plot found out in a *Meal Tub*, or *Petticoat*."[20] In the heady days that led to the emergence of the party system that would define both British and colonial political life for centuries to come, the coffeehouses had served as a vital network in the circulation of the newspapers, pamphlets, and conspiracies, and often as the origins for many of the accusations that led men to the scaffold or rioters to the streets. Thus it was that following the ascension of William and Mary and especially in the relative calm of Anne's reign, the coffeehouse came increasingly to be associated with the instabilities of the previous generation, and the coffeehouse politician was understood as a danger both to home and state. As Mary Astell described this familiar object of scorn in 1696: "He lodges at home, but he lives at the *Coffeehouse*. He converses more with *News Papers*, *Gazettes* and *Votes*, than with his *Shop Books*, and his constant Application to the *Publick* takes him off all Care for his *Private Concern*. He is always settling the *Nation*, yet cou'd never manage his own Family."[21]

Addison and Steele from the start of their collaborations sought to reform the coffeehouse, their own party (the Whigs), and the nation as a whole in terms that were responsive to the critiques of Astell and others. They ridicule the coffeehouse politician Astell describes in terms that will be central for the defense of periodical culture on both sides of the Atlantic in the years to come. Mr. Spectator explicitly offers his periodical in opposition to the foreign news and political intrigue that dominated the newspapers that littered the late seventeenth-century coffeehouse: "Is it not much better to be let into the Knowledge of ones-self, than to hear what passes in *Muscovy* or *Poland*; and to amuse our selves with such Writings as tend to the wearing out of Ignorance, Passion, and Prejudice, than such as naturally conduce to inflame Hatreds, and make Enmities irreconcileable?"[22] The *Spectator* from the start opposed itself to the newspaper, a media only slightly older than the periodical sheet. And it shared with Astell a commitment to family, private life, and manners and a rejection of the traditional coffeehouse topics of intrigue, politics, and public commerce. In both the *Tatler* and the *Spectator*, Steele and Addison set out to celebrate a middle way between the disengagement of a wholly private life and the flames of public business. As Steele puts it in *Tatler* no. 172, "To manage well a great Family, is as worthy an Instance of Capacity, as to execute a great Employment."[23] The coffeehouse they reimagine is modeled in the periodicals themselves: a place of moderation and balance, where the managing of private and public affairs, families, and business, are intimately connected at every turn—and where the rules, manners, and tastes (now fallen into a "desperate State of Vice and Folly") which Mr. Spectator will "recover" for them will help restore the vital relationship between public and private concerns and the balance and moderation necessary for success in both spheres.

Addison and Steele celebrated the coffeehouse as the ideal place for men of a certain "Temper," men drawn neither to the pomp of high society nor the anarchy of the lower orders, a place where caffeinated "Conversation" was the primary pleasure and, when properly regulated and judged by a periodical "Censor" (a title Steele claims for himself in the *Tatler*), its own reward. The ideal citizen of the coffeehouse societies are those whose tempers lie between the two extremes, neither "too Active to be happy and well pleased in a private Condition" nor "too warm to make them neglect the Duties and Relations of life."[24] As an example of the ideal "governor" of coffeehouse society, they tell the story of "Eubulus," who serves as judge, executor, and advisor to all around him. In his coffeehouse court, Eubulus exercises as great a power as the queen does over her courtiers—but with the crucial difference that Eubulus's power derives naturally from his talents, his reason, and his judgment and *not* from genealogy, dress, or connections. Eubulus will have a long afterlife in American periodicals of the early national period; in the *New-York Magazine* in 1791, for example, "The Scribbler" describes *his* Eubulus as offering "a pleasing view of the dispensations of providence to the virtuous and the wise. . . . Happy will it be for my young readers if they imitate the virtues of *Eubulus*."[25]

In the pages of the *Spectator*, the coffeehouses are reimagined as a networked society unto itself. The coffeehouse provides Mr. Spectator with his topics, with his readers, with his correspondence; it is a self-circulating world in which a man may hope to "Print my self out . . . before I Die," as Addison writes in the first number.[26] The periodical papers that emerge from and circulate through these establishments serve in print to represent, connect, and extend the various localities into a larger virtual society through imitation and recycling. Like Eubulus in his diurnal court, Mr. Spectator promises in his periodical court to serve the common good and to promote virtue and value wherever it is found. And in this way, Mr. Spectator offers himself as a model for imitation, just as in the coffeehouse "every Man [becomes] *Eubulus* as soon as his Back is turn'd."[27] In the *Spectator*, every reader is invited—indeed, encouraged—to become Mr. Spectator himself as soon as the issue is read, including those denied regular access to the physical space of the coffeehouse and its conversations (for example, women, apprentices, people living in the outskirts of London, or those at the far reaches of the empire).

Of the many issues that Addison and Steele addressed in their periodical essays, one in particular was of great importance to the American periodical culture that would follow: the question of the economy and utility of periodical reading and writing itself. From the start they worked to define their intellectual and creative labors in the periodical marketplace as operating in a sphere that was neither that of the artisan nor the aristocrat while at the same time intimately bound up with both. In many ways, Addison and Steele most explicitly defined their labors as being structurally similar to that of the rising class of commercial traders and investors, those who make value from exchange and speculation. Indeed, the term Addison especially enjoys playing with in this regard is "Speculations"—a term used in the *Spectator* to describe meditations, financial investments, and keen observation (the superpower Mr. Spectator claims to have acquired through his constitutional taciturnity). But the play on the term extends even further: It is introduced, in fact, in no. 3 as being synonymous with "late Rambles," the endless walks Mr. Spectator describes himself taking around the city. This point of introduction is particularly interesting since this is the essay in which Addison's Mr. Spectator visits the Bank of England and has his extended vision of the beauty and power of Lady Credit. But equally influential for American readers, structurally bound by the colonial system to trade and commerce, was the notion that the world of trade, credit, and commerce might *not* be anathema to literary and intellectual exchange.

It is important to appreciate how very much against the grain this argument was at the time. For most observers of early commercial life, the men of the Exchange (linked almost invariably with the coffeehouse politician in the late seventeenth century) were one step removed from barbarians—as one ungenerous but not atypical commentator put it in 1709, the speculator is "a Compound of *Knave, Fool, Shopkeeper, Merchant*, and *Gentleman*," while another still more vituperative author in 1696 labeled the whole class "cruel ill-natur'd Monsters" and "the destroyers and devourers of most Mens

Substance."[28] Associated with deviants and the "foreigners" who made the 'Change their place of both pleasure and business, there were few positive portrayals before Addison and Steele of those who did their business at the Exchange. When Addison therefore declares, as he does at the start of *Spectator* no. 69, that "There is no Place in the Town which I so much love to frequent as the *Royal-Exchange*," and goes on to describe how his "Heart naturally overflows with Pleasure at the sight of a prosperous and happy Multitude, insomuch that at many publick Solemnities I cannot forbear expressing my Joy with Tears that have stolen down my Cheeks," he is offering a radically different response to speculation than would have been found in the pamphlets or the pulpits of his day.[29] Thus "speculations" by Mr. Spectator, this "Lover of Mankind," allow him to see speculators themselves as the force that "knit[s] Mankind together," in ways parallel and inextricably bound to art and culture, and not opposed. It is in the periodical that this redefined "speculator" is first imagined.

For Addison and Steele, the "speculations" of the periodical served a vital role in that work of "knit[ting] Mankind together," here circulating art and commerce along common and mutually beneficial wires. Perhaps nowhere in the *Spectator* is this more fully imagined than in no. 367, where Addison meditates at length about the "two kinds of Benefits which accrue to the Publick from these my Speculations."[30] What he calls the "formal" advantages—the improvements his readers experience as a result of their daily reading—he feels he has sufficiently explored at length in earlier issues; but here he determines to catalogue the equally meaningful "material" advantages that extend even to people who never read a single *Spectator*, or even read at all. He details the amount of paper required for the publication of his periodical and the many economies that are affected by the extent and volume of this trade—even to the point of following the ragpickers and other nocturnal tradesmen of the growing city in gathering and recycling the raw materials that will be transformed into the next issue of the magazine: "In short, when I trace in my Mind a Bundle of Rags to a Quire of *Spectators*, I find so many Hands employ'd in every Step they take thro' their whole Progress, that while I am writing a *Spectator*, I fancy my self providing Bread for a Multitude."[31]

Articulated in 1712, this fantasy would captivate the men and women who would devote unaccountable energy to the periodical form in colonial America and the early United States over the course of the next century: the ideal of a form that could make, quite literally, a business out of literature and a literature out of business, establishing a network along which ideas could travel, connecting diffuse centers of thought and commerce. It is no wonder that this idea was especially appealing to colonial Americans, living as they did at a vast distance from the metropolis and, often, from each other. It was the *Spectator* and the coffeehouse, two forms never easily transplanted to America, that remained the ideal toward which these men and women would work.

Of course, the ideal of London coffeehouse society as a place of rational conversation, of meritocracy and moderation, was always just that—an ideal. The realities on the ground were certainly much more cacophonous, unruly, and decidedly irrational, as many contemporary accounts suggest.[32] But it remains a powerful ideal for generations to come for readers who would never had the opportunity to set foot in a London coffeehouse.

Long after coffeehouses had themselves fallen out of fashion in Britain, the idea of the coffeehouse was still closely associated with the periodical in the colonies. Aitken's *Pennsylvania Magazine*, for example, listed its site of publication as being "opposite the London Coffee-House, Front-Street." Philadelphia's London Coffee House had been established in 1754 to provide a meeting place for merchants and city leaders to gather, to share news, but perhaps most importantly to replicate the coffeehouse culture of London that they or their parents had left behind. Unlike traditional London coffeehouses, however, Philadelphia's London Coffee House was funded by subscription, with the printer William Bradford as the chief promoter and manager.[33] Aitken ran a successful credit business alongside his printing business through connections he made there, and the location of his printing shop across the street from the coffee shop was no accident. Here he sold beautiful calf-bound editions of the *Spectator* to Hopkinson and others and forged the contacts that would converge, however briefly, in the creation of his magazine.[34]

In truth, Philadelphia's London Coffee House was closer to a genteel tavern than a coffeehouse; liquors were sold, and the governor and his men held court there on a regular basis. As David S. Shields points out, tavern culture was much more prominent in colonial America than was the coffeehouse culture of London.[35] Where the coffeehouse ideal that emerged in late-seventeenth-century England was an alternative space to the paralyzing and artificial codes of conduct of the court, in the colonies, tavern culture served in many ways as an extension of the community and power structures outside its doors.

The newspapers of the early eighteenth century are dotted with advertisements for merchandise for sale at neighborhood coffeehouses or announcements of the convening of a bankruptcy court or other official proceeding. So, for example, the *Boston News-Letter* in 1714 advertises that the Crown Coffee House on King Street will be the site of the sale of "Hollands-Duck, several sorts of Sail Cloth, Kentings, Linings, Earthern Ware, Iron Mongers Ware, Grind-stones, Cordage, Broad cloths, and several other sorts of Goods, which are to be dayly seen at the Warehouse of Capt. *Magon* on the New Long Wharff."[36] And in 1716 the same establishment served as the site where "all Persons that have any Debts to receive from the Estate of Mrs. *Susanna Gray* Widow, are desired to bring in their Accounts to the Commissioners for that Affair."[37] The Crown Coffee House had been built in 1711 by Jonathan Belcher, who would later serve as colonial governor of Massachusetts and, later, New Jersey. From the start, therefore, the coffeehouse in colonial America was not apart from but intimately bound up in colonial power.

After all, in colonial America, *every* space was a space apart, and so from the start the ideal of the coffeehouse was different. This explains in part why actual coffeehouse never truly thrived in the colonies. Even in establishments in the colonies titled "coffee-houses" alcohol was often consumed in higher quantity than caffeine, and unlike in Britain, laws governed how much time could be spent in a tavern or who could be prohibited entrance (slaves) or credit (sailors). And these "coffee-houses" served as a kind of neighborhood commons in a way very different from what was set forth in the *Spectator*. The tavern served as a site of entertainment for locals, a resting place for travelers, so frequent in the business of the far-flung colonies, and a makeshift place of business for traveling merchants or various ad hoc assemblies. While these were far from egalitarian spaces, as Sharon V. Salinger has shown, they were spaces that drew clientele from all ranks of society. Far from a space apart from everyday colonial society, the tavern culture of colonial America was a microcosm and a concentration of everyday life, reflecting the social structures and hierarchies of life outside the tavern.[38]

But if the coffeehouse failed to thrive as an economic and social institution, the club, the informal gathering of like-minded men of the mind, remained potent. The image that hovers in the mind's eye of all early American periodical editors and writers is found in the frontispiece to the bound "proceedings" of English literature's most famous "club"—a company of like-minded spirits, bound by taste, wit, and good feeling (as opposed to class, profession, or politics) (figure 1.2). The *Spectator*'s frontispiece represents precisely the kind of space where the ideal conversation would take place. The importance of this homosocial coffeehouse society to the development of modern English middle-class taste and culture was not lost on the empire's American cousins.[39] Yet without the same institutional structures in place where the club could meet and exchange ideas, the *periodical* became the thing itself. Eighteenth-century colonials and young republicans came to invest heavily in the ideal of the periodical as a place where even those denied access to the coffeehouse might join in a kind of virtual coffeehouse.

Just as the virtual coffeehouse of the periodical came to be the idealized form for forging a new literary culture, Addison and Steele served as the ideal for English prose for generations of colonial Americans. This idealization was not unique to the colonies, by any means. It begins as early as John Gay's celebration of their influence on the morals of a decadent nation: "'Tis incredible to conceive the effect his Writings have had on the Town; How many Thousand follies they have either quite banish'd, or given a very great check to; how much Countenance they have added to Vertue and Religion; how many People they have render'd happy, by shewing them it was their own fault if they were not so; and lastly, how intirely they have convinc'd our Fops, and Young Fellows, of the value and advantages of Learning."[40] Despite such pronouncements, in their own day, the *Tatler* and the *Spectator*

Figure 1.2. Frontispiece to the bound volumes of the *Spectator* (1747) by C. Grignion after Francis Hayman.

were not universally admired and were often rightly associated with the political divisions of the day (the authors were both Whigs). But within a generation, the periodicals were held up almost universally as standing above the fray of new fashion, finance, and partisanship. And it was this ideal that was circulated regularly to the colonies in imported British periodicals. As early as the 1730s, we find Addison and Steele celebrated as "the best Prose Writers we have in *English*": "A careful Reading of the immortal Writings of a late Reign, will give you such a compleat Knowledge of the *English* Language in its greatest Perfection, as will make you a Judge and Master of Style."[41] Here the periodicals are revalued as national inheritance, a schoolroom for future generations of writers necessary to continue the important work of the previous generation.

This ideal would only be amplified in the coming decades. In his *Letters from a Nobleman to His Son* (1764), Goldsmith, looking back to the "Last Age," describes Addison as "deserv[ing] the highest regard and imitation. . . . Whatever he treated of was handled with elegance and precision; and that virtue, which was taught in his writings, was enforced by his example."[42] Samuel Johnson's portrait of Addison in his *Lives of the Poets* (1779–81) argued that the "Tatler and the Spectator . . . were published at a time when two parties, loud, restless, and violent, . . . were agitating the nation; to minds heated with political contest, they supplied cooler and more inoffensive reflections."[43] For Johnson, "Before the Tatler and Spectator, . . . England had no masters of common life. No writers had yet undertaken to reform either the savageness of neglect, or the impertinence of civility; to shew when to speak, or to be silent; how to refuse, or how to comply." For those who wish to master what Johnson terms "the middle style" or the true "English style, familiar but not coarse, and elegant but not ostentatious," the only course is to "give his days and nights to the volumes of Addison."[44]

Goldsmith and Johnson knew of what they were speaking, having both undertaken extended periodical projects in the style of the *Tatler* and the *Spectator*, Goldsmith in *The Citizen of the World* (1760–61) and Johnson in *The Rambler* (1750–52). Nonetheless, by the time of the first sustained American periodical experiments, it was understood in the colonies that the ideal of Addison and Steele had been largely squandered by a decadent mother country. As with their Calvinist forebears, the American periodical editor saw the New World as a place where the City on the Hill—or its secular antitype, the virtual coffeehouse—might be restored. Unlike John Winthrop and his cohorts, however, the latter-day Addisons and Steeles in America had little faith in the fitness of their fellow citizens, and they had no illusions about the challenges that lay ahead. Where Addison and Steele confronted a generation of educated Londoners and told them to their face that they were, as Gay put it, "a parcel of Fops, Fools, and vain Cocquets," their colonial descendants had to confront a generation of mercers, farmers, and provincial burghers who cared little for learning and less for manners. But if the challenges were daunting, the reward was too tempting for many to pass up: to become an American Addison—and in the process not only bring credit to colonial (and later, early national) America but ultimately restore the great English republic of letters. In these terms, these early periodical reformers were very much the Enlightenment counterpart to Anne Bradstreet's generation, when she imagined in 1642 in her "A Dialogue Between Old England and New" a purified New England returning finally to redeem and reform the degenerate Old World.

III

The American *Spectator* made its first appearance in colonial America in James Franklin's *New-England Courant*, technically the third newspaper published in Boston but arguably the first "magazine." Unlike its predecessors, which published proclamations and imported news from London gazettes (always weeks or months late), Franklin's *Courant* looked in more like an issue of the *Spectator*, opening each issue with witty meditations on philosophical topics and chastising its readers to reform. In its first issue in 1721, the *Courant* introduces its guiding spirit in much the same playful terms that Steele introduced his Mr. Spectator a decade earlier, promising the future contributions of a club of collaborators. While the *Courant* differentiated itself from the rival *Boston News-Letter* in promising to "*soar now and then with* the grave Wits *of the Age*," almost immediately the *Courant* became embroiled in the smallpox inoculation controversy, making it unique among colonial periodicals for taking strong and controversial positions on local issues of the day.[45] From the start, Franklin's *Courant* set itself up as a secular pulpit and directly challenged the Boston ministers, including Cotton Mather himself.

As Benjamin Franklin famously records in his *Autobiography*, his older brother's efforts to translate the spirit of the *Spectator* to Boston resulted in his imprisonment for mocking religious and political authority in the town, the result of which was that young Ben was nominally put in charge of the paper once James was stripped of his right to edit a newspaper. And it was this promotion, however ceremonial, that famously provided the younger brother the leverage necessary to break his indentures and flee to Philadelphia, a turn that would shape the history of American print culture.

But before Franklin earned his freedom from his apprenticeship, he earned perhaps an equally valuable prize in the pages of the *Courant*. The issue for April 9, 1722, introduces a new correspondent who promises to serve as the "Enemy to Vice, and a Friend to Vertue. . . . I have likewise a natural Inclination to observe and reprove the Faults of others, at which I have an excellent Faculty. I speak this by Way of Warning to all such whose Offences shall come under my Cognizance, for I never intend to wrap my Talent in a Napkin."[46] This is the widow "Silence Dogood," Franklin's first persona and the beginnings of his career as author. As he records it in his *Autobiography*, "being still a Boy, and suspecting that my Brother would object to printing any Thing of mine in His paper if he knew it to be mine, I contriv'd to disguise my Hand, and, writing an anonymous Paper, I put it in at Night under the Door of the Printing-House." The anonymity of the periodical allowed the apprentice the "exquisite pleasure" of hearing James's friends praise the essay and, in guessing at its author, "nam[ing] . . . Men of some Character among us for Learning and Ingenuity."

The "exquisite pleasure" of this moment was one that Benjamin Franklin would seek out for himself many times in the years to come. Print itself was the avenue to this buzz, but it was not *any* print that could provide it: only the strange combination of print and conversation that was represented by the periodical form. It was precisely where periodical and "club" came together—in America a space found not in the coffeehouse but in the print shop where James's friends lounged, debated, and judged the previous week's productions, and then set about writing new entries to fuel the engines for the coming week's conversations. Although biographers have often focused on the "pleasures" of fooling his brother, the deeper pleasure of the scene for young Ben came from his validation by the club. As he records the encounter in his *Autobiography*, it was the discovery of the *Spectator* in his brother's shop that served as his schoolmaster as he trained himself to write by essentially reverse-engineering the essays: cutting them up and then reassembling them: "By comparing my Work afterwards with the original, I discover'd many faults and amended them; but I sometimes had the Pleasure of Fancying that in certain Particulars of small Import, I had been lucky enough to improve the Method or the Language and this encourag'd me to think I might possibly in time come to be a tolerable English Writer, of which I was extreamly ambitious."[47] If the *Spectator* was his schoolroom, the "Silence Dogood" essays were his final exam, and the exquisite pleasure lay in having passed the test, one in which his talents were judged not by his name or his age but by his words and their effects. When Addison praised "the many Letters which come to me from Persons of the best Sense in both Sexes," he made it clear that his judgment was not based on the authors' positions in society or the elegance of their exteriors; instead, "I may pronounce their Characters from their Way of Writing."[48] The amateur, anonymous journalism afforded by the periodical allowed even an apprentice boy to be recognized as a "person of the best sense."

For decades much critical energy has been devoted to disproving the notion "that the [Dogood] *Papers* are little more than imitation" of the *Spectator*.[49] Against this assumption, George F. Horner and many to follow have argued that a unique "American" "vernacular style" marks what was "original" in Franklin's prose. Although this work has contributed to our appreciation of Franklin as a prose writer, ultimately the privileging of individual genius and exceptional "Americanness" has perpetuated the neglect and systematic misreading of the tradition out of which Franklin and the American periodical emerge. The *Courant* in general and "Silence Dogood" in particular mark the beginning of a century-long attempt to resurrect the spirit of the *Spectator* and the *Tatler* in America—not to "Americanize" them, but, Frankenstein-like, to reassemble and reanimate them. Almost all of the notable phrases and vernacularisms in Franklin's "Dogood" essays can be traced back to the materials he found in Addison and Steele. "I never intend to wrap my Talent in a Napkin" (no. 1) references a quotation from Bacon found in *Tatler* no. 267: "I have [not] put [it] into a Napkin."[50] The topic of "Silence Dogood" no. 4, chastising the students at university as so many "blockheads," is one found throughout the *Spectator*, and its form is a direct allusion to the "vision" genre of the periodical essay that Addison made famous. (Dogood even describes herself as empowered by her role as a "Spectator" in this vision, in case any reader might not catch the genealogy being established here.) And Franklin introduces his persona in terms that are meant to remind all readers immediately of the introduction of Mr. Spectator: "[S]ince it is observed, that the Generality of People, now a days, are unwilling either to commend or dispraise what they read, until they are in some measure informed who or what the Author of it is, whether he be *poor* or *rich, old* or *young*, a *Schollar* or a *Leather Apron Man*, &c. and give their Opinion of the Performance, according to the Knowledge which they have of the Author's Circumstances, it may not be amiss to begin with a short Account of my past Life and present Condition, that the Reader may not be at a Loss to judge whether or no my Lucubrations are worth his reading."[51]

When we compare this to Addison's introduction of his persona one decade earlier, it becomes clear that Franklin, while eager to hide his own authorship, is equally determined to have the *Spectator*'s imprimatur be clearly legible: "I have observed, that a Reader seldom peruses a Book with Pleasure 'till he knows whether the Writer of it be a black or a fair Man, of a mild or cholerick Disposition, Married or a Batchelor, with other Particulars of the like nature, that conduce very much to the right Understanding of an Author."[52]

But perhaps the most explicit borrowing from Addison and Steele can be found in Franklin's use of the word "lucubration." Defined in Blount's 1661 *Glossographia* as "a study or work by candlelight," the word came into occasional use in the seventeenth century to refer to nocturnal meditations, mental work completed often after hours, often rough or unfinished. The term might be used self-disparagingly by an author to downplay the pretentions of the work being published, or disparagingly to refer to the pedantic (worse yet, monkish) habits of the scholar. It was in the early eighteenth century, and most visibly in Steele and Addison's periodical essays, that the term began to take on more positive meanings. In fact, despite being up to that point an infrequently used term, "lucubration" shows up well over fifty times in the *Tatler* and *Spectator* alone. Here, the term begins to take on particular meanings that become central to the ideal of periodical culture that is imported to the colonies. As Bickerstaffe (Steele) introduces his project in the *Tatler* no. 4, for example, he explicitly announces that "we . . . are labouring to make our Lucubrations come to some Price in Money, for our more convenient Support in the Service of the Publick."[53] By definition, lucubrations were "profitless" writing: the freelance ramblings of an endowed scholar or an insomniac divine. In announcing a profit motive alongside and inextricably bound up with the goals of public service, Steele is reconceiving the term as one of binding, economically as well as intellectually, author and reader together. And unlike the earlier associations, here lucubrations are always public minded: "I have with great Application studied the publick Emolument: To this End serve all my Lucubrations."[54]

The very term itself becomes suggestive of the strange borderland space of the periodical: somewhere between conversation and writing, between private and public, between embodied and spectral. The exchange of periodical lucubrations is a shadow economy, but it is an economy nonetheless. In *Tatler* no. 270 Bickerstaffe can confidently proclaim that "Notices from Persons of different Sexes and Qualities are a sufficient Instance how useful my Lucubrations are to the Publick."[55] But when the investment of his talents in these lucubrations does not result in an equivalent return from his readers, the whole enterprise begins to fall apart. That the world of these circulating lucubrations in the periodical should become envisioned as a kind of shadow economy, mimicking in many ways the notes being traded and the commodities being valued at the same coffee houses, is not surprising. What is worth noting, however, is that the economic ideal of the periodical lucubration is always one that is based on trade but remains in many ways rooted in a traditional economy of barter and exchange. This is not work for hire, official writing, or courtly writing, but freelance work, and as such the customer, the reader, is always the final arbiter of its worth and value.

If Franklin's success in some real measure emerges out of his chance encounter with the *Spectator* volume, his future success follows from a series of chance encounters with men—governors and leather-apron men alike—who recognize in him a kinship forged through a shared taste for a certain kind of reading and writing the *Spectator* and other early periodicals had taught them to emulate. Indeed, Franklin understood the *Spectator* essays to be so essential to his own education and eventual success that they would feature prominently in his proposal for an English school in 1751, in which he suggests that second graders should work with "some of the easier *Spectators*," fifth graders would be given "the Sentiments of a *Spectator*" to "cloath" in their own words, while the sixth grade would study, among other canonical works, "the higher Papers in the *Spectator*."[56] What the periodical form meant to Franklin cannot be underestimated. It imagined a world where merit triumphed over caste and where reinvention through imitation was not only possible but the fundamental law of the land. Franklin's career can be understood, with little exaggeration, as a series of attempts to reassemble the *Spectator* essays in homespun: Silence Dogood, Busy-Body, Poor Richard, and especially the acerbic persona of the *Autobiography* are all different orderings of the substance and style he learned from reading those essays. Even the quality that most infuriated many of his contemporaries—his stubborn silence in public debate—can be seen to be adapted from the studied "profound Silence" of Mr. Spectator.[57]

What we have been trained by two hundred years of cultural nationalism to see as signs of an inchoate, incoherent, and insecure literary culture—the open borrowing of style, subject matter, and often the substance itself from other periodical sources—is something else entirely. Franklin saw the imitation, copying, and adaptation of the best English periodical essays as the means to gain him access to the idealized club as portrayed on the frontispiece to the *Spectator*; like Johnson and Goldsmith, he also saw his participation in this particular form of labor, these lucubrations, as fundamentally English and of fundamental importance to the preservation of English values and virtue. As with everything in his career, for Franklin personal pleasure (the pleasure of hearing his anonymous work praised by his brother's club, for example) and public good (say, the good of chastising the morals of Harvard students or the arrogance of Mather and his fellow divines) should always go hand in hand. And it was in the periodical form that this marriage could best be imagined.

By the 1730s, Franklin was a successful Philadelphia printer, having launched a newspaper and *Poor Richard's Almanack*. In part due of these endeavors, Franklin would become extremely wealthy and powerful, eventually supplanting his predecessor, Andrew Bradford. And yet by the end of the decade, even as he was fighting for huge stakes, Franklin devoted immense resources in the race for the seemingly dubious distinction of publishing the "first American magazine." We have a strong image in our mind of colonial Americans—and perhaps Franklin most of all—as eminently practical. So what compelled him, at considerable risk and cost, to engage in a literary duel over the claim to the new periodical form of the magazine? That Franklin would vie strenuously with his rival Bradford for the bragging rights to the "first American magazine" is in some ways not surprising. For the colonial printer, the magazine represented their rights to hold the doors to the virtual club, the periodical coffeehouse, and the ability to provide access to a still larger conversation, one that extended beyond the chance encounters and literary cruising that made Franklin's career, beyond even the leather-apron clubs to which Franklin devotes an inordinate amount of time in his *Autobiography*.

Further, the new term that had come to define the form—*magazine*—strengthened the connection already central to the form between the newer networks of trade and commerce and the more abstract and ancient networks of culture, knowledge, and identity. Contemporaneous with its definition as a storehouse for munitions, the term had first come into use in the sixteenth century to describe the commercial warehouse, a structure newly brought into existence by the surpluses of modern trade and speculation. Its most familiar usage today, however, describing a miscellaneous periodical publication, was largely the invention of one man, Edward Cave, who expanded on the periodical sheet formula developed by Addison, Steele, and their contemporaries, and created the first successful multiauthored regular periodical, the *Gentleman's Magazine*, in 1731.

Almost immediately the new *Gentleman's Magazine* was acknowledged as something important by the earliest colonial newspapers. The *Boston News-Letter*, for example, the oldest of the Boston papers, began regularly turning to the *Gentleman's Magazine* as a source for its "advices" about world events, including exchange rates, preparations for war, and other information especially of value to the colonial trader and investor, and within a few years the *Gentleman's Magazine* and its rival, the *London Magazine*, were the primary source in the colonies for intelligence of the world across the Atlantic.

In truth, although the majority of the colonial readers would not know it from the contents reprinted in the papers, the *Gentleman's Magazine* was not devoted first and foremost to international news and economic records. A typical early issue in February 1737, for example, featured an account of the ongoing struggle to measure longitude; a comic tale, "Annals of a Modern Traveller"; a long letter from one Ignis Fatuus to the editorial persona of the *Gentleman's Magazine*, Sylvanus Urban, detailing an encounter with a personification of the *London Magazine*, Cave's Whiggish rival in the field; mathematical essays; a debate about the Swedish constitution; a satirical account of a Parliament of Old Maids; and extensive excerpts from various coffeehouse periodical sheets, including *The Craftsman* and *Common Sense, or the Englishman's Journal*, a new periodical paper that claimed to "take on all Subjects whatsoever, and try them by the Standard of *Common Sense*."[58] Especially in its first decade, the *Gentleman's Magazine* essentially sought to network the various periodicals themselves, compiling, engaging, and debating them, turning the magazine itself into an amphitheater in which the growing cacophony of the four-page sheets could be organized.

In the years since the launching of James Franklin's *Courant*, there had been few other attempts to duplicate the periodical form of the *Spectator* in the colonies. The *Gentleman's Magazine*, however, offered a different model, one disassociated from the physical space of the coffeehouse or the personalities gathered around a particular club. The magazine, unlike the periodical sheet, found its authority and its form in the *editorial function*. Cave's Sylvanus Urban emerged as the epitome of the editor, he who could organize the growing chaos of print voices and the expanding network of information and distill from it the essence of what was truly useful and entertaining. This was especially true in the earliest years of the new magazine, when the bulk of the *Gentleman's Magazine* was culled from the papers and periodicals around London.

In Philadelphia, both Bradford and Franklin followed the practice of the Boston papers in excerpting from the *Gentleman's Magazine*. There was a difference, however, in *what* each chose to reprint from Cave's magazine. Where Bradford's choices of materials were largely those that could have been found in a traditional newspaper—foreign news and market reports—Franklin often focused on the other kinds of materials that made the *Gentleman's Magazine* different from the newspaper form. For example, in September 1737, the *Pennsylvania Gazette* reprinted on the front page "Annals of a Modern Traveller" from the February issue of the *Gentleman's*

Magazine. With so much to choose from, it is interesting that Franklin gravitated to this particular contribution. It tells the story of a young Irish heir who, upon receiving his fortune, realizes that "this was too great a Fortune to be spent in such a Country as *Ireland*," upon which he begins his career as a traveler, turning his back on cultivating his land.[59] In the course of his travels he acquires all kinds of knowledge necessary to the making of a modern gentleman, including skills in cocks and dogs, dueling, gambling, fashion, seduction, and finally speculation—ultimately throwing away what remained of his fortune on John Law's Mississippi Company venture.

Within the context of the *Gentleman's Magazine*, this was pretty standard fare: a country critique of the Whiggish nouveau riche, of cosmopolitan fashions, and especially of the destruction of old money and tradition by newfangled financial instruments such as trading in Mississippi Company shares. The detailing of the erosion of the Traveller's woods and estates in the course of his speculations underscored what was a familiar criticism of modern "economies." And within the London context, of course, the Irishman's pretentions to being a gentleman and a "Man of the World" were meant to be source of ridicule, the provincial bumpkin pretending to a place in the world he could never occupy without being an embarrassment to himself and others.

In reprinting the sketch on the front page of the *Pennsylvania Gazette*, however, it becomes a different thing. Franklin, after all, is no Tory. In 1729, for example, he had published *A Modest Enquiry into the Nature and Necessity of Paper-Currency*, arguing explicitly why paper money was vital to a colonial economy dependent on trade. For Franklin the bite of the piece lay in its critique not of the Traveller's engagement in speculative economy and urban pleasures, nor in the fact that he was Irish, but in the Traveller's belief that he was too good for his provincial home. For Franklin, all the misfortunes that follow stem from the Traveller's conviction that virtue, nobility, and value are only to be found in the capitals of Europe, instead of in an industrious and vigorous life in the margins of the empire. That the Traveller's misadventures eventually led him to America must have surely amused Franklin all the more, as the Irishman finds his final ruin on these shores in imagining he could make his fortune by investing in the labor of others (mediated in this case by Law, a corrupt agent of the French government).

I pause over this one sketch because it reminds us that transatlantic reprint culture was a complex thing, not reducible to source texts and authorial meaning—nor would anyone at the time have imagined it is so. Transposing the sketch from the *Gentleman's Magazine* to his Philadelphia newspaper, Franklin was making of it a different thing for a different audience. But he was also explicit in his citation of the *Gentleman's Magazine* as his source; in this age before modern intellectual property law, such citation was usually a sign that the editor wanted to claim something from the source. In the case of Bradford or the *News-Letter*, the promise that foreign intelligence was coming direct from the *Gentleman's Magazine* assured the reader that the news was already vetted and distilled by the most reputable periodical in London. In addition, Bradford, as the postmaster of the city prior to 1737, could use the specific issue from which he was copying the information to advertise the speed with which he was receiving issues from London.

In the case of Franklin, however, the act of reprinting was intended to make a different kind of statement. In September 1737, Franklin was about to take over from Bradford as postmaster, who had used the power invested in the office to restrict the circulation of Franklin's paper. Franklin, upon assuming the office, must have felt his old rival all but vanquished, and he was beginning to set his eyes on other goals. He no longer sought after the news and information from Europe from the *Gentleman's Magazine*; as postmaster for Philadelphia he would have other ways of accessing such information as all mails now flowed through his office. Instead, what he longed for was to do in America what Cave had done in London: to create a magazine that excerpted the best of the periodical press and, through its network of contacts and associates, worked to flesh out the rest of the issues with original contributions like the "Annals of a Modern Traveller." Just as his brother James had earlier recognized that what made the *Spectator* special was not its news but its form and its conceit of the club, the space for frank critique and reform of manners of the great and the small, so Franklin saw in the *Gentleman's Magazine* the next logical step in the development of the form—and his own claims as its American heir.

It is almost certainly around this time that Franklin first developed the idea of starting his own magazine. But he had many distractions at the end of the 1730s, including the establishment of his post office and the seemingly endless battles with Bradford, who refused to play the part of vanquished rival. In 1740, however, Franklin set out in earnest to bring his magazine to life. As Gordon S. Wood writes, Franklin at this time "found himself caught between two worlds, between that of aspiring artisans and tradesmen and that of wealthy gentlemen, with whom he mingled constantly."[60] He saw the magazine as a way of bridging that gap; after all, Cave had proved the magazine as the ideal place where artisans and gentry, printers and societies of gentlemen, might come together.

Cave, like Franklin, had been born poor, the son of a cobbler, and was almost entirely self-educated. Franklin surely identified with Cave's transformation, which made him one of the most influential men in English literary society. By 1740 Cave could write with fairness that his magazine was "read as far as the English language extends."[61] Despite his own considerable success as a newspaper and almanac publisher, Franklin admired Cave's success in bridging successfully the worlds of tradesmen and gentlemen, and he saw the magazine as a way to emulate Cave's success in America, distancing himself once and for all from his rival, Bradford. In his *Autobiography* he had described Bradford as "very illiterate," distinguishing him from Keimer, the other printer he found in the city when Franklin first arrived in Philadelphia in 1723, whom he derided as "something of a Scholar" but "knowing nothing of Presswork."[62] The ideal for Franklin lay in embodying the two together—the artisan and the scholar. And this ideal was best represented by the *Gentleman's Magazine*, where Cave brought his skills as a pressman and as a man of letters together to create a unique space where all could come together, anonymously, and where even the son of a poor bookseller such as Samuel Johnson might, through his own talents and energies alone, rise to become the most eminent literary voice of his age.

In the preface to the 1740 volume of the *Gentleman's Magazine*, Samuel Johnson celebrated periodicals as "contribut[ing] very much to the Emolument of Society": "their Cheapness brings them into universal Use; their Variety adapts them to every one's Taste: The Scholar instructs himself with Advice from the literary World; the Soldier makes a Campaign in safety, and censures the Conduct of Generals without Fear of being punished for Mutiny; the Politician, inspired by the Fumes of the Coffee-pot, unravels the knotty Intrigues of Ministers; the industrious Merchant observes the Course of Trade and Navigation; and the honest Shop-keeper nods over the Account of a Robbery and the Prices of Goods, till his Pipe his out."[63] The ideal here of the periodical as a space where all walks of life would find common interest was to prove very seductive in America over the next century. For example, Charles Brockden Brown would reprint (without attribution, so universally shared had the ideal become) Johnson's piece in his *Literary Magazine* as late as 1805.[64] And for Benjamin Franklin, the founder of the Junto and the Library Company of Philadelphia, this ideal helps us understand why he was prepared to risk his name and his fortune on a venture that was almost certain to fail.

As it happened, Franklin's plans for his own *Gentleman's Magazine* became almost immediately embroiled in the complicated politics of newspapers, the post, and personal ambition, forces that would affect the fates of American magazines for the next several decades. As Postmaster Franklin after 1737, Franklin had "magnanimously" reversed his predecessor's practice by allowing Bradford's *Mercury* open access to the post (no doubt, believing that in doing so he exercised a measure of control over the content of that paper). But this policy was derailed in late 1739 when Alexander Spotswood, the postmaster for the colonies, ordered Franklin to "commence Suit" against Bradford for revenues owed.[65] Spotswood also ordered that Franklin "no longer suffer to be carried by the Post any of his News-Papers,"[66] obliging Bradford to assume the added expense of bribing the post riders, as Franklin himself had done when Bradford was postmaster.[67] Franklin hired a young Philadelphia lawyer, John Webbe, to handle the suit against Bradford.

Attracted to Webbe's literary sensibilities (and perhaps, despite himself, to his genteel background), Franklin outlined his plans for the magazine to the young lawyer, offering him the position as editor. Webbe apparently found the terms Franklin proposed decidedly ungenerous (Franklin was to claim the first half of all revenues in his capacity as printer, dividing the second half with Webbe as co-editors), and he repaid Franklin by bringing the plans for the magazine to Bradford.[68] On October 30, 1740, Webbe and Bradford advertised the prospectus for their own magazine in Bradford's *Mercury*, citing as inspiration the "Success and Approbation which the MAGAZINES, published in *Great Britain*, have met with for many Years past, among all Ranks and Degrees of People."[69]

While Bradford may well have been motivated in this undertaking by his enmity for Franklin, it is clear that Webbe, who was likely the author of the prospectus, had caught the periodical bug, and his prospectus is as comprehensive an account of the ambitions of the periodical editor as any we will find in the early American magazine, notwithstanding the fact that his own venture would last only three issues. Setting up the *American Magazine* as a journal for the whole of the colonies, including the West Indies, the prospectus promises to explain the laws of the colonies in clear language that all may understand and to communicate the grievances and complaints of the colonists back to England, where Webbe imagines his magazine would be of intense interest for much the same reason that each new issue of the *Gentleman's* or *London* magazines was eagerly awaited by the colonies. Further, he proposes to open up a space within the magazine for free inquiry and debate, where no party or faction can determine the shape of the conversation: "Here any Person, in whatever Colony residing, will find a ready Admittance to a fair and publick Hearing at all Times." The prospectus, in fact, takes up most of the issue of the *Mercury*, serving as one of the longest such documents (rivaled only by the monumental prospectus to the *Port-Folio* at the start of the next century). Its terms will serve as something of a catechism for most to follow: the rejection of partisanship and of libel and slander, the promise of a space for interactive debate and intellectual pursuit, commitment to reform of manners, the defense of freedom of the press, the benefit for future generations of historians, and the measured calm and editorial judgment inherent in monthly periodical publication.

While this "first magazine" is often treated as a historical footnote primarily interesting for its role in Franklin's biography, demonstrating little in the way of the wit and originality of its London models, there are aspects of its goals worth our attention. First, Bradford and Webbe sought to make theirs an "American" magazine; at a time long before anything resembling "national" identity had begun to stir in the colonies, we see the attempt to create something like a national periodical—to assemble the parts of the colonies together in the pages of their magazines into a coherent whole. The first issue of the *American Magazine*, for example, features an account of government in New Jersey, Pennsylvania, and Maryland. And the issue concludes with a reprint from the *London Magazine* citing a galaxy of "British Worthies," among whom is John Locke, which the editor suspects will be especially gratifying to the magazine's readers. In the second issue, the *American Magazine* promises several features that will be continued monthly, including proceedings from the assemblies in Maryland, Pennsylvania, New York, and New Jersey, and affairs from Europe. While the magazine would only last one more issue before Bradford became the first not only to start an American magazine but also the first to fold, with the third and final issue Bradford had begun to add longer essays on miscellaneous subjects, including "The Religion of the Indian Natives of America" and "An Essay towards explaining the Nature of Money." The magazine also opens up a debate with a correspondent about the interpretation of a debate in the Maryland assembly, one that it promises to continue in the following issue.

That issue never arrives, the first of countless interrupted serial conversations in the history of the early American periodical. Franklin's *General Magazine* would be the second. Indeed, Franklin surely knew, the minute he learned of Webbe's betrayal, that his own venture was doomed. He suggested in his advertisement for his *General Magazine* that Webbe had rushed out the prospectus to dissuade him from proceeding with his plans. In truth, giving up his own magazine in the face of Webbe and Bradford beating him to the punch was the logical thing to do, and in most business decisions Franklin was in every way a rational man. Instead, the prospectus for his *General Magazine*, published in the *Pennsylvania Gazette* on November 13, seemed anything but rational. Offering a compressed account of the contents of the proposed magazine, he promised that the first issue would be published in January, two months ahead of Webbe's planned first issue, and that it would not even require subscriptions, as the *American Magazine* did: "We shall publish the Books at our own Expence, and risque the Sale of them; which Method, we suppose, will be most agreeable to our Readers, as they will then be at Liberty to buy only what they like; and we shall be under a constant Necessity of endeavouring to make every particular Pamphlet worth their Money."[70] Franklin's business plan for the magazine was clearly suicidal; the magazine could not hope to survive without capital up front in the form of subscriptions, and it is clear from his advertisement that he is motivated more by vanquishing Webbe and Bradford's magazine than by having his own succeed. As it turned out, while the *American Magazine* would beat his to press by three days, Franklin's magazine would survive its rival by three months.

In many ways the two first magazines are hard to tell apart, but there are some interesting differences that become visible even in the short run of both magazines. While Franklin's makes fewer claims to "national" scope and range, from the first issue the *General Magazine* makes room for poetry, riddles, and correspondence. After March, perhaps emboldened by having the field to himself, Franklin begins to include more of the kinds of essays he most admires in the *Gentleman's Magazine*, including "The Character of a Gentleman" and an early epistolary seduction tale. And the "Historical Chronicle" that concludes each issue works to compile the various happenings around the world into a cohesive feature, in which the happenings in New England and Virginia are put in dialogue with events occurring in Persia and Russia. By the final issue in June, however, it is clear that the magazine is running out of material, and the issue is made up almost entirely of reprints from the newspapers.

The struggle to found the first American magazine did not make its way into Franklin's *Autobiography*; it was, after all, not a triumphant story, or one from which clear maxims or models might be gleaned. But even as he gave up the idea of founding a magazine of his own, he did not abandon his hopes for the form. Franklin's instincts that the magazine was the right medium for him to complete his metamorphosis into gentleman-artisan were on the mark, as he well knew by the 1750s. It was the *Gentleman's Magazine* that would do more to effect the transformation for Franklin than perhaps any other vehicle. After his experiments with electricity were essentially ignored by the Royal Society, it was the *Gentleman's Magazine* that first published them, when Peter Collinson, with whom Franklin had been corresponding, shared his letters with Cave. Cave also published the full correspondence in a separate pamphlet, *Experiments and Observations in Electricity.* The attention the magazine brought to Franklin led to his being awarded the Copley Medal by the Royal Society in 1753, a fact that the *Gentleman's Magazine* celebrated in its December issue. So it is not surprising that we see Franklin's ongoing interest in magazines into the 1750s, when he would contribute his sponsorship and pen to an ambitious periodical project under the editorship of his nephew Benjamin Mecom.

IV

Benjamin Mecom had from a young age demonstrated signs of a constitutional restlessness and "queerness" (as a young Isaiah Thomas would observe about him), and he had a very hard time settling into the model life that his uncle wished for him. He was a constant source of worry and vexation to his family, and given his devotion to Franklin, his failure to imitate the great man's example seems to have been especially baffling. When Benny was twenty, Franklin used his connections to send his nephew to Antigua, to run a print shop in which Franklin had an interest and to reestablish the local paper. The experience was a miserable one for Mecom by all accounts, and eventually he paid off what creditors he could, packed up the press, and sailed back to Boston to attempt to set up shop in what was already an overcrowded field.[71] Despite Franklin's obvious disappointment in his nephew, he recommended, of all things, that his nephew start a magazine in the style of the *Gentleman's Magazine* as a way to make a name for himself in the competitive field of Boston printers. Although it was probably the worst possible advice to give to a young disappointed man, one increasingly prone to bouts of depression that would eventually lead to his institutionalization, it is a sign of how very much Franklin continued to prize his ambition for a viable American magazine, now a full seventeen years after the failure of his own.

The previous years had seen few other attempts to launch a magazine, and only one of them any more successful than were the first forays of Franklin and Bradford. Taking its name from Bradford's late *American Magazine*, the new *American Magazine and Historical Chronicle* modeled itself on the *London Magazine* and had a run of over three years, the longest in the colonial period. Printed by Rogers and Fowle in Boston and edited by Jeremiah Gridley, who would go on to be an influential jurist, this new *American Magazine* focused less on original material (with the exception of some able contributions from Harvard undergraduates) and more on producing a worthy colonial compilation of the best of the London magazines.[72] Part of its relative success also lay in the development of a network of printer-booksellers who would seek to manage subscriptions and sell bound volumes of the magazine. Included in the list advertised were Ben Franklin in Philadelphia; Franklin's New York printing partner, James Parker; and Franklin's brother Peter in Rhode Island. Rogers and Fowle were themselves regular customers of Franklin's side business in wholesale paper. Thus we can see how the magazine early on became a node around which emerged a proto-national network of print—an early space in which an imagined community beyond the circulation of the local papers began to be literalized in American print.

While the second *American Magazine* was notable for being the first American magazine to survive more than a year, it was the *New-England Magazine* that Mecom established in 1758 that stands out for being the first true "American" magazine in the sense of being devoted to the ideal of forging a space apart from the cacophony of politics and business that so dominated colonial life and the local papers. In many ways, it was the job Mecom was born for, and if the magazine only survived a short time, it was not due to any lack of energy or wit on his part as editor.

In the first issue of the *New-England Magazine*, Mecom offers one of the most sophisticated analyses of the formal properties of the magazine form. In "The Quintessence of Books," Mecom's editorial persona, "Urbanus Filter," describes the "infinite Advantage" that authors who publish their thoughts in books have over one, like Filter himself, "who communicates his Writings to the World in loose Tracts and single Pieces." However, in an argument that will be developed over the course of the next half-century, Filter suggests that the advantages of book publication are all at the expense of the happiness and freedom of the *reader*. In a book, an author has the right to lay down the rules in a preface, including the rule "That a Man ought to be dull sometimes," and a reader is bound to submit to the rules governing the volume until finally released by its conclusion. Thus, Filter reminds us (borrowing from the *Spectator*), "*A great Book is a great Evil*."[73] In contrast, Filter defends the art of periodical publication, "that noble Art . . . truly calculated to diffuse Good Sense through the Bulk of a People." Through periodical publication, Filter continues, "Knowledge, instead of being bound up in Books, and kept in Libraries and Retirements, is *thus obtruded* upon the Public; when it is canvassed in every Assembly, and exposed upon every Table." Filter here directs his magazine to the particular attention of each "class" of person in turn, "Persons of all Conditions, and of each Sex," promising them within his pages the opportunity to fulfill their "Obligation to *improve their own Understanding*."[74] As Filter goes on to describe it, this obligation crosses all lines, and it is the primary responsibility of all citizens. Without a sense of this duty, as Mecom will spell out in explicitly revolutionary terms a few years later in his broadside *To the Publick of Connecticut*, all are reduced to "slaves," left impotent and unprotected as the "Monster" of tyranny works his will.[75] If it is "the necessary Duty ... of every Person living to *improve his Understanding*, to *inform his Judgment*, ... and to *acquire the Skill of good Reasoning*," it is the periodical publication alone that will allow him to fulfill this duty.

The very qualities that make the early magazine so frustrating to modern readers are precisely what mark it out as a unique form for the "cultivation" of a new citizenry: The magazine can resist tyranny precisely because it is so haphazardly ordered—because it contains "loose tracts and single Piece." Despite its seemingly random construction, however, Mecom insists that the magazine resists anarchy because of the firm but invisible hand of the editor. And it is through this perfect balance between these two extremes that the periodical will serve as the true engine of the next literary renaissance. For Mecom it is the variety of subjects and their juxtaposition in surprising and provocative combinations that provokes in the readers the imaginative spark: just as "a particular Smell or Colour is able to fill the Mind, on a sudden, with a Picture of the Fields or Gardens where we first met with it, and to bring up into View all the Variety of Images that once attended it," so too "Our Imagination takes the Hint, and leads us unexpectedly into Cities or Theaters, Plains or Meadows."[76]

It is hard not to hear echoes of a modernist manifesto from two centuries later here in Mecom's celebration of the power of the periodical to people new worlds in the imagination—as if reading one of William Carlos Williams's prefaces to his own little magazines. The idea here is that the fragment, the disjunction, the refusal of totalizing narratives and dominant univocal authorship alone can provide room for the reason and imagination of the individual reader to create new knowledge, to complete the conversation that the periodical seeks to inaugurate.

Mecom's *New-England Magazine* opens with the following playful dedication:

> Old-fashioned Writings and select Essays,
> Queer Notions, useful Hints, Extracts from Plays,
> Relations wonderful, and Psalm, and Song,
> Good-Sense, Wit, Humour, Morals, all *ding-dong;*
> Poems, and Speeches, Politics, and News,
> What *Some* will like, and other *Some* refuse;
> Births, Deaths, and Dreams, and Apparitions too;

With some *Thing* suited to each different *Goû*,
To humour HIM, and *Her*, and *me*, and YOU.[77]

This epigraph epitomizes everything in the early American magazine that
has marked it for such pointed critical neglect—a bizarre conglomeration
of hints, fragments, news, and death notices, of "queer notions" and "useful hints," of "politics and news" and "Apparitions too." To make matters
worse, Mecom proudly proclaims his deep indebtedness to British sources
in his choice of editorial persona, "Urbanus Filter," openly adapted from
the *Gentleman's Magazine*'s "Sylvanus Urban." Yet as we have already seen,
in Filter's playful and seemingly nonsensical defense of "all ding-dong"
there is very serious work at hand. "Ding-dong" had multiple meanings
for eighteenth-century readers, including, adverbially, "hammering away
at a subject" or, nominally, a jingle or playful rhyme. All these definitions
would make sense in the context of these lines, and there is every reason
to believe that Mecom intends all of them. But of course the first definition of "ding-dong" references the sound of a bell, and it is in the pages of
Shakespeare, whom Mecom and his contemporaries loved to cite above all
others, that his readers would have heard the allusion, whether in Ariel's
song in the *Tempest*—"hark, now I hear them—Ding-Dong, bell"—or, more
provocatively, in Portia's song in *Merchant of Venice*:

> Tell me where is fancy bred,
> Or in the heart or in the head,
> How begot, how nourished?
> Reply, reply.
> . . . .
> Let us all ring fancy's knell.
> I'll begin it- Ding, dong, bell.
> ALL. Ding, dong, bell.

In both cases, the call and response of the song is what echoes with the
ringing of the bell, whether rung by nymphs or fancy, and it is this we are
meant to hear in Mecom's "all ding-dong"—the stage direction of *Merchant* deliberately misread and transposed into the dedication, the chorus's
response (across oceans, centuries, classes, and genders) incorporated into
the printer's address.

It is the editor who does the work of holding it all together, keeping everything in place, arranging the voices so that each may be heard separately
and together, so that the choice or taste of each reader will be respected,
so that new ideas might form and new arrangements take place. As "Tom

Taciturn" would later put it in Isaiah Thomas's *Worcester Magazine* in 1786:

> [The magazine] is a place for every man to speak his mind in—not like the Mouth of Stone in Venice, into which every Calumniator may throw his private information against particular persons—if so I should be as willing to be dinned by a parcel of slandering gossips, as to read it.—It is more like a *masquerade*; but unless there be a very good master of the ceremonies to prevent base characters from entering and bringing along with them indecency and vice, a masquerade would be rather a publick nuisance than any source of improvement . . . And indeed it is so difficult to regulate masquerades in this respect; they are so like a blind beast untamed, that I would rather not see them introduced in this country; but it is not with a Magazine—the Editor may preserve good order.[78]

Taciturn here is describing what we might call the policy of "editorial federalism," refusing both the tyranny of the book and anarchy of the newspaper that lay at the extremes of the political (and literary) models then coming into being. Thus it is that Mecom's variation on Cave's nom de plume from the *Gentleman's Magazine* is particularly telling and much more than simply a sycophantic gesture. Whereas Cave's "Sylvanus Urban" is meant to convey the bringing together of the rural and the urban in the making of a literary space for the rapidly expanding notion of the "gentleman" in early-eighteenth-century Britain, Mecom's "Urbanus Filter" privileges the urban and the editor's function as *filter*, he who will sift out the sediment and properly arrange the whole in a bouquet—like the one held aloft by a ruffled hand in the magazines' title pages.

In these terms, we might take seriously as well the other telling borrowing that Mecom engages in from Cave's magazine: The motto and engraving that decorated his title page is lifted directly from the frontispiece to the annual bound editions *Gentleman's Magazine*: "E Pluribus Unum" (figures 1.3 and 1.4). The borrowing is explicit, and yet, as with Franklin's borrowing of the tale of the Modern Traveller, the effect is not the same. For the *Gentleman's Magazine*, the motto referred explicitly to the binding of the individual issues themselves, collected into a leather-bound edition that transformed the ephemeral periodical publication into a piece of furniture worthy of a "gentleman's" library. But Mecom used the motto and the symbol in each of his three individual issues, thus the "many" being collected refer explicitly to the various "queer notions" within the pages of the magazine, allowed to arrange themselves randomly but held in place by the firm and ruffled hand of the editor.

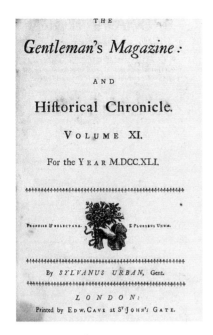

THE

Gentleman's Magazine :

AND

Hiſtorical Chronicle.

VOLUME XI.

For the YEAR M.DCC.XLI.

By *SYLVANUS URBAN*, Gent.

LONDON:
Printed by EDW. CAVE at ST JOHN'S GATE.

Figure 1.3. Volume title page for the *Gentleman's Magazine* 11 (1741).

Figure 1.4. Image from title page for each of the individual issues of the *New-England Magazine* (1758).

There is evidence to suggest that Mecom's short-lived magazine provided another more lasting model for the nation itself. Among the committee who sat down in Philadelphia in 1776 to design the seal for the new nation was Benjamin Franklin, uncle and sponsor of Mecom. Although the most visible source for the motto was the immensely popular *Gentleman's Magazine,* it is equally likely Mecom's short-lived *New-England Magazine* provided its inspiration through Franklin: *E Pluribus Unum*. In either case, however, we must take stock of the fact that the nation's founding motto, one that received the approval of Franklin's fellow committee members Adams and Jefferson as well as Congress as a whole, traces its source to the ideal underwriting periodical culture in the eighteenth century, and the model of citizenship it sought to inscribe into the foundation of the new nation was a periodical one—one in which Addison, Bickerstaffe, and Mr. Spectator would all be very much at home.

CHAPTER TWO

The American Magazine in the Early National Period

Publishers, Printers, and Editors

"We connect the ideas of *failure* with the very name
of a magazine in America."
—Benjamin Rush to Noah Webster, February 13, 1788

I

The pioneering historian of the American magazine, Frank Luther Mott,
described the obstacles facing the earliest magazine as "(1) Indifference, (a)
of readers, and (b) of writers; (2) lack of adequate means of distribution;
(3) losses in the collection of subscription accounts; and (4) manufactur-
ing embarrassments."[1] To these we might add a host of attendant risks of
magazine publishing in eighteenth-century America, including physical and
mental stress, and the loss of profitable business while the press is tied up
in a decidedly unprofitable periodical. Almost a half century after the first
colonial magazines, essentially quoting in his own periodical the bleak advice
from Rush cited in this chapter's epigraph, Noah Webster would declare
that in America "the expectation of failure is connected with the very name
of a Magazine."[2] But the occasion of Webster making this declaration is
not in burying his magazine (as he would do twelve months later) but in
launching it, whistling in the wind as he staked his reputation on a venture
guaranteed to "fail." All of which brings us to arguably the most urgent question surrounding the early American magazine: why? Why would otherwise
rational, ambitious, economical, and pragmatic individuals devote their
energies, finances, and reputations to such a seemingly hopeless enterprise?

Of course, there is no universal answer to the question, as the individuals
who took on such magazines in these tumultuous years brought different
fantasies and ambitions to their periodical ventures. But the early editors

and publishers did share sufficient qualities to present something of a profile, one more consistent than might be expected from a literary form that is, by definition, miscellaneous and collaborative. Unlike other literary, economic, and political ventures available to the men and women who pioneered the American magazine, periodical work offered no real prospect of success. It was something of a literary suicide mission. No early magazine succeeded, a fact well known (and even advertised) by those who began the process anew in the early national period. But the possibility that the next one *might* succeed was held out by each in turn as a kind of litmus test (or, perhaps a better metaphor, a canary in a coal mine) as to whether the atmosphere was at last right to allow such a venture to, if not thrive, at least survive. In the pages to follow, I consider in detail *why* the magazine was invested with this cultural and national significance, especially after the Constitutional Convention of 1787. But I begin first by examining in some detail an example of the kind of individual inclined to risk all on its behalf.

Webster is fairly typical of the early editors of the national period: federalist, ambitious, patriotic, committed to the education of the nation's youth and the youthful nation. And he is also fairly typical in his realism about the counterintuitive (some might even say perverse) impulses that motivated him to take on a magazine at a crucial juncture in his young career. After all, in late 1787 Webster had better prospects. He had earned his law degree in 1781, and in 1785 he completed his *Grammatical Institute of the English Language*, which was frequently reprinted by the time he sat down to begin the *American Magazine*. He had just wrapped up a successful lecture tour and met some of the most prominent men of the day, including Benjamin Franklin and George Washington. He was looking to get married and make his way in the world. A magazine was clearly the least likely of the many options that fanned out before him in 1787. So, again, why?

In his introduction to the first issue of the magazine, Webster somewhat coyly evades the question, insisting only that "among several motives which actuate him on this occasion, there is not a *bad* one."[3] We might guess at what such "bad" motives would be in the republican worldview of 1787: partisanship, desire for personal gain, vanity. But what are the "good" ones that brought Webster to this project? Mott attributes the impulse behind the early magazine editors largely to a kind of starry-eyed "enthusiasm," and yet Webster, like most of his fellow editors, was temperamentally as far from an enthusiast as can be imagined. And still less romantic was the man who first suggested to Webster that he undertake a periodical in the first place, Benjamin Franklin, who was nonetheless still dreaming of the successful American magazine almost a half century after his first attempt.

And so we must look elsewhere for the "motives" that brought otherwise practical individuals to the early American magazine.

When Webster launched his magazine, he had recently tossed his hat into the constitutional debates, contributing to the federalist cause an influential pamphlet, *An Examination into the Leading Principles of the Federal Constitution* (1787), dedicated to Franklin and seeking to refute the various charges of those arguing against ratification. Much of the pamphlet looks rather unremarkable when compared to the longer and more eloquent *Federalist Papers* to follow, but in addition to laying the early groundwork for much of the federalist defense, Webster's *Examination* is notable for working against the grain of several republican pieties of the day. Instead of virtue and republican disinterest, Webster argued that it was *property* that served as the "basis of national freedom." For Webster, "*Virtue*, patriotism, or love of country, never was and never will be . . . a fixed, permanent principle and support of government"; instead, common self-interest in the distribution of property must be the glue that binds the new nation. The proposed constitution, he argues, is the instrument best suited to achieve this goal.[4] And "while *property* is considered as the *basis* of the freedom of the American yeomanry," he continues, "there are other auxiliary supports; among which is the *information of the people*," supports that will ensure that the new federal system serves the property rights of its citizens.[5] Under the confederacy, property and information had been quickly monopolized by a few powerful states and landowners, while the vast majority was disempowered. When all do not have equal investment in the success of the enterprise, Webster argued, faction, rebellion, and oppression must surely be the result.

This model of liberal federalism that Webster articulated in *An Examination* is something of a founding faith shared by the vast majority of the first periodical editors of the national period, men who were, like Webster, called to periodical duty in these heady days of constitutional indecision. Webster, proud of the positive reception of his *Examination* and eager to capitalize on its success, sought advice from Franklin on where next to direct his energies. Instead of encouraging Webster to take up law, politics, or pamphleteering, Franklin advised him to carry on the fight for federalism in a magazine, where he might bring together his instincts as editor, educator, and political theorist. The idea made immediate sense to Webster. His former Yale classmate Josiah Meigs was at the time presiding over the Connecticut Wits as editor of the *New-Haven Gazette*, and in Philadelphia not one but two new monthlies (the *Columbian Magazine* and the *American Museum*) were at that time featuring some of the most important literary figures of the day. Webster took the suggestion and ran with it, scouring Connecticut for subscriptions and selling his publishing rights to the profitable *American Spelling Book* to raise startup funds.[6]

He opened his periodical doors with an invitation, perhaps the broadest one in the American magazine to date, to all readers and contributors, proposing the magazine as a virtual commonwealth where divines and philosophers would rub elbows with laborers and merchants, and where even women would "be found in the number of his correspondents."[7] And not surprisingly for a man who had already devoted himself to defining and defending a uniquely "American" language, Webster concludes his introduction with what will become a familiar call for homegrown literary production and custom: "In a country where people generally read, and where their governments require them to be informed, Magazines must be well received if well conducted."[8]

But behind the prophecy that the magazine *must* be well received is the clear knowledge that in fact it likely won't be. There is no logical reason, Webster insists over and again in his introduction to the first issue, why the magazine *should* fail. Its editor is dedicated and intelligent, its subscribers are some of the most prominent men in the new republic, its doors are open to everyone, and it is arguably the best conducted magazine of 1788. Yet within a year the magazine had folded and Webster was forced finally to take up the legal career he had been dodging for some time. And long before that—as early as the second issue, in fact—Webster knew this fate was inevitable.

The story of the failure of the *American Magazine* was, even in 1788, already an old and familiar one. Quickly it became clear that many of the contributions Webster had been promised were not going to arrive, and he found himself writing the vast majority of the original contents of each issue. More disastrous and equally familiar, subscriptions were not paid, and Webster, bound to fulfill his contracts with printers and paper mills, quickly ran through the capital he had secured to launch the magazine. Further, as he bemoans in his third issue, he was finding his magazine's contents plundered and plagiarized by rival editors, often without attribution. For an early advocate of copyright law, this last fact was especially galling, and Webster complained at some length: "The Printers throughout the United States are requested to observe, that this publication circulates as the Editor's property." While "the rights of literary property have not yet been clearly ascertained and established in this country," he insists that, in the absence of a national copyright law, printers should respect intellectual labor to protect the infant literary culture from costly court battles. Doing so is not only "common justice" but common *interest*—as the inevitable legal reprisals will only disadvantage all parties.

Yet, in the very same issue wherein Webster was decrying the rapacity of his fellow editors for his wares, he himself published a piece from MacKenzie's *Lounger* and an installment of Smith's *History of Virginia*. And like all of his peers, he was forced occasionally to "borrow" pieces of domestic or foreign manufacture without acknowledgment, as when he prints "An Anecdote of a Nun" in the June issue, a sketch that had circulated widely in newspapers since 1785.[9] This is not to accuse Webster of laziness or want of originality. After all, his magazine was one of the most scrupulous of the day in terms of attribution and one of the most energetic in terms of original content, much of which came from his own pen. Nor is it to label his laments about the abuse of his property at the hands of fellow editors hypocritical. After all, Webster does not claim the magazine's contents to be entirely the product of his own pen. Indeed, he does not claim them to be the product of *his* pen at all. Like the vast majority of the early American magazines, Webster published (and edited) anonymously, allowing his name to grace the pages of the magazine only in connection with a series of somewhat surprisingly inaccurate speculations on "Antiquity," published as if they had crossed the anonymous editor's desk along with other contributions.

Instead, what Webster asks for from his fellow editors is an acknowledgment of the editorial *labor* involved in making a magazine. It is not the content he is protecting but the editorial vision responsible for assembling the pieces into a coherent whole: "A man who has devoted the most valuable period of life to the acquisition of knowledge; who has grown 'pale o'er the midnight lamp;' who labors to decypher ancient manuscripts, or purchases copies at three thousand per cent. above the usual price of books, is indubitably entitled to the exclusive advantages resulting from his exertions and expenses."[10] This insistence of the rights of "the property of the Editor" is not the defense of "literary property" we might have in mind when thinking about issues of intellectual property in our own day. Even though Webster is the author of a remarkable amount of the magazine's content, it is not in terms of his original authorship that he stakes his property claims (and in fact he had temporarily surrendered financial claims to his own spelling book to take on this anonymous editorial work). After all, Webster's own magazine was made up, by his own acknowledgment, of large portions of borrowed and reprinted material. But this was not a source of shame for the eighteenth-century editor, however. Far from it: It was as "compiler," as selector and arranger of the very best materials from the crush of information washing over the average American in this first information age, that Webster and other magazine editors staked their claims and literary identities.

This is perhaps the hardest concept for the modern reader to fully grasp, so schooled have we been by a literary history defined by authors and great books—this alternative notion of literary culture, one predicated not on the authorial but on the editorial function and the careful arrangement of fragments and data. Webster's primary contribution to the magazine form in America during his one year as editor was to bring categorization, departments, order—precisely the same features that he believed were necessary for the country as a whole. When Webster takes on his rivals in the pages of the *American Magazine* over their appropriation of his intellectual property, it is not his *authorship* he is defending but his editorial labors—not the originality of his material but the original genius of their arrangement. As he writes (as "Giles Hickory") in the first issue of the magazine, "One half the people who read books, have so little ability to apply what they read to their own practice, that they had better not read at all."[11] It is the task of the editor who *can* read well to discriminate, arrange, and organize the material so that it will be more usefully (and agreeably) consumed by the vast majority. Thus, even as he opens the doors to his new magazine in the first issue to all classes of society, he "reserve[s] to himself the right of deciding the merit of the Essays communicated, and the propriety of admitting them into the work."[12]

It should therefore come as no surprise that the vast majority of publishers and editors of the early magazine were committed federalists. The very logic of the magazine depended on a celebration of the importance of not only unity but of centralized authority. As the early magazine developed over the course of the next decade, the serial essay often became the place where the politics of this literary federalism were developed most fully. For example, "Modestus Mildmay," a correspondent to Judith Sargent Murray's "Gleaner," calls upon Congress in 1792 to appoint "a committee of persons duly qualified, to examine every literary pretender" and to provide federal financial support "according to the wants and degrees of merit" of each would-be author.[13] There is nothing disingenuous about Murray's fantasy here, however impractical she knows it to be, and the fears that inspire it are deeply felt. As Mildmay writes, "if Pope Addison and Swift flourished in America, their merit would be almost entirely disregarded, and . . . there would scarce be found a single wight, who would acknowledge their superiour claims."[14] And so it is that, in the absence of a federal "Department of Taste and Merit," it must fall to periodical editors to guarantee that Mildmay's fears do not come to pass—that *someone* will be there to acknowledge and celebrate the superior merits of any future American Popes, Addisons, or Swifts.

Like others advocating for federalism at this time, Webster had come to believe that republican ideals and lofty values alone were not sufficient to serve as the foundation for national stability. Self-interest would always win out over idealism, as the factionalism and competition between states under the confederacy had proved. But if excessive self-interest could lead to corruption and tyranny, then self-interest, properly managed, could also be the glue that could bind the nation together. The trick, Webster came to believe during this tumultuous decade, was to encourage self-interested individuals to make common cause with each other—to recognize the ways in which one's own property, ambitions, and desires were intimately connected to those of their fellow citizens. As Franklin had no doubt counseled the young Webster, only if the majority found that their self-interest was also their *common* interest would the republic survive. Demanding uniformity and republican disinterest was fine in spirit, but in practice, unity would come from shared individual interest.

The magazine became the literary model for this ideal. Here self-interest was encouraged, contributors invited to lay their claim to the laurels of the American Addison. But the magazine was by definition a risky venture, one doomed to failure without the combined efforts of all—subscribers, correspondents, printer, and booksellers. The magazine would succeed only when all found common interest in its success, when all understood that their own interests were served by its continuance. And hovering over the enterprise as a whole stood the editor, who exercised executive authority, made decisions as to worth and merit, and worked to ensure that all remained organized and disciplined to serve the literary republic.

In these terms, it is worth revisiting Webster's complaint about the theft of his literary property by rival editors. Looking to the pages of other magazines for evidence of this theft, one is hard pressed to find it. Although there were at this time a record number of periodicals being published in the United States, inspired by patriotic enthusiasm, only the *New-Haven Gazette* seems to have borrowed material from the *American Magazine* (and Meigs most likely did so with his friend's blessing). Newspapers, however, were another story, as almost immediately after its first issue the magazine's features became regularly reprinted in papers across the country. It is not rival magazine editors Webster is complaining of here; it is the *newspaper* printer whom he accuses of indiscriminately raiding his magazine, disordering the arrangement he had worked so hard to achieve, and placing his property in unseemly disarray among the sordid wares and poisonous atmosphere he associated with the early republican newspaper. For periodical federalists of the day, the newspaper stood in stark contrast to the magazine, and it was as a refuge from the former that the magazine imagined itself. In fact, Rush and Franklin had both recommended that Webster name his new magazine the "Monthly Asylum"—a space *apart* from the politics, business, and violence of the everyday press.[15]

The newspaper, as Bernard Bailyn and others have shown, had helped to galvanize revolutionary spirit during the years leading up to the war with Britain. As David Ramsay, one of the Revolution's earliest historians, put it in 1789, "The fire of liberty blazed forth from the press," and "In establishing American independence, the pen and the press had a merit equal to that of the sword."[16] American newspapers and the Revolution had come of age together, and the newspaper emerged as the primary tool by which to galvanize the support of the far-flung citizenry into a sense of the wrongs they had suffered at the hands of the British government and into a course of action that few would have considered in the years preceding the Stamp Act. For the printers and politicians who came together to found the revolutionary newspapers, it was "assumed that there would be no conflict between the views of the mass of the people and those of their representatives, once the people were properly informed and proselytized in print."[17]

But now, only a few years after the end of the Revolution, newspapers were viewed with mounting anxiety by some of the very men who had made their political names and fortunes in the revolutionary papers just a decade earlier. And the memory of even the revolutionary papers was now not as rosy as it had been just a few years ago. For example, far from remembering the revolutionary press entirely in heroic terms, John Jay, in the second installment of the *Federalist Papers*, reminds his readers how, in 1774, "the press began to teem with pamphlets and weekly papers against those very measures" recommended by the First Continental Congress.[18] Now in 1787, even as they controlled an overwhelming majority of the nation's newspapers, federalists began to look to the papers with growing concern, seeing them not as a mode for dissemination of information and the education of the masses, but as "teem[ing] with party zeal" and pandering to "Pale envy, faction, falsehood, hate."[19]

The federalist magazine offered critiques and parodies of the newspaper, designed to distinguish their periodical efforts from those of their fellow printers (even as many of these magazines were printed by men who themselves also ran newspapers). The *American Museum*, for example, offered sardonic suggestions for how "to conduct a newspaper dispute, according to the most approved method now in practice," including instructions to "rail, defame, and vilify" following the "dictates of passion, slander, and revenge."[20] Events in 1788 had furthered Webster's distrust of newspapers' ability to capture "the collective sense of the nation."[21] For Webster, dragging random materials from his carefully organized *American Magazine* into the disordered pages of the newspaper was to expose to ruin the whole federal fantasy upon which the magazine had been erected in the first place.

But it was not only as a metaphor for national unity that the magazine captured the imagination of literary federalists such as Webster. If the magazine was conceived of as standing in contrast to the factionalism of the newspaper, it was also understood by many of its adherents as offering an alternative to the *book*. If the danger of the newspaper was that it was factionalist and fragmenting, encouraging a kind of literary anarchy, the danger of the book as a literary model for the new nation was that it tended toward a kind of authorial tyranny, offering fixed text and placing the reader always in a passive relation to the ideas of the writer. Although Webster clearly was less worried on this score in 1788 than he was about the dangers of the factionalism and competing self-interests represented by newspaper publication, in his staunch defense of the mutability of the proposed constitution in the pages of the *American Magazine* we can see how he understood the magazine as serving as a metaphor for his ideal federal system in these terms as well. Webster devoted much energy in the *American Magazine* to refuting calls for a bill of rights and for an unalterable constitution, both of which he understood as an illogical contract to protect "against our *own* encroachments on *ourselves*."[22] Webster believed that, however excellent the proposed constitution might be understood to be today, and however ideally suited for the needs of the moment, it would of necessity require revision for the future. A government of the people must have the ability to change and adapt with the habits of the people; it must be, that is, an editable, interactive document. Constitutions are documents created by "*fallible* men," as he writes in the *American Magazine*, men "consequently not competent to make *perpetual Constitutions* for future generation."[23] A bill of rights, for Webster, by placing restrictions on government, effectively ties the hands of future generation of citizens—who are the only legitimate source of power—to revise and edit. For Webster, a bill of rights proceeds from the assumption that the people's interests and the government's are not one (like the factional newspaper press), while provisions to make the constitution unalterable transform what should be a changing, *periodical* contract into a static, unalterable document (in this way, like a book).

The proposed constitution, therefore, was to be understood as a document very much like the magazine Webster had launched to defend it.[24] Founded by men of considerable talents and qualifications who had common interest in its success, it must remain always open to revision and input from the readers. The constitution should be a dynamic text, constantly being updated and rewritten to address the common needs and interests of the age. In this way, the magazine would be the ideal literary form for the new federal nation. If the unalterable constitution called for by some was the book, forever sacrosanct in closed covers, growing increasingly obsolete (and tyrannical) on the library shelves, the magazine was to be a living document, forever responding to the needs of the moment.

The magazine was to be a very different space from both newspaper and book: orderly, dispassionate, rational, interactive, open to all political persuasions. As the ideals of the Revolution quickly gave way to a rising tide of factionalism in the years following the ratification debate, the periodical would become invested with even greater hopes and fantasies as a refuge, an asylum, where the best possibilities of the republic could be nourished and sheltered until the storms had passed. After independence and for the next generation, the periodical remained a vibrant model of a literary nationalism, one that would offer a very different set of possibilities from both the revolutionary newspaper and from the novel, which would eventually displace it in the nineteenth century.

In a sense, then, the answer to the question of "why?" is a fairly simple one. While the early magazine would never prove a financial success (although several would indeed achieve some notable longevity in the years to come) and while all would eventually fail to achieve their ideal, the magazine remained the model of the literary nationalism that many of the best minds of the day believed was the proper foundation for the new nation. That it failed, again and again, proved to successive editors and publishers only the need to redouble the efforts of their predecessors, as they promised with each new venture that they would. That this endless string of failure never seems to have dissuaded any of its practitioners of the potential of the form itself suggests how deep was the faith in its possibilities, despite the harsh realities arrayed before them.

And those realities, it must be reiterated, were very harsh indeed. For all his initial optimism, Webster almost immediately despaired of making the magazine a success. Despite his sense that the city would soon serve as the epicenter of the new nation, in 1788 New York remained too provincial, and, despite his rather immodest sense of his own abilities, the labors of running a magazine almost single-handedly proved too Sisyphean. But instead of giving up after one or two issues, as many of his predecessors had done, Webster decided to use the problem before him as an opportunity to put his model of federalism to the test.

Instead of scaling back his ambitions for the magazine, he devised a plan for taking the magazine national, a vision of the periodical that was ambitious beyond anything ever attempted before. As he described the plan to Jeremy Belknap in February, "I now superintend the publication of a magazine in this city, the plan of which I wish to enlarge so as to comprehend every species of useful information in the United States,—in short, so as to make it a federal publication. My plan is this: to divide the property of the work into ten shares, to have a proprietor in Boston, another in Connecticut, a third in Philadelphia, a fourth in Virginia, a fifth in Charleston, and the editor with the principal superintendence in New York and four shares. The other share to be disposed of in New Jersey, Maryland, or Georgia, as we can find a suitable person. . . . Such a plan well executed would remove prejudices and gradually cement the union."[25]

This plan would allow Webster to focus his energies on "arrang[ing] the materials, and dispers[ing] the copies to every part of America."[26] The fantasy of a network of national editors, a kind of editorial joint stock company, was on one hand a practical solution to the problem facing American magazines. Whereas in Britain magazines were supported "by societies of literary gentlemen," in America such societies as existed were in general populated by men who had too many other professional commitments to devote sufficient time to a magazine to fill out its contents.[27] In appealing to Belknap to take on a share of the responsibility for this "federal publication," Webster believed he had arrived at a solution that would make such productions not only useful but profitable to its proprietors.[28]

Webster's concerns were by no means primarily financial. He had already sunk considerable resources in the magazine, and he felt the need to prove himself to older men like Franklin, Rush, Belknap, and Isaiah Thomas. As he wrote to his fiancée, Rebecca Greenleaf, the next day: "The eyes of America are upon me, and, having made my appearance upon the stage, I must act my part well or lose both my reputation and my prospects."[29] And the part he saw himself called to play was to create an editorial model, one that could scale to national proportions, thereby binding the new nation together. But his correspondents did not reply as he wished. In fact, his correspondents responded with precisely the provincialism and self-interest that Webster hoped the magazine would make obsolete: Benjamin Rush expressed his doubts about New York as the home of the magazine, insisting that Philadelphia was and would remain "the primum mobile of the United States"[30]; terms could not be reached with Isaiah Thomas for a merger with the printer's planned *Massachusetts Magazine*; and Belknap threw cold water on the whole endeavor, following the advice of his friend, Ebenezer Hazard, who had taken a personal dislike to the "literary puppy."[31]

Thus provincialism, competition, self-interest, and petty jealousies combined to do what they so often do, and by the end of the year Webster abandoned the magazine and the city. What the failure of the plan revealed to Webster were important lessons that would dissuade him from ever taking up a magazine project again: The group of literati to be counted on was simply too small, self-interested, and regionally grounded to make the goal of a national magazine viable. There seemed no way to make a magazine that was not, ultimately, a "one-man show."[32] And a one-man magazine was not the literary model for a federal United States that Webster had in mind. In the early issues, 40 to 50 percent of the *American Magazine*'s contents were written by Webster himself. Toward the end, he was exhausted of the project and his contributions fell markedly. In early November 1788, Webster made one last attempt to save the magazine, attempting to "form a Society" to take over "the publishing the American Magazine & Universal Register," but he no longer cared whether it succeeded (it did not).[33] By the time Webster folded the magazine, he could calculate his losses at upwards of £250, and he was clearly ready to leave magazine publishing behind forever.[34]

In an irony typical of the period, a few years later, supplied with capital from Alexander Hamilton and his allies, Webster took on the editorship of a partisan newspaper, the *American Minerva*. By the early 1790s, as Jeffrey L. Paisley describes in detail, an arms race had launched between the warring parties over control of the press, and many of those who just a few years earlier had expressed their contempt for the partisan press were now raising funds to support it. But Webster, though burned by the magazine, seems to have at least initially invested the hopes he brought to his earlier periodical venture to his newspaper. As he wrote in the first issue of the *Minerva*, newspapers "are the common instruments of social intercourse, by which the Citizens of this vast Republic constantly discourse and debate with each other on subjects of public concern," and in a time of crisis they are the vehicle whereby "a unanimity of opinion is formed, from Maine to Georgia."[35] But if he truly believed it (and taking on an explicitly partisan appointment, such claims are a bit hard to swallow), his faith in the newspaper would not be long-lived. When he annotated this "Address" many years later, he wrote, "Events have very much weakened my hopes that newspapers might prove useful in America."[36] Indeed, by the middle of the 1790s, there were few who would have defended the newspaper as a moderating and unifying force in American life. It was not surprisingly at this time that the magazine went through its great period of efflorescence as the asylum from partisan politics and the daily hornets' nest of the newspaper.

II

When Webster initially wrote in 1788 to Belknap that "periodical publications are almost the only lucrative ones, as you probably may know from experience," he likely had little idea how very little force such an assertion would have with his correspondent.[37] After all, Belknap had the year previous declined an offer from William Spotswood and Mathew Carey for the editorship of Philadelphia's *Columbian Magazine*, and Spotswood had subsequently kept Belknap well informed of the financial hardships he had escaped by saying no. In April 1787, Spotswood claimed as many as 1,500 subscribers, a heretofore unheard of number; but even with that success, Spotswood complained to Belknap, the expenses of running the magazine are such that "every idea of profits to the proprietors has been relinquished."[38] By February 1788, Spotswood reported that, as predicted, the first volume had been produced at a "considerable loss," conditions not at all "satisfactory to persons in business." Despite the financial hardships (which included the breakup of the original partnership), however, and despite mounting competition from Carey's new periodical venture in the city, the *American Museum*, Spotswood decided to continue for a time with the journal. Again, Spotswood is no idle visionary or well-heeled romantic; a bookseller and printer, like all other Philadelphia printers of the late eighteenth century, Spotswood was a businessman first and last. He maintained his communication with Belknap in the hopes that Belknap would continue to provide installments of his popular comic allegory, *The Foresters* (another strong contender for the title of first novel, had it in fact been completed within the pages of the *Columbian Magazine*) and other invaluable support to the struggling magazine. And yet, his esteem for Belknap and his recognition that their collaborations would likely extend beyond the inevitable demise of the magazine required of Spotswood honesty that might seem surprising from an editor vainly steering a sinking ship into its second volume.[39]

In truth, Spotswood knew that appeals to pecuniary rewards were beside the point. The real issues that drove these men to devote their energy to these magazines lay elsewhere. As the editors of the *Columbian Magazine* put it in the preface to the first volume, "However superior the wisdom of succeeding generations shall prove, posterity may at least be taught to venerate the purity and virtue of their fathers."[40] Such pronouncements, coupled with the spectacular artwork and the patriotic name, point to the ambitions of the magazine's founding: It sought to create not an ephemeral periodical production but a lasting monument upon which a national literary culture might be built.

Yet this same preface also speaks to the other side of the coin of such ambitions, as the editors conclude by recounting the costs of publishing their magazine ("a monthly expense of one hundred pounds") and pleading for prompt payment of subscription fees to help keep the magazine above water. Although the *Columbian Magazine* proved one of the longer lived of the periodicals of the early national period, from the start it is clear that the magazine was just barely holding on, a condition that would lead editors and publishers to withdraw for economic reasons, only to be replaced by new volunteers.

Like most of the magazines, the *Columbian* sought to avoid the partisan debates of the day, instead representing the best ideas and knowledge of the age. The stance the editors articulate for themselves, that of curators in a literary museum, seems to call upon the nation to embrace its magazine as representative of itself. Indeed, the miscellaneous nature of the issue pointed toward a refusal of a unified program, as the magazine instead sought to celebrate the diverse productions and knowledge of the day. The magazine begins with great optimism for the future progress of the nation, both as an empire and as a culture, an optimism that is reflected in numerous pieces in the first volume. For example, the first issue contains a "Chronicle of the Year 1850," in which the author (magazine cofounder Mathew Carey, in what he later identifies as one of "the earliest articles I wrote after my arrival in this country") reads a newspaper dated over a half century in the future.[41] This "news" details what will develop as some of the hobbyhorses of the magazine in the next couple of years: among the various intelligences from the future he reports are word of the complete destruction of the Algerian pirates; the expansion of American economic empire throughout the Atlantic world; and the transportation of 10,000 African Americans "back" to Africa and the end of the institution of slavery.[42]

Tellingly, the optimistic prophecy of the "Chronicle" is followed immediately by "The Shipwreck. A Fragment," which describes the fate of ship of immigrants bound for America that, after an encounter with a brutal storm, is left an unnavigable hulk with no provisions and no prospects for relief. A father begs of the captain some water to save his child who is dying of thirst, but the captain refuses, as the shares of the remaining provisions have been distributed. In desperation the father attacks the captain and kills him, at which point "disorder and confusion ensued in the vessel. The sailors plundered every thing they could lay their hands upon: and such was their irregularity and carelessness, that they ran the vessel aground at *******, in the state of *******."[43] Having finally made it to America, to an unnamed state, the few remaining survivors find themselves stripped and robbed by the inhabitants, "reduced to beggary in a strange land, without hope for redress." "The Shipwreck" reads quite clearly as an allegory for the perilous state of the nation in 1786, and the images of rebellion, anarchy, and shipwreck after the loss of a central authority would have been immediately recognizable to the readers of the day as speaking to the logic that was at this time underwriting the efforts to secure a stronger federal union than the confederation had provided. But perhaps most importantly for our purposes, the juxtaposition of this bleak allegory with the utopian prophecy of the "Chronicle" points to the divided sensibilities and the alternating fears and fantasies that underwrote the earliest attempts at a national periodical during these tumultuous years.

The magazine makes its most direct address to the debates surrounding the Constitutional Convention in "Thoughts on the Present Situation of the Federal Government," in which PRO REPUBLICA cautions his readers against "excessive jealousy, entertained by a people of their rulers," which "is the surest foundation of anarchy and ruin; or despotism and slavery."[44] The appeal to visions of anarchy and slavery uncharacteristically engaged the political passions of the day in explicit terms, and this departure from policy points to the desperate straits in which the editors found their nation as they launched their magazine: "our political difficulties have been principally occasioned by the want of powers in Congress, adequate to the government of the United States." A more common intervention into the political debates of the time was through satire and parody. For example, one deadpan correspondent, playing on the numerous essays the magazine typically offered on scientific classifications and discoveries, claimed to offer technical definitions of the different kinds of "manias" plaguing mankind. Among these are "negro mania" (whereby southerners are convinced they cannot labor for themselves), and "republic mania" (in which someone tries to introduce republican government "where the people are not prepared for it by *virtue* and *knowledge*").[45] A more substantial and significant satirical contribution to the political debates was found in the serialized publication of Belknap's "The Foresters," which uses allegory and satire to argue for natural hierarchy and the need for a strong federal government.

The magazine officially was wary of the novel and of sentimental fiction in general; what fiction did get published in the first volume of the *Columbian Magazine* tended toward "fragments," "eastern tales," and short "moral lessons" about the masochistic trials and tribulations of young unmarried women.[46] A representative example of this last genre would be "Constantia, or, Unexampled Magnanimity," transplanted (without attribution) from the British anthology the *New Novelists Magazine* of that same year. "Constantia" tells of a young woman who sacrifices her marriage portion and ultimately her prospects of future happiness so that her sister can marry an aspiring gentleman; here the reward for her "unexampled magnanimity" turns out to be a lonely death and, presumably, the graces of heaven. The amount and the length of fiction in the magazine increases during the second half of the first year of publication, most importantly with the original long fiction "Amelia: or, the Faithless Briton An Original Novel, Founded upon Recent Facts." Explicitly identified as "an American novel," "Amelia" was published in the issue immediately following the magazine's publication of the Constitution, then under consideration at Philadelphia (figure 2.1).

How we are asked to read "The Foresters" or "Shipwreck" in relationship to the constitutional debates seems clear, but "Amelia" is a more challenging text to read allegorically and is in many ways more characteristic of periodical fictions of the period. "Amelia" is, at least at first glance, a fairly conventional seduction tale, the story of a virtuous young woman during the Revolution who is tricked into a mock wedding by a British solider whose life had been saved by her father. As the first installment in the October 1787 issue ends, Amelia has just learned that she is to be abandoned and that she is not in fact married, and she has sunk into a stupor in the face of this news, resulting in the premature delivery and death of her infant. All of this is standard fare for the seduction plot, but what is perhaps surprising here is the "To be continued" at this point in the story: abandoned, baby dead, surely, by the dictates of the seduction plot laid out by Richardson and his imitators, Amelia should quickly follow and the story come to its moralizing end. What more is there to "continue"?

Much of the second part of the tale, published two months later, focuses on the events that lead to the father's arrival, just in time to prevent Amelia from drinking the fatal draught (figure 2.2). Going back in time, we follow the father's heroic struggles to find out where his daughter has been taken, his determination to stand by her even after the worst has been made clear, and his nursing of her through her long, and ultimately unsuccessful, recovery. Contrary to the traditional seduction novel, in which parents are either ineffectual or tyrannical and ultimately play little direct role in either the redemption or the downfall of the daughter, in "Amelia" the father stands by the daughter and, we are assured, could have prevented her ultimate fate if only she had confided in him. For a magazine promoting the ratification

THE

COLUMBIAN MAGAZINE,

For OCTOBER, 1787.

AMELIA: OR THE FAITHLESS BRITON.

An ORIGINAL NOVEL, *founded upon recent facts.*

THE revolutions of government, and the subversions of empire, which have swelled the theme of national historians, have, likewise, in every age, furnished anecdote to the biographer, and incident to the novellist. The objects of policy or ambition are generally, indeed, accomplished at the expence of private ease and prosperity; while the triumph of arms, like the funeral festivity of a savage tribe, serves to announce some recent calamity—the waste of property, or the fall of families.

Thus, the great events of the late war, which produced the separation of the British empire, and established the sovereignty of America, were chequered with scenes of private sorrow; and the success of the contending forces was alternately fatal to the peace and order of domestic life. The lamentations of the widow and the orphan, mingled with the song of victory; and the sable mantle with which the hand of friendship clothed the bier of the gallant Montgomery, cast a momentary gloom upon the trophies his valour had atchieved.

Though the following tale then, does not exhibit the terrible magnificence of warlike operations, or scrutinize the principles of national politics, it recites an episode that too frequently occurs in the military drama, and contains a history of female affliction, that claims, from its authenticity, at least, an interest in the feeling heart. It is the first of a series of novels, drawn from the same source, and intended for public communication, through the medium of the Columbian Magazine: but as the author's object is merely to glean those circumstances in the progress of the revolution, which the historian has neither leisure nor disposition to commemorate, and to produce, from the annals of private life, something to entertain, and something to improve his readers, the occasion will yield little to hope from the applause of the public, and nothing to dread from its candor.

HORATIO BLYFIELD was a respectable inhabitant of the state of New-York. Success had rewarded his industry in trade with an ample fortune; and his mind, uncontaminated by envy and ambition, freely indulged itself in the delicious enjoyments of the father and the friend. In the former character he superintended the education of a son and a daughter, left to his sole care by the death of their excellent mother; and in the latter, his benevolence and council were uniformly exercised for the relief of the distressed, and the information of the illiterate.

His mercantile intercourse with Great Britain afforded an early opportunity of observing the disposition of that kingdom with respect to her colonies; and his knowledge of the habits, tempers, and opinions of the American citizens, furnished him with a painful anticipation of anarchy and war. The texture of his mind, indeed, was naturally calm and passive, and the ordinary effects of a life of sixty years duration, had totally eradicated all those passions which rouse men to opposition, and qualify them for enterprize. When, therefore, the gauntlet of the Constitution, which received its first votes in the month "Amelia" was concluded, the force of the allegory becomes clearer. In Britain, there would have been no "to be continued" after the first installment: seduced, abandoned, dies. While our heroine's fate is ultimately the same (significantly, Amelia dies in England), she is *not* abandoned. Her father stands by her, defends her, and with his son, the soldier, avenges her. The serial form, with the two-month delay while the constitutional debates are reaching a fever's pitch, encourages readers to combine their speculation over Amelia's fate with their agitation over that of the Constitution—and to see in the generosity and authority of the father all they might hope for from a strong federal government.[47]

For literary historians, the *Columbian Magazine* has perhaps garnered most attention for marking the beginnings of Brockden Brown's career, with the publication of his four "Rhapsodist" essays in 1789 (his first published works were two poems published in Webster's *American Magazine* the previous year). Although at the time still a law student in Philadelphia, Brown worked in these essays to define a model of literary vocation explicitly positioned against the utilitarian model of authorship privileged by the magazine, most prominently in the person of its other major essayist in the *Columbian Magazine*, "The Retailer," whose pen name bespeaks the anti-literary model of the writer so widespread in periodical culture of the time. The Rhapsodist in his first number admits that he has always had a "despicable idea" of the character of a "retailer."[48] Unlike his colleague, Brown's Rhapsodist is a romantic, a dreamer, a loner, refusing consideration of use value and of material concerns (by contrast, much of the rest of the issue in which the first number of the Rhapsodist appears is focused on decidedly utilitarian concerns: "Chemical and Economical Essays," "Chronological Extracts," and so forth). As he defines his vocation, "A rhapsodist . . . pours forth the effusions of a sprightly fancy, and describes the devious wanderings of a quick but thoughtful mind"; "he loves to converse with beings of his own creation, and every personage, and every scene, is described with a pencil dipt in the colours of imagination."[49]

This is the Brown that critics celebrated for generations, finding in his earliest work, "The Rhapsodist," the ideal of the romantic man of genius in a culturally threadbare world of merchants and clerks. But such a reading requires us to read "The Rhapsodist" essays entirely straight, which several signs in the text suggest we might be wise not to do. The Rhapsodist describes his earlier rural life in utopian terms that closely resemble Crevecoeur's agrarian fantasy in the early chapters of *Letters from an American Farmer* (1782); however, material realities have now forced him to leave

Frenchan Delineate & Sculps. d

Amelia: or the faithless Briton.

Figure 2.2. *Columbian Magazine* 1 (October 1787): 676.

his pastoral state for the city in order to earn a living. Once enveloped by the hustle and bustle of the city, he is increasingly forced to admit that "I am indeed at present little more than a Rhapsodist in theory. There was a time when I sustained that character in all its vigour: but it was in the midst of a wilderness."[50] Within society, on the other hand, compromises must be made. The very act of writing—of attempting to turn one's visions into acts of communications—is a necessary dilution of the ideal: "Every person who commits his writings to the press has by that means voluntarily parted with his ancient liberty and becomes the general vassal."[51] The discussion of voluntary servitude—of the surrendering of ancient or natural rights— was everywhere in the air during this tumultuous period of constitutional debate, issues that could not have helped but fascinate a young law student. The Rhapsodist has given up much; as he describes his earlier rural life, he had seemingly unlimited access to a universe of reading and was allowed to follow his own whims. Entering the city and print (which are explicitly equated here), he has surrendered his ability to maintain his isolation. Demands now can and will be made on him.

Such demands are represented in "The Rhapsodist" by a letter from a correspondent. The Rhapsodist, this anonymous correspondent charges, is not whom he claims: He is not the older rural exile but an educated and ambitious young man. The correspondent takes the liberty not only of chiding the Rhapsodist for putting on false appearances but also of assuming the role of collaborator in future entries. The intrusion of the correspondent throws the Rhapsodist into despair and confusion, and he questions his own decision to publish the letter in the first place. In the end, he confesses, he realized that "in this my favourite art"—the periodical essay—he could not succeed alone. "The assistance of another was therefore necessary and proper in the present instance."[52]

It is a strange partnership indeed: the Rhapsodist giving over half of his own column to another anonymous correspondent who sets himself up not only as critic of the Rhapsodist's performances but as an author in his own right, demanding equal access to the space the Rhapsodist has carved out for himself in the *Columbian Magazine*. And in the end it does not prove a successful one, as the series comes to an abrupt end following the second installment from the anonymous correspondent. Very quickly it becomes clear that the correspondent has taken over the enterprise: "In this disquisition, and in every work proceeding from my pen," the correspondent announces, "my chief demands are the liberty of judging for myself, and, as a necessary consequence of such a primary request, entire freedom with respect to composition, and the qualities of stile." After only four install-ments, the Rhapsodist ceases.

This abrupt silence could be a consequence of other demands on Brown's time or of the impending collapse of the *Columbian Magazine* (which ceased publication just a few issues later). But given the issues Brown is wrestling with here, it seems more likely that the abrupt ending is intentional and integral to the "plot" of "The Rhapsodist": Ultimately, the Rhapsodist can-not accept the compromises of periodical publication, his "favourite art." Despite acknowledging those compromises—including collaboration with the reader—he is unwilling to surrender his fantasy of himself as solitary Rhapsodist or to share the periodical stage. With one final petulant insult at his anonymous correspondent's "medical knowledge" (he "seems particularly unacquainted with the distinctions that maintain between 'mania phrenitis, and delirium'"), the Rhapsodist withdraws. Indeed, by this time, the reader is much more likely in any case to want to hear more from the anonymous correspondent who has seized the Rhapsodist's soapbox for himself.

Beginning with the assessment of Brown's friend and biographer, William Dunlap, the autobiographical nature of these first essays has always been taken at face value; as Dunlap said of the Rhapsodist essays, "the title was assumed, [but] the *character* was not."[53] But while Brown was certainly drawing on some aspects of his own temperament in the portrait of the Rhapsodist, it is equally clear that he was here creating a *character* of a writer unprepared to take on the unique challenges and responsibilities of periodical publication. Indeed, insofar as we can see the autobiographical in Brown's first published prose, we might see his recognition of his own unpreparedness at this time to commit to the compromises and voluntary vassalage that periodical authorship demanded. Instead of reading his turn from the novel after 1800 as a retreat from his proper literary vocation, we might well understand his turn *to* the novel as an extended apprentice-ship to prepare him for his true career in the periodical form with which he launched and concluded his literary career. The novel, not the magazine, was retreat for Brown: a chance to hold on a little longer to the Rhapsodist's youthful desire to remain in constant and uninterrupted contact with the voices of his own fancy, unimpeded by demands for correspondence and the attendant interruptions and challenges from readers and collaborators.

And surely the young man, who would soon turn his back on the law in order to launch his literary career, was aware of the fact that both of the venues of his earliest publications, the *American Magazine* and the *Colum-bian Magazine*, were out of business by 1790. Despite this harsh reality,

Brown, like so many other editors and contributors, would continue to devote considerable energy to periodical production throughout his career, including while in the midst of the remarkable period of productivity that resulted in his major novels. For although the Rhapsodist claims to find distasteful the self-presentation of the Retailer, the *Columbian Magazine*'s most prolific serial essayist, Brown also recognized that what made the Retailer successful were precisely the qualities that made the periodical form the ideal model for the social contract required by the new nation. When, in his second installment, the Retailer celebrates having already gained a regular correspondent "who promises to furnish me with his future lucubrations," he literally turns over the rest of his column to this correspondent's meditations.[54] Far from being a threat, as it is to the Rhapsodist, for the Retailer the arrival of a collaborator "not a little flatters my vanity." In the third installment, the Retailer falls into a dream—as he points out, seemingly an occupational hazard of periodical essayists—and encounters none other than the "shade of the immortal *Addison*" who takes him on a tour of the "*city of literature*" where, in keeping with the metaphor of literature as "food of *the mind*," departed authors prepare foodstuffs appropriate to their literary talents.[55] Addison vends roast beef, while lesser lights prepare ketchup or beer entirely made up of the leftovers in customers' cups. But the item that most strikes the Retailer's fancy is a punch he discovers in Addison's house, one "made only at particular periods, though never to be sold," a collaborative endeavor made up of contributions from all of Addison's particular friends, "each supplying some part of the refreshing beverage": "Thus you see what an agreeable compound can be made from tempers so opposite and absolutely contradictory, when united by friendship; but even here, when any ingredient predominates, it injures the whole, although we can sometimes remedy it; as, for instance, by correcting the acidity, with a little water or sugar." This is the ideal of the periodical form to which the Rhapsodist aspires but cannot quite bring himself. In fact, the Retailer himself seems to have been a collaborative persona much like Addison's punch, with at least two correspondents assuming the name.[56] But even this corporate author surrenders his column regularly to other correspondents. For example, in the very issue where Brown's Rhapsodist abandons his column for good, the Retailer turns his columns entirely over to his correspondents, "claim[ing] to myself no other merit in this number, but that of handing the letters to my readers, and furnishing the motto."[57]

The identities of contributors to the Retailer are lost to posterity, identified in print only by a series of initials, "Q," "P.," and "H." In his Rhapsodist essays, Brown came as close as any periodical essayist of the period to spelling out his actual name, signing each of his four entries with a single initial: B., R., O., W. The promised fifth entry never arrives, and had it done so it would have constituted, as Brown well knew, a fundamental violation of the rules of the periodical. If he turns to the novel in part so that he can spell his own name out, only a little more than a decade after "The Rhapsodist," Brown would wish that the productions of his pen could never be traced back to his name, bringing him back to the periodical form once again. As a reader and occasional contributor to the *Columbian Magazine* and the *American Magazine*, Brown served his apprenticeship for the model of literary culture and career he would later come to believe was that which was most appropriate for himself and the young nation. It may well be, if "The Rhapsodist" is any clue, that he believed it already in 1789.

III

The magazine occupies a liminal place at best in the history of print in the early republic. The book and the newspaper dominate far more space in the story of the print's rise, and rightly so, if circulation numbers are to direct our attention. Newspapers reached circulations well beyond those magazines could hope for; and books routinely were printed in runs of 2,000 (with best-sellers like school texts and almanacs often printed in much larger runs). A magazine like the *Massachusetts Magazine* of Isaiah Thomas and his Boston partner Ebenezer Andrews rarely saw circulations much above 800, and Andrews suggests that 700 is likely closer to the truth. And the *Massachusetts Magazine* was one of the lucky ones—indeed, the longest running American magazine of the period. So it is not surprising that for historians Thomas's newspaper the *Spy* is more likely to be valued as a repository of the political concerns and daily struggles of late-eighteenth-century Massachusetts. The magazine, in contrast, seems dominated by random posturing, by armchair moralists with neoclassical pseudonyms offering their opinion on everything from fashion to dueling. It is no wonder that modern readers have favored two forms—novel and newspaper—whose genealogies are more immediately traceable into the twentieth century.

The genealogy of Isaiah Thomas's interest in magazines is obscure and deeply personal, but like his fellow printers Franklin and Carey, it has much to do with his ambitions for himself, his profession, and his nation. As a child, Thomas's father had abandoned the family, forcing his mother to indenture her son to the Boston printer Zechariah Fowle: "He promised my Mother he would take care me as his own, as he had no children," Thomas later recalled. However, "after I was bound and he had absolute power over me, he put me to all the servile employments in his family that I could perform." "His office was the only school I ever had—I was left to teach myself, he never once attempted to learn me either to read or write or caused it to be done."[58] Fowle's failures as a printer and a man were perhaps Thomas's most urgent lesson. Thomas recalled Fowle as a printer of ballads and "pedlars pamphlets." In the person of Benjamin Mecom, however, Thomas saw another model. In his *History of Printing* (1810), Thomas would recall the striking impression Mecom first made on him when he met him at Fowle's shop: "He was handsomely dressed, wore a powdered bob wig, ruffles and gloves; gentlemanlike appendages which the printers of that day did not assume, and thus apparalled, would often assist . . . at the press."[59] Mecom's visits to Fowle's print shop offered Thomas an alternate model, an alternate genealogy, much as the chance encounter with the *Spectator* did for Thomas's fellow pioneering printer Franklin—the European ruffles and gloves (an affectation Mecom had picked up during his time in the West Indies) combined with the leather apron: "I viewed Mecom at the press with admiration. He indeed put on an apron to save his clothes from blacking, and guarded his ruffles; but he wore his coat, his wig, his hat and his gloves, whilst working at press; and at case, laid aside his apron. When he published his magazine with Queer Notions, this singularity, and some addenda, known to the trade, induced them to give him the appellation of *Queer Notions*. Mecom was, however, a gentleman in his appearance and manners, had been well educated to his business, and if *queer*, was honest and sensible, and called a correct and good printer."

The "queerness" of Mecom was directly associated with his *New-England Magazine* described in chapter 1, whose cover represented that ruffled hand prominently; in working throughout his career to make certain that he would not grow up to become Fowle, Thomas seems to have set his ambitions after the model represented by Mecom. And yet Mecom's magazine was a "failure" by any financial measure, whereas Fowle, who Thomas recalls with all the understandable contempt of a former apprentice, was a fairly successful printer over the course of more than two decades in the business. Nonetheless, even after the demise of his own two magazines, Thomas would recall Mecom with fondness and respect in his history of American printing, celebrating that "queer" something that Mecom and the magazine brought to the business of printing—a queerness that had finally little to do with business at all.

In its inaugural issue in 1789, the *Massachusetts Magazine* presents a meditation on the "utility of well regulated Magazines." Here Thomas's "correspondent" first enumerates the advantages for the infant national culture—"It would both gratify and excite the natural inquisitiveness of the human mind. . . . It would give birth to literary emulation and effort. . . . It would improve the taste, the language and the manners of the age." But his most euphoric vision he reserves, as did the *Columbian Magazine* in its opening issue, for the benefits that will accrue to future generations: "It would serve as a repository for the preservation of many valuable fugitive pieces—the bold, though short flights of fancy, and the mature and weighty, though concise sentences of the judgment. It would be esteemed a rich treasure, constantly accumulating, supplied with new veins continually opening like the mines of Peru or the diamonds of the east."[60] Such visions are found in most of the publications after 1787 and the metaphors by which they sought to define themselves—as a "repository" for the present and a "museum" for the future—reveal both the seriousness of the project and the sense that it is to posterity that they must look for their rewards.

This was indeed serious work, and by 1792, Andrews, Thomas's junior partner and the man responsible for overseeing the day-to-day running of the magazine, was tired of it. On November 3 of that year, Andrews sent an accounting of the finances of the *Massachusetts Magazine* to Thomas's office in Worcester, which he annotated carefully to make clear his larger point: "By this is appears that we do not get paid for it by £100 per year. . . . Indeed, it appears to me that if you should sell or give up the Magazine we could make as much again money by other work."[61] As he underscored in the letter accompanying these calculations, "I sometimes have a wish to [be] rid of the Magazine, especially if we could get a compensation for it. I have been making a calculation, by which it appears that we do not get nearly so well paid for doing the Magazine as for other work that we do. . . . [I]f you think my calculation right perhaps you will think it best to dispose of the work, (if we can), in preference to carrying it on ourselves."[62] Indeed, Andrews had cause for concern, as he reiterates in later letters to Thomas: the hundred pounds per annum that the press was losing on the magazine was chickenfeed compared to what was being lost in tying up the press and the apprentices in magazine work when there was much more profitable work being turned over to their competitors. A year earlier, Andrews had written Thomas regarding the need to expand operations in Boston: "We have in hand," he writes, "as much as 13 or 14 hands, and three or four presses could do," and he goes on to offer estimates of the print runs for the titles in production that gives a true sense of the place the magazine occupied in the bottom-line accounting that Andrews was trying to get Thomas to acknowledge: 30,000 spelling books, 4,000 copies of Watts, 800 of the magazine.[63]

It is not surprising, therefore, that Andrews increasingly announces himself "heartily sick of the Magazine, and so thoroughly convinced, that as we conduct it we do not make any thing by it (because we might do much better work) that I would give it away, rather than continue it."[64] What *is* surprising, and what merits careful consideration, is why Thomas, a man who was highly conscious of the bottom line and hard-pressed at the time for cash, did not see things in precisely the same light as did his junior partner.[65] We do not have Thomas's replies, but Andrews's increasing impatience on the subject suggests that Thomas was certainly not responding as he had hoped. By the middle of 1793, it is clear that Thomas has given Andrews leave to search out potential buyers for the magazine; Andrews, after failing in two attempts to turn the magazine over to new proprietors, pronounces himself "sick" and "tired" one last time and then lets the matter drop. There is every reason to believe that Thomas, against his own pecuniary interests, did little to encourage Andrews's plans to dispossess the press of the magazine.[66]

We return then to the question that governs this chapter: Why did Isaiah Thomas, one of the most successful and influential printers of his age, continue with a magazine that was by any calculation costing his business money? Thanks in large measure to the longevity of the magazine and to the repository of papers Thomas left with the American Antiquarian Society he founded in Worcester in 1812, we can come perhaps closer to a direct answer to this question in Thomas's case than we can with many of the other printers and editors of the period. But these answers apply in equal measure, I am confident, to others who set out with similar energy and against the advice of both history and their bookkeepers to build a literary museum for the new nation. It will help us understand the deep melancholy Mathew Carey expresses over the 1792 demise of his *American Museum* when thinking back on this event in his 1834 autobiography, even as he admitted to the trials and embarrassments the magazine had brought him: "Never was more labor bestowed on a work with less reward. During the whole six years [of publishing the magazine], I was in a state of intense penury. I never at any one time, possessed four hundred dollars,—and rarely three or two hundred. My difficulties were of the most embarrassing kind. I was, times without number, obliged to borrow money to go to market, and was often unable to pay my journeymen on Saturday; which sent me to bed sick with vexation."[67] Despite the fact that he confesses to being "now astonished how I was able to muster the perseverance and fortitude to struggle through" six years with the magazine, he remained "much attached to the work, and had a great reluctance to abandon it, unproductive and vexatious as was the management of it." Even at a distance of forty-odd years, it is clear Carey remains proud of the "unqualified approbation" the magazine received from "some of the most distinguished citizens of the United States," including Rush,

Washington, and Hopkinson. And he concludes his wistful "requiem" to his magazine with a 1788 letter from Washington testifying "that a more useful literary plan has never been undertaken in America, or one more deserving of public encouragement."[68] Even as the magazine was by any measure a financial failure and a considerable drain on Carey's prospects and energy, his attachment to it remains, seemingly irrationally, unbowed.

The traditional account of the early magazine is the story of a remarkable inability of otherwise fiercely intelligent editors, publishers, and writers to learn from the dismal failures of their predecessors. Even the most loving historians of the early magazine have a hard time not winking condescendingly at the apparent naive energies that are repeatedly summoned for each new literary miscellany, energies that inevitably dissipate in the coming months (or, rarely, years) in the face of the obstacles the early magazine faced. And these obstacles *were* considerable; to enumerate only the most obvious as they are recited, in what becomes almost a catechism in the editor's address "To the Publick": subscriptions, contributions, and distribution. The last of these concerns is actually touched on only rarely in the editors' addresses to their subscribers, but it figures prominently in their personal correspondence: distribution continued to be a primary obstacle, as postal regulations and policies made the transportation of magazines often vastly more expensive than newspapers. Even those printers, like Thomas, who were also postmasters had a difficult time in getting post riders to accept their magazines for regular delivery. It is not surprising that Carey gave up the magazine after 1792, when new policies made explicit what had already been general practice, marking an official distinction between newspapers and magazines—where newspapers were charged for up to a hundred miles at only 1 cent each (and 1–1/2 cents each for longer distances), magazines were charged 1 cent a *sheet* up to 50 miles, and 2 cents a sheet over 100 miles. For a 64-page octavo, like the *Massachusetts Magazine*, such policies drove up the costs of distributing its magazines nationally—and all the important magazines had explicitly national ambitions, despite the often local nature of their titles—consequently turning the magazine into something of a luxury item.[69]

Of course, as Carey's memoir makes clear, a primary and immediate concern facing all magazine printers, even large concerns like that of Thomas, was cash. Printing was a complex credit economy, as Thomas's account books make manifest, and magazine subscriptions consistently proved a remarkably unreliable credit risk. Perhaps the most common complaint found in periodical publications of the period is the demand that subscribers return their subscription fees for the publications they had received. That said, and contrary to the conventional accounts of the early magazine, in comparison to their "first cousin" the newspaper, the failure of subscribers to send in their cash seems to have been a relatively secondary concern. Whereas in the *Spy* Thomas would familiarly plead and even threaten his dilatory readers, in the *Massachusetts Magazine* he repeatedly expresses general satisfaction with his readers on this score.

Where his readers fail most consistently, according to the jeremiads that were a recurring feature in this and all magazines, is not in returning their cash but in returning their *correspondence*. When Thomas announces, on the eve of the Revolution, the suspension of his first periodical venture, the *Royal American Magazine*, it is not his "large Out-Layings" he points to first but the "embarrassment" caused by "those Gentlemen . . . who kindly promised to assist the Editor with their various Lucubrations"—fully vindicating, as Thomas says, "the Propriety of the ancient Observation, that 'Art and Arms are not very agreeable Companions.'"[70] Although Thomas might have hoped that conditions facing the editor in 1774 would prove unique, the problem turned out to be perennial, as complaints about the failure of correspondents to send original material continue in virtually every literary magazine of the early national period. Throughout the course of the *Massachusetts Magazine*, the editors make frequent apologies on behalf of their correspondents for the failure of the magazine to fulfill its promise to provide more "originality" than any other domestic magazine.[71]

While the editor prized originality in his magazine and from his correspondents, he absolutely refused any claim of it in himself. The job of the editor, it was insisted, even in cases where we know the editor wrote large portions of the material, was merely as curator of the genius of his readers and his nation. It was to the brilliance of their contributors that the editor laid claim and to the wisdom and system of their arrangement of the miscellaneous materials that made up their museum. And yet even as the correspondents were encouraged to seek fame within the halls of the museum, it was by necessity of a stamp that looks strange to modern eyes: However famous Thomas's most prominent correspondents might have been, it was as Philenia, the Gleaner, Constantia, the Lay Preacher, or Colon and Spondee that they were most recognized, not as Sarah Morton, Judith Sargent Murray, Joseph Dennie, or Royall Tyler.

Further complicating the model for the modern reader, in their own columns and series, these writers set themselves up as "editors," offering "repositories" *within* the magazine. Murray, for example, introduces her popular persona, the "Gleaner" (see chapter 3), as a "plain man" of limited talents, who promises no more than to "ransack the fields, . . . deeming myself privileged to crop with impunity a hint from one, an idea from another, and to aim at improvement upon a sentence from a third."[72] Tyler and Dennie's "Colon and Spondee" set up shop as "wholesale dealers in verse, prose, and music" offering "a fresh Assortment of *Lexographic . . . Goods*, Suitable for the Season."[73] As Constantia, another persona Murray performed within the *Massachusetts Magazine*, she introduces the "Repository" as a series of observations lifted from her commonplace book, claiming "that for myself, neither my leisure, nor my abilities, permitted me to add a single ray, to the brightening era."[74] Similarly in the *Columbian Magazine*, the "Trifler" introduces himself as one "who collects facts and compiles materials" for the greater good, "but whose abilities to do good are enfeebled by irregular studies and imperfect acquisitions."[75]

In the complex exchanges between serial essayist and reader, we have in miniature a version of the larger economy that organized the magazine itself. It is in similar terms that we must read the lamentations and apologies the editors offered their readers in their proposals and addresses that recur so deliberately throughout the run of all the magazines of this period. Not that this play isn't quite serious play—or that the concerns about credit and contract that Thomas and Andrews articulate when asking for contributions and subscriptions are not real. After all, the stakes as these editors describe them could not be more grand: in the balance hangs "the honour of Massachusetts, her sister States, and the Union at large."[76]

For those who set out to build these literary museums, neither the newspaper nor the novel was the proper foundation for a literary culture in the new nation. Newspapers were necessary to democracy; this no individual felt more strongly than Thomas, himself the founder and editor of arguably the most influential paper of the revolutionary era. Newspapers might offer a space for some imaginative literature, and they did so, especially after the Revolution and before the political crises of 1786–87 began to dominate the public space completely. But newspapers were inadequate for the job for three primary reasons: They were not generally preserved, they were responsible first to political concerns, and they were not generally places in which correspondence took place—that is, they were first and foremost a repository of fact and the political attitudes of the editor and his associates, not a space in which a community of conflicting and multiple voices might be heard. This is made manifest in the appendix to Thomas's *History of Printing*, in which he catalogues the political positions of all the newspapers then published in the United States, marking whether they are federalist, republican, or neutral. His catalogue is illustrative in revealing how few could be justly termed "neutral."

His catalogue of magazines, however, demands no such classificatory system, and in his history of the magazines of the pre-revolutionary era, Thomas marks out for particular disdain those few titles that took explicitly political positions. The vast majority of the magazines of the age explicitly eschew political debate, avoiding "local" politics and any attempts at a unified ideological program in preference for representing the best ideas and knowledge of the age. The position the editors claim of curators in a literary museum seems to call upon the citizenry to embrace its magazine as representative of the nation and to give of themselves as representatives of their nation. The miscellaneous nature of the magazine was therefore not a fault but a virtue, celebrating the diverse productions and knowledge of the day in as many voices as possible.

The economy that the magazine depended on is examined in detail in chapter 3 with regards to the Gleaner, who emerges from the mass of readers in response to a plea for new correspondents, and in turn pleads with *his* readers for response, correspondence, and remittance of credit due. And the Gleaner even describes new correspondents emerging in response to his appearance on the public scene, correspondents who in turn use his column to appeal for still further correspondence from others. This is the fantasy of the early American magazine: a perpetual if cacophonous conversation out of which will be born a literary culture not founded on the unities of novel or newspaper but out of the uniquely democratic space the magazine longed to be.

It is certain that Thomas and other editors did lay some short-term hopes in their own periodical publications, but for the most part they understood themselves to be part of a larger ongoing conversation that included many current magazines (all of which borrowed openly from each other) and as part of a larger tradition of magazines past. In the editors' address "To the Publick" that begins the fifth and final volume of the *Massachusetts Magazine* published under the auspices of Thomas and Andrews, the editors cast their gaze on the departed shades of their former colleagues and contemporaries who have recently abandoned the field:

> Death, though the destroyer of human hope, often invigorates the confidence of the living. The *American Museum, Columbian Asylum, New Jersey Repository* and *Novascotia Magazine*, are now no more. The period of their dissolution, we account as the dawn of vitality, as the morn of our existence. Their features, variously beautiful, we shall attempt to harmoniously unite, and from thence to form a perfect, an admired whole. . . .

[A]n affectionate tribute is rendered to the virtues of the dear departed. Their passing shades move silently along, and beckon the *Massachusetts Magazine* to follow: Fond of life, and anticipating length of days, she bids them a tender adieu.[77]

Even as they write these words, Thomas and Andrews were completing final arrangements to divest themselves of the magazine, which they turned over to Weld and Greenough the following year (after which it passes through a variety of editors and printers before finally meeting its demise two years later in 1796).

But that does not mean that we should read these words as disingenuous. Even as Thomas surely knew that his magazine career was coming toward its close, he nevertheless did anticipate for it a substantial longevity. And all the evidence points to the fact that in this important regard, at least, these magazines did fulfill their proprietors' ambitions; far from ephemeral, like the newspaper, the editors and publishers of the magazine were right in imagining that their volumes "will be preserved in the LIBRARIES of men of taste and literature, and that they will find it a useful repository."[78] The copies of the *Massachusetts Magazine* housed at Thomas's American Antiquarian Society provides one measure of the value in which these "repositories" were held; in the first bound volume is inscribed "Nathaniel Paine his Magazine," and he marks almost each issue of the volume "Nath Paine's"; the second volume was apparently owned by Judy Myers, and she has colored some of the engravings; but volume III contains perhaps the most interesting inscription: appended to "Ledyard's Eulogy on Women" in the November issue is a handwritten note, "versified in Salem Gazette March 1803." This last note suggests that readers took pleasure in identifying original sources for materials, amateur antiquarians and bibliographers all; and it suggests as well that this magazine was preserved and studied twelve years after its publication, identified now as the source of later productions, as a foundation for a future literary production.

Further, in the correspondence of Isaiah Thomas and Mathew Carey, we get a sense of how these magazines circulated and were valued as a kind of currency among the printers themselves. If they did not bind the nation into the literary republic its proprietors imagined, the magazine did succeed in binding the printers themselves into a national network. From 1788 to 1789, Thomas served as Carey's agent in New England for the *Museum*, and it is clear that even as he was setting out to found his own magazine in 1789, he already knew well the odds against him; as Carey wrote, "I thank you for your exertions in favour of the Museum, & regret they failed of success."[79] Even after the launching of his own magazine, Thomas continued to serve as agent for Carey's magazine; and Carey suggested as well a new arrangement: "I shall forward the Museum in return for the Massachusetts Magazine, the success of which & every other publication promotive of public virtue & public happiness is sincerely wished." The printers assiduously kept track of the exchange of their magazines; as Thomas complained to Carey in October 1789, "We sent you a Magazine Monthly, and should be glad to have your Museum in return, but have not rec'd any for some months past."[80]

The following year, Thomas appealed to William Young, the new publisher of the *Columbian Magazine* after Spotswood had sold his interests, asking after a missing issue of that magazine. In the same letter, Thomas then asks Young, a man he had never met, to look in on a relative of his residing in Philadelphia "who has been unfortunate in her affairs, and needs the tender Arm of relief to be extended": "I am loth to trouble you, but as I am at a great distance from her, and have not the *direct* means of assisting her, but thro' the medium of Stranger I never saw, and consequently through doubt and uncertainty, you will I hope more readily forgive my application."[81]

In very real terms, it was their shared status as publishers of magazines that bound these printers together, separated them from the Fowles of the trade, and allowed them to create a network of exchange and value around the peculiar currency of their periodicals. They bound each other's magazines, promoted them along with their own, and used them as currency to secure both credit and access to markets far beyond the reach of their local agents. The magazine allowed them to imagine a *national* literary culture for the first time, and if the realities on the ground lagged behind the vision, it did not prevent them from inhabiting this brave new world together. Even such seemingly mundane acts as reaching out through a "Stranger I never saw" via the medium of the magazine exchange to help a relative in distress was a reminder of how these printers and editors themselves utilized the literary network they were working to create in these first magazines of the national period.

These correspondences also serve to remind us that, unlike the newspaper, the magazine was not fully a creature of modern "print culture." As Richard Brown and Sandra Gustafson both point out, word of mouth and handwritten transmission continued to be the primary means of communicating information well into the early national period, and as we will see in chapter 3, the magazine was always about conversation and correspondence as much as, or more than, print.[82] If, as Trish Loughran has persuasively argued, we have overemphasized the role of print culture in our commitment to a narrative whereby the nation was literally "printed into existence"—anachronistically imagining national networks of print where none existed—we have perhaps another explanation for the challenges we face in trying to bring the magazine of the early national period into focus.[83] Itself a hybrid of modern print culture and older and ongoing cultures of correspondence, conversation, and manuscript exchange, the magazine sought to use print not to eradicate the spaces between the voices, but to make them productive, communicative. The magazine was never first and foremost about profits, in the way that the spellers and almanacs always were. But neither was it simply about vanity or prestige. The magazine was a medium for a kind of exchange that those dedicated to its service believed was vital to the future of the nation.

Around the time Thomas began finally to give up on the *Massachusetts Magazine*, the two projects that would consume the last decades of his life were beginning to take shape. His correspondence and accounts reveal the energy Thomas was investing at this time in collecting the periodical publications of his nation and its colonial past. Part of Andrews's task throughout the 1790s seems to have been to keep up Thomas's collection of current magazines, and he reports meticulously on his successes and failures in procuring the issues that Thomas requires to complete his sets. Thomas's diary for 1808 records some of his purchases made while researching his *History of Printing*, including "48 vols. of Newspapers. Purchased about 46 Vols. old Papers, Boston Evening Post, nearly complete, of Mr. Eliot" for fifty dollars; and a few months earlier he had written to Thomas and Thomas in Walpole in search of copies of the *Farmer's Museum* needed to complete his collection. "I would not hesitate to give 3 or 4 dollars per Vol. for those that are deficient," he writes, adding, "It was a great oversight not to keep a complete file for ourselves."[84] The footnote to the 1810 edition of the *History* records Thomas's sense of bemused wonder at the investment he has made in his most recent endeavors, investments that can by no measure ever be called "profitable" in the sense of the word that Andrews would have preferred. "An entire sale of the edition of this work," Thomas writes, "would barely defray [the expense]. The purchase of volumes of old newspapers alone, has required a sum amounting to upwards of a thousand dollars. It is true, however, these volumes are valuable; and, together with the collection previously owned by the author, probably, constitute the largest library of ancient public journals, printed in America, which can be found in the United States."[85]

It is clear that by this point Thomas had already conceived of the literary museum he would build next, the American Antiquarian Society. In his description of his new museum, it is impossible not to see the continuities with his earlier efforts with the *Royal American Museum* and the *Massachusetts Magazine*: "The American Antiquarian Society is . . . different from all other societies established in the United States. Membership is restricted to no state, or party. There are no members merely honorary, but all have an equal interest and concern in its affairs and the objects of this institution, whatever part of the United States they may reside in. It is a truly national institution. It has no local views nor private concerns. Its objects (to collect and preserve) embrace all time, past, present and future. . . . The benefits resulting . . . will be increased by time and will be chiefly received by a remote posterity."

These words, from Thomas's final will and testament, echo the aspirations etched into the frontispiece for the first volume of the *Massachusetts Magazine* in 1789. There, Thomas's engraver, Samuel Hill, portrayed Apollo handing a bound volume of the magazine to a young woman who seems simultaneously to represent Science, Hope, and Columbia. Overhead an angel unfurls a "sacred Scroll" bearing the prophecy: "It shall increase in Fame." The pronoun referent remains deliberately ambiguous—does "it" refer to the magazine or the nation?—as does the nature of the "fame" to come. But what is manifest in Thomas's ambitions for both his periodical museum and the one of bricks and mortar he built at the end of his life is that he continued to believe that the proper foundations for the future of the nation lay in an "institution" in which all would "have an equal interest and concern," one in which investments of time, talent, and capital would be made in the interests of a "remote posterity."

CHAPTER THREE

The American Magazine in the Early National Period

Readers, Correspondents, and Contributors

> Shall I then compare your Magazine to the *General Court*,
> where every member has a right to speak his mind freely without
> being amenable in any other Court whatsoever—but there is
> this difference; the members there usually shew their faces and
> their names, *if not their hearts*; here they usually shew their
> hearts and not always their real names; but I will submit it to
> any thinking man if it would not be an improvement could the
> publick debates be carried on in such manner.
> —Tom Taciturn, *Worcester Magazine* (1786)

I

One of the central ideals governing the early magazine, as we saw in chapter 2, was that the magazine should create a space whereby readers could themselves participate as writers. The "Retailer" opens up shop in the *Columbian Magazine* and within a couple of installments, one of his readers joins as a correspondent and collaborator. And the Retailer, or so went the conceit, was himself just another reader until he answered the call found in almost every inaugural issue of an early magazine to become himself a contributor. It is important to recognize how deeply collaborative and interactive the periodical space was meant to be, how very much it worked to collapse the distance between author and reader and create a space where both could converse as equals, overseen by the careful guidance of the editor.

But who *were* the readers of these early magazines? Routinely, the magazines would trumpet testimonial letters from high-profile subscribers, such as Washington or Adams. These were the best advertisement available at the time to demonstrate that the magazine was a very different space from the novel, which would never be graced by such illustrious endorsements. Jefferson, who openly expressed his disdain for novels, crafted a special category in his library for magazines. And we know that Adams did indeed treasure his collection of the *American Museum* sufficiently to inscribe each bound volume with his name and to preserve them in his library. But such names constituted only a minority of the hundreds who subscribed to the leading magazines in the early republican period. Getting a sense of the rest is a more challenging affair.

In his important study of the subscriber list to the first volume of the *New-York Magazine*, David Paul Nord recovers a sense of "the forgotten readers" of the early magazine, demonstrating that magazine readers were far more diverse socioeconomically than might be suggested by the relatively elite content, especially of a magazine like the *New-York Magazine*. As Nord's analysis clearly shows, periodical editors were at least partially successfully getting across their message that magazine reading was a vital form of participatory democracy, a tool of citizenship and self-improvement.

As Bryan Waterman has described in detail in *Republic of Intellect*, the New York of the 1790s was a world of clubs and associations, and the *New-York Magazine* thrived on the connections brought about by this "cluster of male bodies that crisscrossed the city in one another's company."[1] This explains in large measure the fact that, as Nord pointed out, the *New-York Magazine* was somewhat more elitist in its contents than its contemporaries, focusing more on an imagined audience of literary societies than on the broader cross-section of the city's population that actually made up its subscription list. The *New-York Magazine* is somewhat anomalous—but all of these experiments are unique in different ways. In the case of the *New-York Magazine*, it was supported heavily by a society of gentlemen, the Calliopean Society, whose contributions provided the regular correspondence that other magazines struggled for. In part because of this built-in company of readers and contributors, the *New-York Magazine* was able to survive a previously unprecedented eight years with only about 400 subscribers, roughly half that of the *Massachusetts Magazine* and a quarter that of Carey's *American Museum*. Further, the *New-York Magazine* charged the cheapest subscription rate of any of the major magazines of the period: $2.25 a year. The magazine's printer-editors, the Swords brothers, had recently returned to the United States after fleeing with their Loyalist compatriots during the Revolution and were certainly not the ones keeping the magazine afloat on their own, so it is reasonable to assume that this was a magazine that was benefitting greatly from private subventions either from the Calliopeans or from another source within New York society.

Carey's *American Museum*, which was the most expensive magazine of its day, boasting more than 1,500 subscribers from across the nation and as far away as the Caribbean and Europe, is anomalous in another way. Whereas the *New-York Magazine* focused much of its energy on pleasing its base in the city, where over 80 percent of its subscribers resided, Carey's *American Museum* sought to be a magazine for the whole of the Atlantic world. Its national reach better represents the ambitions of the early magazine. The *American Museum* began by publishing their list of subscribers broken down by state. But by the sixth volume in 1789, Carey had decided to run all the names together, separating out only Washington and the senators and congressmen who happened to be subscribers. This long list shows the ambitions of the magazine to secure a *national* audience, and for the modern researcher it provides a useful insight into the backgrounds and biographies of some of the readers of America's first "national" magazines.

The *American Museum* subscribers included some of the most influential men of the day. For example, among the twenty-one subscribers from Connecticut listed in volume 5, we find David Daggett, who would go on to become a Connecticut senator and chief justice, and who was in 1789 a young Federalist on the rise, recently married and admitted to the bar. Another subscriber from the state was Oliver Elsworth, then in his late thirties; having served Connecticut in the Constitutional Convention, he had recently been elected to the Senate. David Humphreys, one of the Connecticut Wits, also subscribed; he had recently served as Washington's private secretary and was just beginning his diplomatic career. Others included Richard Law, a delegate to the Continental Congress during the Revolution and currently chief justice of the Connecticut Supreme Court; Oliver Wolcott Jr., who would go on to succeed Hamilton as secretary of treasury; and Ebenezer Huntington, a revolutionary war hero and scion to a powerful mercantile family, who would himself later be elected to Congress. What we see here is a powerful group of Federalist elites, many of them intimately connected to Washington's administration.

And yet along with this veritable Who's Who list for 1789, we find somewhat more modest names. Leman Stone, for example, had just moved to Derby from Litchfield and was setting up his commercial trade business, which extended from Boston to the West Indies. Like his more famous colleagues in the subscription roster, Stone was a fiercely public-spirited man, devoting much of his energies around this time to the development of the local turnpike. Another subscriber, Peter Sherman of Washington, Connecticut, was involved in a lawsuit over the sale of his farm at the same time he was subscribing to the magazine. And we find his name not only as a subscriber to the pricey *American Museum* but also on the subscription list for Noah Webster's *Collection of Essays and Fugitive Writings* (1790), a volume of Webster's periodical writings.

A survey of the broader list shows similar patterns, with a higher concentration of elite subscribers the further the individual state is from Philadelphia, where Carey published the *Museum*. As Nord found in his survey of the *New-York Magazine*, no subscribers came from the among poor, but in Philadelphia a fair number of the subscribers are significantly more modest in their means than the majority of those found in Connecticut. We need also to be cautious in putting too much stock in these published subscription lists as a reliable snapshot of actual readers. This is especially true when trying to get a sense of the magazines' women readers. Nord discovered in the subscription data for the *New-York Magazine* that 98 percent of the subscribers were men.[2] Those numbers are only slightly less lopsided even for magazines explicitly dedicated to women readers. The pattern suggests that subscriptions were for the most part taken out in the man's name, and if there was a male in the household it was his name that would appear in the list.

Within the pages of the magazine, however, it was quite clear that its readers (and correspondents) were understood to come from the entire household—and letters to and annotations in the magazines suggest that this was indeed the case. The magazine explicitly set itself up for family reading, promising something for the whole family. As a result, the disproportionately male subscription lists mask a much more complex reality. This is even more explicitly the case in the subscription roll of the *Museum*, where, in 1790, only three women are to be found named under the list of subscribers: Mrs. Anne Emlen of Philadelphia; Mrs. Hyatt of Port Penn, Delaware; and Mrs. Eliza Whiting of Berkley County, Virginia. Looking more closely at these names and the history of their public association with the magazine, we get a somewhat clearer picture. For example, in the previous volume Anne Emlen's name is not to be found, but that of her son Caleb is. In 1790, both Emlens are subscribing, suggesting perhaps that the mother had grown tired of waiting for her son to share his magazine, and as a well-off widow she was in a position to purchase her own subscription. While such a supposition cannot be proved, it does resonate convincingly with what we know of the sharing and circulation of magazines within the extended family.

It is also likely that there were many subscribers who either requested not to have their names listed or had their names removed by Carey for failure to remit their subscription fees. In the Carey papers, we get a glimpse of one such reader whose name would not be published in a note from a

Mrs. Wardell requesting a subscription to the magazine. "I have a great desire to take them for the improvement of my children and for the value I set on some peaces in them," she writes; however she has "not the cash at present," but promises she will "pay the[e] in the coarse of the summer the price of them." Even that promise, however, proves quickly attenuated by some backpedaling, as Mrs. Wardell writes that "if the[e] does not dispose of all of them it may be as much profit to let me have them as for them to lay by."[3] Mrs. Wardell's somewhat circuitous request for a free subscription was apparently not an unusual occurrence. Even as Carey's subscription list was filled to overflowing with some of the most illustrious names of the day, as he bemoaned of his subscribers in his 1834 memoir, "their remittances were so extremely irregular, that I was obliged to hire collectors to dun them, at a heavy expense." "It is painful to relate," he continued, that even the "wealthy citizens of Philadelphia, were, in many cases guilty of the gross impropriety, of obliging me to send half a dozen or a dozen times for the paltry annual subscription!"[4]

Mrs. Wardell's diction strongly suggests her to be a Quaker, likely personally known to Carey from the community; further, the irregular spelling also suggests a woman of relatively modest education but with aspirations, for both her children and herself, that extend beyond her ability to support them directly. That her name does not appear on the subscription list is not surprising; if Carey acceded to her request (as he likely did, since he preserved her note in his ledgers), he did so out of friendship or charity, as her name was unlikely to bring prestige to the enterprise. But that she sought it out for herself and her children suggests the value that readers of more modest means also invested in the magazine.

Ultimately archival evidence about the demographics of magazine readers is all but impossible to pin down. In many ways the clearest story about the role of different readers is to be found in the pages of the magazine itself. A remarkable amount of attention is not surprisingly paid to readers in the magazine. After all, the readers were expected to serve both as subscribers *and* as potential contributors. Carey's magazine was in this regards an exception, focusing much of its energy on appealing to the kinds of public men he advertised in his subscription lists, worrying less about "originality" than about his avowed ambition "to *preserve* for posterity—as well as to *disseminate* among the present generations—valuable fugitive publications, hastening to oblivion."[5] Established in the nation's capital at Philadelphia, Carey specifically set up his magazine as a piece of well-made furniture for a gentleman's library, and his subscription roles suggest he was successful, at least for a while, in selling it in these terms.

From his own relatively provincial base in Worcester, Massachusetts, Isaiah Thomas knew that Carey's approach would not work for him. Instead, he sought to lay claims to the "originality" Carey eschewed, and to the attention and contributions of a diverse audience—especially women readers. Explicitly positioning his own magazine in relation to Carey's, Thomas insists that "*Originality*, as far as the infancy of their work rendered it possible, has been their aim," inviting a wide range of contributors.[6] Still, a problem emerges almost immediately: How do you get contributions when you can offer neither money nor fame? As the *Columbian Magazine* worries, while "men of superior abilities may be plenty, yet few of them are possessed of independent fortunes, as in Europe; or have sufficient leisure . . . to write and communicate elaborate essays." Where then "shall we find those disinterested, benevolent geniuses, who shall be willing to exhaust their lamps, their spirits, and perhaps their lank purses, to entertain and amuse the publick, without acquiring to himself either a solid dinner or empty praise?"[7]

It is, indeed, a difficult economy. Readers are called upon to become themselves authors, but as the anxious author of "On the Utility of Well Regulated Magazines" (likely Thomas or Andrews) suggests, the magazine depends necessarily on the voluntary contributions of anonymous contributors. Most men of talent lack either "leisure, patience," or "benevolence" to "throw their lucubrations into a promiscuous heap." As a rule, contributors were unpaid and unnamed—the rewards, as the editors were well aware, were of a different order and one not easily identified or appealed to. In place of more familiar rewards or enticements, the editors hope that "a spirit of emulation, and of liberality which partakes of benevolence, will give birth to profitable communications."

As if to assuage the anxieties of the magazine's proprietors, this "spirit of emulation" inspires the very next contribution to the magazine, the first installment of the magazine's first recurring series, "The General Observer" (likely by Nathan Fiske, a local minister who had appeared in Thomas's earlier *Worcester Magazine* as the "Worcester Speculator"). The Observer's anonymous timely entrance into a correspondence with the magazine promises that there are indeed such "disinterested, benevolent geniuses at hand."

The magazine depended on and encouraged "emulation" in its readers, just as it depended on their "benevolence" in sharing their contributions. A version of what the rewards of such benevolence might look like is allegorized in the story with which the *Massachusetts Magazine* opened its inaugural issue, "Harriot; or the Domestick Reconciliation," an anonymous sketch by William Hill Brown, author of *The Power of Sympathy*. Unlike the tragic stories in that first "novel," this is a tale of seduction averted through the timely correspondence of Harriot, a young woman of "natural genius" "cultivated by a polite education, and reading the best authors"—in other words, precisely the kinds of readers the *Massachusetts Magazine* hopes to attract and promises to produce. By writing to the wayward husband at the moment of crisis, Harriot intervenes just in time to bring the man back to his senses and his family (figure 3.1).

As a model of the kind of fiction the *Massachusetts Magazine* will promote, "Harriot" serves well: Its moral lessons are clearly etched. But the story equally serves to provide a model for the correspondence that is being called for in the magazine itself: spontaneous interventions from "natural geniuses" in every walk of life, whose words can, through the medium of the magazine, touch their neighbors, "though personally unknown," and reform the community through their letters. Indeed, one of the serial essayists introduced in this first issue is the "Philanthropist" (also likely Fiske) who sets up his column as a place where the sufferings of others might be relieved through writing and correspondence. In contrast, shortly after, the "Reformer" critiques newspapers for offering no possibility of either charity *or* correspondence, instead encouraging readers to take pleasure in "seeing the reputations of . . . neighbours stamped with some odious opprobrium."[8]

The magazine promised readers a different kind of public exchange, a virtual space where neighbors could come together to share, collaborate, debate. The magazine offered the fantasy of this textual commons because it had no other capital to offer, and it is likely for this reason that the early magazine paradoxically found getting readers to turn in subscription fees so challenging. After all, like the internet in our own time, devoted readers felt an *ownership* in the magazine, whether explicitly in their contribution of correspondence or implicitly in the idea of the magazine as a commons. The success of the form in creating a space where such citizenship could be imagined ran into explicit conflict with a business model that asked readers, somewhat schizophrenically, to also view the magazine as private property that must be purchased with hard currency. The failure of magazines has much in common with the failures of so many dot.com enterprises; two centuries later, no one has found an effective way to create a viable business model for the ideals represented by the early magazine or the early World Wide Web. Magazines died because the "benevolence" of printers could only go so far; in the end, business had to be attended to and the experiment was done. But as with the internet, the community moved easily and effortlessly to new commons, new magazines.

We see a version of this everywhere in the pages of the early magazine, the exchange of seemingly random scraps of insight, inquiry, and entertainment, the invitation to transform them into something "profitable" through

Nᵒ I] *Engraved for Massachusetts Mag. for Jan. 1789.* [Vol. I.

S·Hill Sculp.

Harriot. or Domestick Reconciliation.

Figure 3.1. *Massachusetts Magazine* 1 (January 1789): 2.

emulation and benevolence—that is, through correspondence. One small but representative example is found in the *Columbian Magazine* of 1789, beginning with a note from a correspondent:

> Sir,
> Your inserting *A new Simile for the Ladies*, in a late magazine, induced
> a correspondent to send the following,
>> Is there so whimsical a creature
>> As an old bachelor in nature?
>> Yes—I'll recall what I have said,
>> And, 'stead of *bachelor*, write *maid*.[9]

Here the correspondent, "D. L.," is responding to a contribution in the March issue of the *Columbian Magazine* from "A Friend to the Ladies," who shared "A New Simile for the Ladies" (unattributed here, but by Sheridan more than a half century earlier) with the following introduction: "I perceive in your Parnassiad of last month an Evening Thought and its Similitudes; perhaps the following Simile of a lively writer, drawn from a subject which the other has but slightly touched, may prove entertainment to your readers." The "Simile" extends predictably the supposed "likeness" of women to stormy clouds and is itself offered to the readers by the "Friend to the Ladies" in response to a poem published in a still earlier issue.[10] This call and response was the bread and butter of the magazine, as one text inspires another, which it turn inspires further responses, retorts, accusations, and imitations.

One reader who early answered the *Massachusetts Magazine*'s call for correspondence was Judith Sargent Murray. In the January 1790 issue, Murray contributed "Lines, Occasioned by the Death of an Infant," a long and sorrowful meditation on her own loss of the previous year.[11] The poem begins with the speaker describing the baby she hoped to hold and the role as mother she had planned to assume. "But agonized nature trembling sighs!/ And my young sufferer in the struggle dies"; and now the speaker must come to terms with her grief and the loss that the community will not acknowledge:

> To the absorbing grave I must resign,
> All of my first born child that e'er was mine!
> And though no solemn train of mourners bend,
> Or on thy hearse with tearful woe attend,
> Too insignificant thy being view'd,
> To be but by thy father's steps pursu'd

Having died in delivery, her stillborn son is accorded no funeral, no community of mourners save her husband who alone accompanies the babe to the graveyard. The speaker is left to come to terms with a solitary grief that she knows her community—the "censurers" she addresses in the poem's conclusion—would "smile" at. Thus this lyric is about profound isolation and loss, about being sundered not only from her infant child but also from a community that offers no consolation.

At the same time, however, the lyric is framed by a correspondence from "B" to the editors and readers of the *Massachusetts Magazine*: "if yourselves and readers, should discover any thing of a similarity to my taste, by feeling more pleasure in attending to the language of the artless heart, than to that of the head, I may, perhaps, be able to prevail on my pensive friend, to become, herself, your correspondent."[12] This epistolary introduction provides an opportunity for the reader and the speaker to overcome the isolation of the poem itself through both shared sympathy and shared taste. The magazine form cures the horrible solitude and lonely grief that the lyric speaks. The invitation to readers to return the grieving mother back into the fold, by inviting the poet to contribute again, perfectly represents the social economy that the *Massachusetts Magazine* hopes to engender.

The poem is signed "Constantia," which, with the "B" of the framing letter, renders the lyric doubly anonymous. "Constantia" was a name Murray had first used six years earlier in her very first periodical essay, "Desultory Thoughts upon the Utility of Encouraging a Degree of Self-Complacency, especially in Females" (1784), and it was also a name she at times used in correspondence. For readers of the *Massachusetts Magazine*, however, it was also a name they had seen in earlier poems beginning a few months earlier. In July 1789, another "Constantia" had offered her own poem, also with an introductory letter: "The following imperfect Lines are with diffidence offered to your attention—they are from the heart—and if you consider them worthy an appearance in your useful Miscellany, the imagination of those who can feel will easily supply the deficient stanzas; and the misfortunes of an individual may possibly excite regret and compassion, even in the happy few whom destiny has placed upon 'a bed of roses.'"[13] The poem, "An Invocation to Hope," like Murray's "Lines," is about isolation, loss, a prayer for a response from the goddess Hope, who strews "fictions in thy train" "sink[ing] in *fancy'd* bliss the *real* pain."

This rival "Constantia," as it turned out, was Sarah Wentworth Morton, who in 1789 had real pain enough. Her husband, Perez Morton, had been engaged the previous year in a widely publicized affair with Sarah Morton's sister, Fanny Apthorp, whose tragic end was fictionalized in *The Power of Sympathy*, written by the Morton's neighbor, William Hill Brown.[14] Rumors at the time suggested that Perez Morton had attempted to suppress the publication of *The Power of Sympathy* to avoid reopening the scandal just when it was dying down.[15] Far from underplaying the connections between the novel and the scandal, Thomas went out of his way to underscore them—first having Fanny's suicide graphically represented in the frontispiece to the book as "The Story of Ophelia," and then excerpting sections of the novel explicitly devoted to "Seduction" and "Suicide" in the first issue of his *Massachusetts Magazine.*

It might therefore seem surprising that Sarah Morton, sister to Fanny, wife to Perez, begins her career in earnest in the magazine of the man who had published the novel that publicized the shame and tragedy that had befallen her family. But clearly, having remained silent throughout the long ordeal save to her closest friends and family, the promise of correspondence and community offered by the magazine was a powerful lure. In fact, in many ways, the magazine gave her an opportunity to respond to Brown's book, however indirectly, in a way the novel form explicitly denied. Morton wryly comments on those "happy few whom destiny has placed upon 'a bed of roses,'" an allusion to the poetic epigraph to *The Power of Sympathy*, which begins, piously, "Fain would he strew Life's thorny Way with Flowers." Not all of us, Morton replies to her neighbor, have found destiny quite so generous with the roses, but perhaps those who have might shut up and listen to what "*real* pain" sounds like, as opposed to the "*fancy'd* bliss" of your "deceptive" fictions.

Both Morton and Murray struggle with private grief at this time and both offer as their first contributions lyrics about incommunicative and seemingly irredeemable pain; both frame their poems with epistolary pleas for readers capable of collaborating on making meaning out of the exchange. Morton's plea for correspondence was immediately satisfied, first by the editors, who lauded her early submissions as "animatedly elegant" and "sublime"; and then by her admirers, who began writing poems in her honor, beginning with Euphelia's rhapsodic poetic appreciation in the October 1789 issue: "Accept fair Poetess whoe'er thou art / These free effusions of a '*feeling heart*.'"[16] In naming herself as the reader of "feeling heart" whom Morton's Constantia had called for, Euphelia enters the stage as a correspondent, describing how Morton's poems have moved her to offer her own contribution. Two issues later, Euphelia returns to the magazine, now as a poet writing her own invocation, here to the Harmony that Constantia had mastered in her own poetry:

> CONSTANTIA, daughter of the tuneful Nine
> Invokes fond HOPE! I bow before thy shrine.
> Inspir'd by thee, her verse enchants my ear,
> For sure *thy smiles* in *her soft lays* appear.[17]

Thus the poetry of Constantia inspires the poetry of Euphelia, which in turn summons forth another poem from *Morton*'s Constantia: "Lines to Euphelia" in the January 1790 issue, the same issue that saw the first appearance of *Murray*'s "Constantia." It is, in truth, a strange response from Morton, opening as it does with an articulation of the failure of Euphelia's verse "to heal the bleeding heart with praise." Morton's "Constantia" declares her own heart a lost cause—"Grief has made this breast its own." But even as she calls on Euphelia to stop wasting her talents on trying to heal her, she asks her to focus her powers as "Sweet soother of another's ill" on those who can be saved. "The social heart, the smiling friend," she concludes, is where "The charms of virtue, and the muse" can best be diffused.

But the protestations of Morton's Constantia only seem to elicit more response from other admirers desperate to heal her pain and soothe her "plaintive notes."[18] And so by the time Murray's Constantia makes her claim to the name in the pages, Morton's Constantia has already summoned forth the complex and potent chain of correspondence that is at the heart of the magazine's enterprise. Murray knew from the start that she had no chance to compete with Morton's popularity as a poet, but she wanted a role in the magazine similar to what Morton had carved out for herself in such a short time. And she wanted her name back, as she informed Thomas and Andrews. The editors attempted to adjudicate the conflict as best they could: "A second *Constantia* (who claims prior right to the signature, as having made use of it some years ago, in various pieces which were printed in the Gentleman and Lady's Town and Country Magazine, printed in Boston, and whose productions are known to her friends under that name) has appeared this month. Her truly Poetical Lines merit every attention. . . . The authoress of Invocation to Hope; Philander, a pastoral Elegy; Lines of Euphelia, &c. will in future have her name decorated with a Star (*) at the end of it, unless one of the other of the fair competitors in poetic fame, should be pleased to alter her signature."[19]

If anything, by calling attention to this conflict, so "delicately embarrassing to the Editors," Thomas and Andrews were explicitly staging a rivalry between the two women, but Morton, or "Constantia*," was indisputably the winner, receiving further poems celebrating her gifts. Nonetheless, it was Morton who would cede the name to Murray, adopting as her new pseudonym first "Philenia Constantia," and then simply "Philenia." In exchange, Murray writes her own lyric letter to Morton in "Lines to Philenia": "Ah lovely mourner! Why should you refuse, / To lend effulgence to a humbler muse?" Here Murray cedes the laurels to Morton, and suggests that she had assumed the name "Constantia" in part with the hopes that Morton's rays might reflect upon her and summon forth her own gifts, as they had for Euphelia:

And while around the splendid orb I move,
My lowly verse its genial rays may prove.
Thus slyly arguing, while I sought for fame,
The two *Constantia's* might be thought the same,
For 'tis not every reader can decide,
The multitude but on the surface glide[20]

But now, Murray's Constantia complains, Morton's Constantia is "fled," replaced by "Philenia":

Its cheering influence no more is spread,
The animating fair ceases to guide,
Alone I venture on the impetuous tide;
Groping my opaque way, and wandering fair,
Without the disk of my sweet polar star.

Murray has surrendered the field but, interestingly, not the name. At around this time, Constantia has begun to appear gracing not poems, traditionally in the magazine the primary site for women correspondents to contribute, but essays. In the March issue had appeared the first installment of "On the Equality of the Sexes" unsigned, but in the April issue in which she surrendered the poet's laurels "To Philenia," Murray signed the concluding installment of her essay "Constantia."

II

That the *Massachusetts Magazine* had realized that much of its readership and potential contributors were women became clearer in the frontispiece to the third volume for 1791, which depicts a young woman reading the magazine while she is crowned for her efforts by Minerva and Cupid (figure 3.2). As the editors gloss the image: "The Fair Daughters of Massachusetts, are collectively represented by the symbolical figure of an elegant and accomplished young Lady, seated in her study, contemplating the various pages of the Magazine. Their general acquaintance with the necessary branches of reading and writing, and the more ornamental ones, of History and Geography, is happily depicted, by those instruments of Science, which adorn the Hall of Meditation. *Minerva*, the Goddess of Wisdom, assisted by *Cupid*, crowns her with a chaplet of Laurel: *Hymen's* burning Torch is displayed aloft—a delicate intimation, that knowledge, combined with beauty, enkindles the purest flame of love."[21]

This reading of the frontispiece mirrors many of the central arguments of Murray's "Essay on the Equality of the Sexes" and "Desultory Thoughts":

Figure 3.2. Frontispiece, *Massachusetts Magazine* 3 (1791).

the value of education, especially for women, historically denied its bless-
ings; the proper relationship between the sexes that might result from giving women equal access to knowledge. Indeed, in the general preface to the
volume, the editors cite among the "celebrities" who have emerged over the
previous two years in the magazine's pages three women: Philenia, Constantia, and Lavinia.[22]

The following year a new figure enters the field of the magazine, the
"Gleaner." He introduces himself in his first installment as "rather a plain
man, who after spending the day in making provisions for my little family,
sit myself comfortably down by a clean hearth, and a good fire," normally
with little ambition beyond a brief period of comfort before his night's re-
pose.[23] But now, we are told, the *Massachusetts Magazine* has violated his
former tranquility by infecting him with the desire to be a "scribbler." He
had resisted the urge bravely for three long years, finally succumbing after
an appeal for new contributors from the editors in the previous issue.

For, we are reminded again and again, from a certain perspective there *is*
no rational reason why anyone should contribute to the magazines. How
then to account for what the Gleaner calls this "this unaccountable itch for
scribbling?" The Gleaner admits, with unusual candor, to being motivated at
first by an ambition for "applause," and for being recognized as possessing
"unequaled" excellence in the field: "The smoothness of Addison's page, the
purity, strength, and correctness of Swift, the magic numbers of Pope—these
must all veil to me." "Audacious as I am," he confesses, he even sought to
"snatch the bays" from Philenia herself. Simultaneous with these ambitions,
however, comes the realization that he might well not possess "abilities
adequate to the furnishing a paragraph in a common newspaper!"[24]

If the alternating currents of ambition and humility sound familiar, that
is because Constantia and the Gleaner are one and the same. In her new
role as the Gleaner, the *Massachusetts Magazine* provided Murray with a
chance to reinvent herself, now not as a poet competing with Morton, but
as a serial essayist. Even more than the periodical poet, the essayist enters
into a contractual correspondence with her readers, and the new "Gleaner"
column provided Murray with an opportunity to achieve the kind of periodical fame Morton had achieved through poetry.

The serial essayist in the early magazine almost always introduces himself as sharing at least some of the contradictory characteristics to which
Murray's Gleaner confesses: literary ambition, a desire to contribute to the
public discourse, a self-consciousness of a lack of polished literary skill, and
a strange and unaccountable "mania" or addiction for "scribbling," one
that is summoned into existence by the medium of the magazine itself. So

much is the admixture of qualities and ambitions part of the form that the "Friend," for example, introduces himself in the *Farmer's Weekly Museum* by assuming both shared familiarity and boredom with the conventions on the part of his readers: "It is common in periodical papers to fill the first number with the author's motive for writing, the method he designs to pursue, and perhaps some apologies for rashness of his undertaking, with a request or two for the candor of the publick, &c. For brevity's sake, I shall suppose all this previous ceremony past, that I have already written an introductory number of sufficient merit to excite publick attention, and that my readers are as cordially disposed to advance my fame as, I am to increase their happiness, or contribute to their amusement."[25]

What was looked for in the introductory column, which served in many ways as a kind of audition, first for editors and then for readers, was wit and originality within the confines of the contract. That Murray was by no means confident of the reception she would receive for her first installment is made clear when the Gleaner suggests that, having "adjusted preliminaries," the editors might choose whether to publish or reject. The Gleaner asks only that he not be forced to "see the Gleaner among your list of acknowledgements to correspondents, set up as a mark for the shafts of wit." And indeed this was a risk that all correspondents undertook. Every issue the editors opened with "Acknowledgements to Our Correspondents," in which the contributions they received were discussed briefly. Given how hungry the magazine was for contributions, it is not surprising that many of them are favorable: "*Philenia*, is respectfully thanked, for her late favour," the October 1791 "Acknowledgements" begin, while "*Philaparthenos*, deserves attention next month." But clearly part of the pleasure for the reader lay in what the Gleaner identified as the "shafts of wit." In the same October issue, for example, we learn that "*The Son of the Sock*" is "more pregnant with ill nature than wit," and to "*A Rod for the Fool*," "remember, there's a whip for the Ass."[26] Or, in the same issue in which the Gleaner makes his first appearance: "*A Harvardian Love Letter*, never won fair lady" and "The *Occasional Visitor*, if engaged, is not bound to write every month."[27]

How many of the contributions were genuinely submitted anonymously, as Franklin had described sliding his "Dogood" essays under his brother's door in the middle of the night, we cannot know. But evidence suggests that the majority of them soon became personally known to the editors. Especially in the opening advances of a new contributor, anonymity served multiple ends here: providing a shelter to the reputations (if not the feelings) of the amateur authors summoned from the body of the magazine's readership, and providing license for the editors to exercise their wit in casting judgment on those whose offerings they found wanting. After all, it was the exercise of judgment that was the editor's one claim to authority. Further, anonymously exposing those whose correspondence was found unworthy of publication only served to augment the prestige of those whose contributions *were* printed.

Murray must have been well pleased by the acknowledgment she received in the issue, not only in the publication of her first appearance as a serial essayist but also in the "Acknowledgements to Correspondents": "Future correspondence is solicited." Even more flattering, no doubt, was appearing as the lead in the following issue, where, after bowing her thanks to the "Editors of the Massachusetts Magazine," the Gleaner begins a tale that will be continued, with countless interruptions and digressions, over the course of many months: "Bless me, cried Margaretta, while in the hope of meeting something from the pen of Philenia, she threw her fine eyes in a cursory manner over the index of the February Magazine. But pray, it may be asked, who is Margaretta?"

The story of Margaretta, the Gleaner's adopted daughter, and their collective adventures in bringing her from orphaned childhood to the safe harbors of married life will quickly become the most popular element of the series. It has, after all, the armature of a novel, and it is in these terms that it is been identified by critics eager to put Murray forward as a pioneering "novelist." Jennifer J. Baker, for example, refers to it as Murray's "novel"; Marion Rust refers to *The Story of Margaretta* as "Murray's only novel"; and Davidson refers to "her novella, *Story of Margaretta* (1798)."[28] Perhaps most influentially, Sharon M. Harris, in her important edition of Murray's work, describes *The Story of Margaretta* as "an important early American novel . . . embedded . . . in a series of non-fiction essays."[29]

Of course, no novel, or book, entitled *The Story of Margaretta* was ever published. In 1798, Murray did publish a greatly expanded version of her Gleaner essays from the *Massachusetts Magazine* in book form, but the work of rescuing the "novel" within the periodical dross has been entirely that of early American scholars of the past generation. Murray certainly teases her readers with some of the stuff of a novel, and the background to Margaretta's arrival in the Gleaner's family sets up expectations that more along these lines will follow. And it will, in fits and starts, but always inseparably bound up with the practices and miscellaneous forms of the periodical.

After the first installment of this story, the Gleaner doubles back to the scene of Margaretta's discovery of the first Gleaner in the *Massachusetts Magazine*, encountered when she was looking for a new poem from Morton's Philenia. Margaretta's suspicions are immediately drawn to her father:

"'Dear sir, did I not lately hear you say that if you ever appeared in the world as an author, you would certainly be known by this appellation?'—I was still silent—'I protest, sir, I am sorry you are forestalled, for I had promised myself a fund of improvement, whenever you should employ your talents as a writer—I expected also, much entertainment, from the various conjectures which I imagined would have been hazarded, relative to the real character of the Gleaner.'"[30] Aware that his daughter is on the verge of recognizing him as author of the new series in the magazine she holds in her hand, the Gleaner distracts her with a lengthy disquisition on the price exacted by "that hangdog scoundrel *Procrastination*," which, he claims, has now robbed him of the possibility of claiming the name of "Gleaner."

Having thus deflected his daughter's suspicions as to her father's secret, he then goes on to deny the readers the pleasure of their would-be novel, beginning a tour in the next several issues of the dominant topics and modes of periodical serials then found in the magazines: a political diatribe on those who see government and its costs as an infringement on their natural liberties, a celebration of the present age as opposed to the virtues of antiquity, a lay sermon on a text from Sterne. Each time the Gleaner rambles in one generic direction or another he concludes by bringing himself up short, and reminding himself, as he does at the end of his sermon, "Whether it may not be well to account for his being induced thus to wander, in a field where, the soil having been so often trod, he could expect to glean so little?"[31] Or, as he ironically concludes his advice on procrastination, "but it is time that I recollect myself, it may be thought that I encroach too far upon a department which may be considered as already filled."[32]

Indeed, these concerns that he is not pleasing his readers with these performances are soon borne out by the new voices that begin to intrude on in his column, beginning with the sixth installment. Here the Gleaner describes a business trip to Boston during which he stopped in at a public house. There, as is his habit, he silently listens in on the conversation, which soon turns literary, as many wordsmiths past and present are called up for "invidious censure." In the course of the discussion, the Gleaner himself soon becomes the subject of discussion. As an anonymous essayist ("he was *any body—every body—or nobody*") debate ensues as to his true identity—a parson, Harvard undergraduate, or Connecticut Wit—and regarding his merits. The general agreement is that the while "his Margaretta" was indeed interesting, no sooner was she introduced than, "whip, in a moment, she was gone."[33] Instead of giving them the story of Margaretta they so clearly desire, his readers complain, the Gleaner bounces from topic to topic with little rhyme or reason.

One in their company does rise to the Gleaner's defense, arguing persuasively that the reason that the Gleaner has withheld the story of Margaretta
has been to avoid "giving to his productions the air of a novel." The silent
Gleaner confesses he "could hardly forbear taking my advocate in my arms,"
and so delighted is he to have found one reader of sympathy and understanding that he suffers little from the slings and arrows that dominate the
assessment of his merits. But he does return home determined to do more
to meet the demands of the majority of his readers for more Margaretta, a
change of heart that is only strengthened when he finds waiting for him a
series of letters that join the chorus of protest against the turn his series has
taken. All his correspondents take the Gleaner to task for abandoning the
story of Margaretta so abruptly, and all request, for very different motives,
that he continue it immediately. One man is looking for advice as to what
to do with his own daughter; another reader, a young woman, is looking
for access to novels, which her father forbids her, forcing her to find them
where she might in magazines; still another seeks wisdom and insight on the
difficult and troubling issue of education for women, hoping to benefit from
Margaretta's example. The Gleaner responds that such demands "forerun
both my plans, and my ability," but he promises to do his best to obey them.[34]

In the next installment, the Gleaner follows through on his vow to please
his readers, describing the education he and his wife provided Margaretta
upon first taking her into their home, an education that revolves around
correspondence. His wife establishes an internal post in the house by which
"they might with the greater convenience open a correspondence by letter."[35] The seemingly strange mode of communicating mother to daughter
within a single house by letter becomes less strange when read in the context of the broader discourse in periodicals on the role of correspondence:
Correspondence was the periodical's ideal mode, each installment a letter
from a contributor with the editor essentially serving as postmaster to the
community. For Murray, who was deeply interested in the topic, letters are
an ideal pedagogical tool, as a child, writing daily "to the parent, or fictitious characters," becomes adept at languages and literature. Although the
Gleaner here had promised to submit to the readers' demands for more
of the "story of Margaretta," the pedagogical model offered in his essays
is in many ways opposed to the education offered by the novel form. The
novel is ultimately dangerous not because of its subject matter (after all,
"The Gleaner" shares many topics with the average novel of the period) but
because it is read in privacy, alone. All the reading and writing that takes
place within the Gleaner's house (and by extension, within the magazine
itself) is social, premised on the contracts of correspondence. Even "fictitious

characters" are to be written to. And when novels *are* read in the Gleaner's house, they are read aloud and in the presence of a parent with whom they can be discussed and debated. The disciplines of correspondence and conversation not only counteract the potentially dangerous, isolating effects of the novel, but they also serve to turn the closed book into a text that is open to the reader's "suggestions, remarks, and observations."[36]

Ultimately it will be these disciplines that save Margaretta from the typical fate of the heroine of the typical eighteenth-century seduction tale. As the Gleaner details the system, in addition to the improvements to writing and language brought about by the regular letter-writing to her mother, perhaps the greatest advantage was in the way that "Margaretta was early accustomed to lay open her heart." Systematically "habituated to disclose, without a blush, each rising thought to her," Margaretta becomes an "exact copiest" of her mother—as if the act of transparent written communication within the household has the ultimate effect of making it so that the heart Margaretta lays open is her mother's heart after all.[37]

This education is soon put to the test when their daughter goes to New Haven and is immediately becomes ensnared in the designs of a rake, Sinisterus Courtland. Fortunately, from her first entrance into the city, Margaretta continued her former practice of writing her mother and immediately confesses her attraction to Courtland: "the epistolary correspondence with which I have for such a length of time . . . been indulged, hath given me the habit of expressing myself to you, in this way."[38] The Gleaner, it turns out, knows much about Courtland, more than Courtland himself is aware—thanks to his own networks of correspondence and information: "I know him to be base, designing." At first, he responds to the news with horror and despair, but then, "hand in glove" with his wife, they begin their collaborative "operations," a series of letters and staged scenes designed to bring Margaretta to a proper realization of her situation.

In many ways "The Gleaner" seems to have given in to its readers' demands by becoming a seduction novel, one that bears the outline of the features found in all such productions of the day: a virtuous young woman of good parentage whose only weaknesses are youth and novel reading; a worthy suitor, rejected; and a relentless rake. But there are some notable differences even within the "novel" sections of the series that are worth underscoring. This seduction "novel" is told from the perspective of the *parents*, who prove both vigilant and brilliant in outmaneuvering the efforts of their daughter's would-be seducer. What saves the day, in the end, is the Gleaner's remarkable restraint: Though he knows the truth of Courtland's past crimes and present circumstances, he does not overtly interfere in his daughter's inclinations.

Instead, he helps her see Courtland as he really is by admitting him into their company, until finally, inevitably, the rake exposes himself.

How he does so is itself significant. After a poem appears in the local *Gazette* dedicated to the beauties of Margaretta, Courtland allows it to be believed about town that he was the author of the verse. When he is publicly exposed as a fraud by a friend of the true author, the Gleaner stages a performance designed to expose Courtland by producing documents that reveal the truth of Courtland's nature, at which point the mask of dissimilitude breaks down entirely. This episode in Margaretta's career ends with a series of letters between our heroine and her friend in New Haven in which the aftermath of her narrow escape is revealed—letters that, like those exposing Courtland, are now safely in the possession of the Gleaner. The story concludes with the Gleaner, now armed with documents and correspondences from all quarters, encountering Courtland in jail, and by carefully and deliberately presenting his texts to his audience, he demonstrates how "our gentleman had become as wax in my hand." An entire reformation of the rake's character is brought about, as Courtland is made dutiful husband to a woman he had earlier abandoned, his relations with his creditors are reestablished through the offices of the Gleaner and his friends in New Haven, and peace and order are restored to the land.

Having performed his part of the contract with his readers, in providing these chapters of the story of Margaretta, the Gleaner now heads out into the city to check up on the progress of his fame and his readers' gratitude to him for his pains. Six months after his previous survey, to his disappointment he discovers that "upon the ear of *the many* . . . the name of GLEANER had never vibrated," while most of those who had read his pages "seemed more occupied in detecting the *real name of the author*, than in essaying to investigate the merit of his productions!"[39] One reader accuses him of being an unmarried young man, and thus an imposter; another young woman assures her companions that no one in New Haven had heard the name of Margaretta "until they saw it in the Magazine"; still another reader promises that he personally knew Margaretta at New Haven. The Gleaner is despondent over this "*hunting after names*," which he insists is "descriptive of the frivolity of the human mind: No sooner does an anonymous piece make its appearance, than . . . conjecture is upon the rack—Who is he? Where does he live? What is his *real name*?"[40] Murray has reason to wish her identity left out of it. As a woman essayist, a field long dominated by men, and as the author, under the name Constantia, of poetry and a feminist essay that had attracted a good deal of attention, her identity would only encourage further speculation about her and her family, detracting attention from the words on the page. As the Gleaner argues, "if the writing is in no sort personal . . . a knowledge of the author can be of no moment, neither can a name designate a character. . . . The business of the reader is to scan the *intrinsick value* and *general tendency* of the composition."

In this definition of the business of the reader, Murray makes manifest the larger stakes involved in the practice of the magazine; by offering up her name, the essays would be read as being about her. What she would gain in "celebrity" she would lose in her ability to make demands upon the *readers'* business. That is, just as the larger institution under whose auspices she writes, the *Massachusetts Magazine*, is built upon an elaborate system of credit, so is the work of the magazine's contributors. Celebrity requires from the reader only laurels, and in the face of celebrity—in the presence of a name of celebrated genius—the reader will inevitably become passive, tyrannized. Instead, readers and writers alike must remember that reading is a mutually creative act, in which each party brings "something" to the table.

Thus the failures of his readers to respond correctly to the story he has just told is not finally debilitating for the Gleaner, for they have at least responded, and their words—however much they might not be those he would have scripted—provide the stuff that makes up much of the twelfth number of the series. As if to underscore this point, the Gleaner inserts at the end of the series copies of letters from two (fictional) readers, Balamour and Timothy Plodder, who had earlier offered themselves as suitors for the hand of Margaretta. These letters are offered out of sequence, following an elaborate back and forth in the previous issues in the correspondence between editors and contributors that occupies the inside cover of every issue, in which the editors claimed to have lost the two letters the Gleaner wished to have inserted earlier and begged him to try and locate new copies of these documents. Thus the Gleaner and the magazine sets up a dizzying correspondence, in which exchanges of letters and responsibilities between the various parties seems always on the verge of breaking down and yet, in part because of its fragmentary, interrupted nature, it continues to provide the material that keeps the enterprise afloat—and "original."

Upon leaving the story of Margaretta, the Gleaner writes: "Reader, though we bid adieu to Margaretta for the present, I would not have thee lament it too seriously. I know thou art tenderly attached to her; and I therefore give thee my word, that if thy acquaintance with me continuest, we will, occasionally, peep in upon her, and thus learn, from time to time, how matters go on."[41] In setting up the terms of the contract for the coming year, the Gleaner is not setting his terms as easy as might appear. If his readers have disappointed him, he too will frustrate them in turn, as he directs his attentions over the next several installments to precisely those *"musty morals"* and "long winded remarks" that his readers pronounced against so loudly over the course of the first year of the series. The next installment of "The Gleaner" is a long sermon about the "general ingratitude to that *August* and *self existent Being* from whom they originate."[42] And yet, the Gleaner can safely feel himself entitled to such sermonizing, knowing that at least for a time he has his readers' attention safely in hand, holding out the promise of more Margaretta only if they maintain their "acquaintance with me."

The series, as it continues, plays on this game of imperfect but not entirely broken contracts, in which editor/author and reader/correspondent each gives to the other not exactly what the other one had asked for, and the continued circulation of this material keeps the enterprise afloat. No sooner does the Gleaner turn from his family "novel" to the kinds of miscellaneous moral lectures with which he began (and which so tried the patience of his readers) than his readers begin to intrude once again. "I have for some months formed the design of ushering my little narrative to publick view, through the channel of your paper," writes one new correspondent; "but observing you engaged in a regular detail, I have waited until you have conducted your account to a convenient pause."[43] This is the mise en abyme of the periodical form, as the editor makes space for correspondents to set up their own shop as essayists, who in turn must make room for correspondents of their own (both real and fictional) within the space of their individual series. It is, in a sense, the Gleaner's household writ large, as correspondence passes ceaselessly to characters real and fictitious, where readers became contributors and contributors became columnists, all presided over by the editor who, like the Gleaner, can distinguish a Sinisterus (the rake) from a Hamilton (the good husband, named in high Federalist fashion) and will always use his quill to reform the one and reward the other.

III

Along with Brockden Brown and Murray, perhaps the writer who would stake the most on a periodical career was an individual in many ways not temperamentally suited to the anonymity, neutrality, and cacophony of the form: Joseph Dennie, As a young man struggling for employment in the small New Hampshire town of Charlestown in 1791, Joseph Dennie wrote to his mother: "Periodical Essayists plume themselves not a little, upon the delight their papers afford *the million*, upon the day of publication."[44] At the time, Dennie was hinting at ambitions that would take him (as they did his contemporary—and later friend—Charles Brockden Brown) far from the legal profession he had been trained into. In fact, it was not until 1794 that he would openly confess to his parents that he had been, since 1792, publishing a series of essays in the local periodicals:

> In moments of dreary vacancy, I have amused myself & enlarged my knowledge of English style, by writing at different times & in various vehicles The "Farrago." This is a miscellaneous essay which was first commenced in the Winter of 1792, was printed originally at a village in Vermont on the *Cumberland* calculation. In the press of Obscurity, I knew that I should risque nothing either in censure or praise. The Public, however saw or fancied some merit;—and, as American essays have been hitherto unmarked except for flimsy expression & jejune ideas, they have allowed me the praise of reviving in some degree the Goldsmith vivacity in thought & the Addisonian sweetness in expression.[45]

What Dennie meant by the "Cumberland calculation" is spelled out earlier in the letter, in describing how Richard Cumberland, the English essayist and dramatist, had published his earliest "Observer" essays "at a Rural press wth the calculation if his essays were jejune, the obscurity of their birth place would save the author [.] if, on the contrary, they had the stamp of Genius, they would soon be current in cities."[46] But in originally detailing the Cumberland plan for his parents, he suggested that he meant it as the model for his legal career, starting out in rural New Hampshire in the hopes that his "Genius" would soon be "current in cities." On the face of it, it makes little sense to imagine that a modest legal career in rural New Hampshire could work according to the "Cumberland calculation." The trajectory Dennie was here imagining for himself would follow not from law or from his other nascent career as a clergyman, but from a literary career as an essayist, an ambition he could only bring himself to admit to by increments.

By the following year, he is able to lay the whole before his mother, writing from Boston where he was making arrangements for the publication of the *Tablet*, his first periodical venture. Assuring his mother that "Authorship" can indeed be "the ways & means" to financial reward, he describes the attentions he has received in the metropolis from the rich and powerful: "The Gay were pleased with the vivacity & originality of the Farrago[,] the Aristocracy were pleased that the satire of Colon & Spondee was leveled against the foes of Federalism."[47] The result was that he was able to gain the sponsorship of his new friends for the establishment of a periodical, to be printed by Spotswood (recently established in Boston following his periodical disappointments in Philadelphia) and built around Dennie's "Farrago" essays.

Like so many young writers turning from traditional career paths for the uncertainties of literature, Dennie is eager to assuage his mother's concerns, reminding her that "The Essays of Addison & Johnson were published in this manner, . . . and shall I be ashamed to tread the path they have pursued [?]. Belive [*sic*] me, my dear Mamma, it leads to property, it leads to political to my legal & to my literary eminence." Predictably, however, the periodical folded after only thirteen issues, dashing the fond expectations Dennie had outlined to his mother of securing through this vehicle £150 annually. Writing to Royall Tyler, his friend and collaborator in the "Colon & Spondee" series, Dennie complained that, despite the support of the Boston elite, "alack, the tasteless or mercenary Bostonians suffered that to die and me to starve."[48] In a later letter to his mother, he describes the failure of the *Tablet* as "the death of my *child!*": "I never felt the inconvenience of being poor and the anguish of disappointment, till then. For if I had been in possession of property, neither the waywardness of the times, the dullness of the Bostonians, nor, the infancy of my *savage* Country would have repressed the growth of my miscellany."[49]

In many ways, Dennie's is an anomalous periodical career, although also one of the most distinguished and influential. Unlike the majority of his contemporaries, Dennie avowed explicitly partisan politics in his periodical writing and editing, and he preached a strident conservatism so very different from the moderate federalism of Thomas or Murray as to make for uncomfortable bedfellows—a divide within Federalism that would contribute to the breakdown of the party after the election of 1800. But it was more than his politics that marked out his difference from colleagues like Brown. As the correspondence above suggests, Dennie was not content to wait for posterity to determine the value of his periodical offerings. Nor was he willing to countenance the limitations of his readers, whose failures to respond to his periodical endeavors as they merited only served to underscore everything he had come to despise about his native country.

Dennie invested the periodical form with all his ambitions, not just for monetary reward and fame but more urgently for a way out. Ultimately, Dennie's dream from the start of his literary career was to write himself (imaginatively at least) back to England, mourning, in his outrage following the "death" of his *Tablet*, the career that might have been his "had it not been for the *selfish* patriotism of that hoary traitor, Adams": "I might now, perhaps, in a Literary Diplomatic . . . Situation been in the service of my rightful King and instead of shivering in the bleakness of the United States, felt the genial sunshine of a Court."[50] Such attitudes would end up making

Dennie an easy target for those Republicans eager to portray Federalists as crypto-monarchists.

Dennie was in truth one of the more partisan periodical writers of the age, rivaled only by William Cobbett and, on the other side of the political spectrum, Philip Freneau, editor of the *Time Piece*. But whereas Freneau would ultimately find his vocation within the partisan newspaper of the period as editor of the Jeffersonian *National Gazette*, Dennie only briefly pursued such opportunities, all too plentiful in this period of intense factional divide. In 1799, finally abandoning provincial New Hampshire in response to numerous invitations from literary and political admirers in Philadelphia, Dennie accepted work as Pickering's secretary and as a contributor to Fenno's archfederalist *Gazette of the United States*. But he quickly found the "absurdity and inaccuracy" of the *Gazette* distasteful and tried to keep his distance as much as possible from the world of newspaper politics. Instead, he quickly began planning what would prove his most successful periodical venture, the *Port-Folio*.[51]

Why a man of such fierce political convictions with admirers among the most powerful federalists of the day would have resisted offers of newspaper work is worth pausing over, because it helps us see the model of literary citizenship the periodical offered in distinction from that to be found in the newspaper. For Dennie, much of the appeal of his chosen line as a periodical essayist was in the imaginative connections it forged for him to predecessors in the field from across the Atlantic—Addison and Steele, Goldsmith, Cumberland. His maddening visions of the future he might have had—"Had not the *Revolution* happened; had I continued a subject to the King, had I been fortunately born in *England* or resided in the City of London for the last 7 years"—find relief only in the fantasy that through the periodical he might somehow be restored to his rightful place in history.[52] In his important study of Dennie's *Port-Folio*, William C. Dowling has argued persuasively for reading the magazine as an attempt to offer an alternative imaginary community to that which was represented by America, as Dennie found it, especially after the ascendancy of the Jeffersonians in 1801. The citizenship Dennie and his collaborators wished to achieve was one that would bind them to a moral community that crossed not only national boundaries but temporal ones as well, allowing them to claim kinship not just with the British across the ocean but also with the literary communities of generations past.

Dowling ultimately sees the *Port-Folio* and Dennie's attempts to forge a model of federalism whose "values will be literary rather than political" as "a long and complex withdrawal in which Federalism, banished from the civic sphere by a triumphant Jeffersonian ideology, seeks an alternative home in . . . the republic of letters."[53] Yet in imagining a spiritual and moral kinship with Addison or with Johnson and his circle, Dennie was doing nothing after 1800 that other periodical dreamers had not been doing at the height of Federalist power in the previous decade. For Dennie, it was indeed a retreat, but it was one he had been seeking his whole career—a retreat into a borderless, timeless society that the periodical form seemed to promise, one where he could be a citizen of the nation he so desperately longed for.

But Dennie is no easy representative of the average periodical federalist. Dennie's retreat ultimately has more to do with his inability to accept the compromises and correspondences inherent in periodical publication. Dennie had been initially attracted to the periodical precisely because of the genealogical connections it maintained to an earlier age and another country. He never accepted that the early periodical was also premised on a model of compromise, correspondence, and ultimately failure. For most of his early essay writing career, Dennie went it alone, making little space in his columns for correspondence from readers or for collaborators. Even his one ongoing collaborative feature, "Colon & Spondee," was divided neatly between himself and Tyler, each of them signing his own entries. Writing as the "Farrago" in the *Tablet* in 1795, for example, Dennie challenged anyone who might "censure me for sameness of sentiment" to keep in mind that "I am a *lone author*." Here in America, he argued, worthy collaborators were few and far between: "In the periodical publications of Great Britain, the papers are usually furnished by the members of a literary society, who assemble at some coffee-house or tavern, and club their genius to amuse the public, as they club their cash, to discharge the reckoning. Those speculations, which have improved, and have gladdened life, were rarely the fruit of a single brain, but the offspring of wit in conjunction. This union of abilities is almost as essential to the perfection of a miscellany, as the union of sexes to the formation of our being."[54] In New Hampshire, by contrast, Dennie found few collaborators, no club, little society, and certainly no peers. He was instead, as he titled his next series, a "Lay Preacher," sermonizing to the rabble who happened, unfortunately, to also be his countrymen.

His work on the *Farmer's Museum* is an excellent case in point. Arguably one of the most influential periodicals of the period, despite its relatively isolated place of origin in Walpole, the success of the *Museum* owes everything to Dennie's remarkable energies and talents. And yet the *Museum*, like the *Port-Folio*, was a strange and uncharacteristic periodical: a hybrid of the newspaper and the magazine. The closest predecessor I have been able to find is Thomas's short-lived *Worcester Magazine*, which itself came into being as a sly end-run around new postal regulations that temporarily crippled Thomas's ability to circulate his newspaper, the *Spy*. In the end, however, once the regulations had loosened sufficiently for Thomas to return to his newspaper, he did so, and the *Spy* resumed with the end of the *Worcester Magazine*. The unique pleasures and possibilities Thomas rediscovered in the magazine format, he would revive with his *Massachusetts Magazine* a few years later.

When Dennie's contributions first began appearing to the *Farmer's Museum* in 1794, co-owned at the time by Thomas and New Hampshire partner David Carlisle, it was a modest production. Unlike Thomas's earlier *Worcester Magazine*, here the decision to edit the *Museum* as a hybrid periodical was based on the practical consideration of the smaller New Hampshire marketplace: large enough to support neither a newspaper nor a magazine, the hybrid format—in many ways closer to earlier weekly papers such as the *New-England Courant*—seemed a tenable compromise. In the inaugural issue, Thomas promised that his long involvement in periodical publication "causes him to keep open an extensive correspondence, in the line of publick information, throughout the United States, and in Europe;—a stream from this channel will flow to nurture The NEWHAMPSHIRE JOURNAL Or, the Farmer's *Weekly Museum*."[55] But while promising the most current news, Thomas and Carlisle also called on readers to provide intelligences and original contributions to the four-page weekly.

As Dennie began to become more central to the management of the *Museum* after 1795, he developed an extended network of correspondence, inviting contributions from various corners of the far-flung literary republic. As Catherine Kaplan puts it, "Dennie's genius lay in understanding how to create . . . a persistent network for creating and circulating his *Museum*. That network included all those who read, wrote for, solicited subscriptions for, extracted, or even quoted the *Museum* in conversation. Their efforts brought Dennie more readers, which potentially brought him more content; their efforts also brought Dennie more content, which potentially brought him more readers. Each issue of Dennie's paper provided new fodder for conversation, new material to read and, given Dennie's penchant for extracting, new volumes to seek out."[56]

Ultimately, however, Dennie's success as America's "first professional man of letters" depended in every way on his success in summoning forth a network of correspondents who were willing to remain both anonymous and amateur writers.[57] What made Dennie unique among the periodical editors of the period is that he longed for *his* voice, and not just his editorial vision, to predominate over the conversation. Whereas almost universally the other periodical editors of the period went to great lengths to perform the ritual sublimation of their own political opinions, their own talents, their own egos to the editorial function, Dennie sought to use the periodical form to argue for a natural cultural aristocracy: "Daring and impudent as it may appear in this leveling age, to avow respect for birth or talents, . . . [m]y own head is so weak, that I cannot help fancying some difference, in the capacity of those of other men."[58] Dennie concludes this "Lay Preacher" column with a vision, in which he is entrusted with the care of "the head of Genius, whose ancestry can be traced beyond William the Conqueror." In his original version he briefly contemplated consigning it to the museum at Harvard, but he rejected that option for fear that the head would "sustain a rude kick from some of the *animals* of the place, or have its fine features marred by the fogginess of the atmosphere," ultimately consigning it to the care of *Philenia* (his friend and supporter, the poet Sarah Morton). A decade later, in revising the same "Lay Preacher" column for his *Port-Folio*, Dennie is notably less optimistic that an American repository might be found for his "head of Genius": "I, at first, thought of wishing it a place in the Museum of Mr. Peale, but was apprehensive, that either the Prairie dogs, or the vasty Mammoth, might intercept the view. I therefore consign it to the munificent patronage of British generosity, and instantly it seems to exhibit all the glorious lineaments of classical statuary."[59]

In both cases, Dennie's Lay Preacher will *not* consign the "head of Genius" to the museum, whether Harvard's or Peale's. In the earlier case, still smarting from his own treatment as a student at the university, Dennie cannot imagine the "*animals*" of that place treating the "head" as it deserves. In the second, Dennie ridicules the American natural curiosities that dominate Peale's museum as taking away from a proper appreciation of genius and culture. Despite the title he had inherited—*The Farmer's Museum*—the periodical Dennie imagines was never the "literary museum"—the periodical analogue of the museums of Bowen or Peale—that so many magazines took as their model. He was never to be the anonymous editor Charles Brockden Brown was at that time transforming himself into.

In many respects, Dennie bears more in common with the magazine form that would follow in the nineteenth century than with the anonymous and cacophonous world of eighteenth-century magazines. That Dennie was one of the only individuals actually to make a living writing and editing magazines speaks to the unique talents and energies he brought to the enterprise. Magazines were a money-losing enterprise for printers and an exercise in voluntary literary association—or virtual clubbing—for most readers and authors. Ultimately, however, the editorial position Dennie imagined for himself bore closer resemblance to the editor's armchair of the nineteenth-century magazine, with the man of genius at the head of his periodical society, his voice speaking first and deferred to at all times.

In the first volume of his *Port-Folio* in 1801, Dennie lauded his old editorial persona, even as he assumed his new one as "Jonathan Oldschool": "No country *of its age*, has so many newspaper bantlings to provide for, as America. Every petty village has its printer. . . . From a mass of dull or frivolous papers, from the country, the Walpole paper must be excepted. Its Editor is a gentleman of learning, and taste; and of his wit, propriety of sentiments, and felicity of allusion, we are always happy to exhibit . . . specimens."[60]

By this point, his readers well knew that the editor of the *Port-Folio* and the former editor of the *Farmer's Museum* were one and the same: He had announced it clearly in his "Prospectus of a New Weekly Paper" "submitted to men of affluence, men of liberty, and men of letters": "A young man, once known among village-readers, as the humble historian of the hour, the conductor of a *Farmer's* Museum, and a *Lay Preacher's* Gazette, again offers himself to the public as a volunteer-editor. Having, as he conceives, a right to vary, at pleasure, his *fictitious* name, he now, for higher reasons than any fickle humour might dictate, assumes the appellation of Oldschool."[61] In celebrating the editor of the *Farmer's Museum*, he is openly celebrating himself, his wit, and his talents. But in doing so he is only demanding that genius be recognized, that his achievements be distinguished from the mass of country editors and village pressman.

In his prospectus for the *Port-Folio*, Dennie goes further in distinguishing himself from both the newspapers and magazines that have come before. His *Port-Folio*, he insists, will be "not quite a *Gazette*, nor wholly a *Magazine*" but something in between—pretending to neither the impartiality of the magazine nor the leveling tendencies of the newspaper. In searching out models that might vouch for the likelihood of his prospects, Dennie can only point to his own *Farmer's Museum* or, more promising but significantly more distant, the grandfathers of the periodical press, Addison and Steele. Like the model of the *Tatler* or the *Spectator* (and unlike the *American Magazine*), Dennie insists he "will not make his paper 'a *carte-blanche* on which every fool and knave may scribble what he pleases.'" Only a select few, or what Dennie goes on to identify as "the *Master-Spirits* of the nation," need apply for admission to the pages of the *Port -Folio*, and most certainly not "the lower classes of our motley vulgar, too often composed of the scoundrels of all nations."[62]

Only at the end of his abbreviated career does Dennie allow himself to feel at home among a community of like-minded peers that gathered around him in Philadelphia, men such as Brockden Brown, John Blair Linn (Brown's brother-in-law), and the various writers, doctors, and lawyers who participated in the Tuesday Club. As he wrote to his mother in his last letter home in 1809, "The circulation of the Port Folio augments, and the Literary Club, who assist me, includes some of the most distinguished characters in the Country. I am now very powerfully supported."[63] And, most important of all, the end result for which Dennie had been working his whole career—his recognition by *English* critics and men of genius— seemed finally close at hand. The "old school" to which Dennie devoted himself was first and foremost the Old World—the world of British letters and culture to which he desperately sought to tie himself through the periodical form. These were ultimately the only readers from whom Dennie had been truly waiting to hear, and so one cannot help but hear the relief in his voice when he wrote to his mother that he had heard "from authentic sources, that my efforts, as a man of letters, are very candidly appreciated at London, Edinburgh and Paris."[64]

It would be Washington Irving, who in 1801 began writing under the pen-name "Jonathan Oldstyle" in a clear homage to Dennie, who would prove the first American author to claim the audience abroad that Dennie had so long imagined would be his. But if Irving was the first successful American author, he was also the last major figure to emerge out of early American periodical culture. Those who would follow Irving would be pursuing a very different model of literary career and culture, one in many ways that had at least as much in common with Dennie's ambitions as it did with Irving's nineteenth-century career.

CHAPTER FOUR

The Early American Magazine in the Nineteenth Century

Brown, Rowson, and Irving

I

The parallels between Susanna Rowson's and Charles Brockden Brown's careers are worth considering. Before 1800, Rowson and Brown had secured their places as the two leading novelists of the early national period; after 1800 they both moved away from the novel and from their own literary fame. And for all the differences between their early novels, there are some notable similarities: Both were interested in transatlantic themes, and both saw their writings as serving a pedagogical function. They also shared concerns about the novel form itself, an ambivalence that is lost to history when we focus exclusively on their novel writing (and, in each case, too often on only *one* novel). Both wrote in a variety of forms: poems, essays, dialogues, geographies, histories, and political economy. And even within their novels themselves, there is a remarkable range of formal and generic approaches. Brown experimented with gothic and psychological fiction but also with epistolary forms and seduction plots. Rowson's generic and formal experimentation in the novel is even more striking: Although she is associated most closely with *Charlotte Temple*, with its unified narrative voice and didactic address, in some ways *Charlotte Temple* is an exception in an exceptional career. It is indeed hard to find two books from among her many productions that closely resemble each other formally, from the Byzantine wanderings of *The Inquisitor*, the anti-novelistic structure of *Mentoria*, the sweeping historicism of *Reuben and Rachel*, or the epistolary sufferings of *Sarah*.

Looking at Rowson's career as a whole, only a handful of her many books are what should properly be considered novels. Here I refer not only to her schoolbooks (*Youth's First Step in Geography* [1818] or *Spelling Dictionary*

[1807]) or anthologies (*A Present for Young Ladies* [1818]) but also to several of the books often categorized as novels, including *The Inquisitor* (1788) and *Mentoria* (1791). *The Inquisitor* is narrated by a man who acquires a ring that allows him invisibly to visit his fellow citizens, encounters he describes in a series of "rambles, excursion, characters, and tales."[1] *Mentoria* even more aggressively refuses any novelistic plotting. The book begins with a series of letters from a governess of a boarding school to her former charges and then moves into a series of short stories. Like *The Inquisitor*, *Mentoria*'s structure bears much closer relation to the periodical form than to the novel. Mentoria writes letters to her former charges upon various subjects—filial duty, proper society—and highlights each one with an anecdote, a story designed to give force to the moral lesson. One story leads to another—stories within stories, letters within letters, until the conceit of Mentoria as letter writer gives way completely after a long epistolary story of Agnes, whose story, Rowson tells us in a footnote, is "authentic and not the offspring of fancy."[2] Rowson then immediately moves into a story of "Marian and Lydia," which itself is composed of stories within stories. The book concludes with an "Essay on Female Education," followed by two stories, an oriental tale about vanity entitled "Urganda & Fatima" and a moral essay on envy and gossip entitled "The Incendiary," both of which, Rowson tells us, have "formerly appeared in a Magazine."[3] While the original source is not known, both appeared in the British periodical *The Polite Repository or, Amusing Companion* in 1791. In addition to these two (unattributed) tales, the first volume of *The Polite Repository* also featured Rowson's poem "Lydia," a selection from her first novel *Victoria* (1786), and a sketch from *The Inquisitor*, indicating Rowson's close connections with the periodical community at the start of her career in Britain before moving to America two years later.[4] *The Inquisitor* and *Mentoria*, meanwhile, soon became part of the great textual commons in the late eighteenth and early nineteenth centuries, excerpted frequently on both sides of the Atlantic.[5]

It is the Rowson who wrote outside the novel, who resisted and even explicitly critiqued the novel, who remains to be recovered—not just for a fuller sense of Rowson's career but also for a more accurate picture of the literary culture of the period, one that was far less invested in the novel than literary history might suggest. If many of Rowson's books look somewhat motley and even formally unrecognizable to us today, it is because many of them were working out of models that bore no direct relationship to the rising novel. (Even *Reuben and Rachel*—with its multiple plotlines, documents, stories within stories, and blend of history, travelogue, and fiction—shows the influence of the schoolbook and the periodical miscellany as much as any novelistic model.) And as with Brown, a fuller recovery of Rowson more accurately contextualizes her work in a literary history that does *not* revolve entirely around the novel—or at least not around the definition of the novel that would be codified in the nineteenth century. This magazine work complicates in important ways the familiar stories we tell about the rise of the novel, and for this reason critics have historically, until quite recently, worked to marginalize and even ridicule the turn to periodical form. For Rowson, as for Brown, the turn to anonymous periodical work in the first decade of the nineteenth century was in large measure due to increasing doubts about the politics of the novel form. Their periodical writings and projects help us understand some of these concerns and the possibilities of another model for a national literature that the magazine form sought to provide.

Throughout her career, Rowson expressed concerns regarding novels. In *The Inquisitor* (1788), for example, she ridicules the conventions of "the modern novel": "It is indeed shocking . . . to see so many reams of paper expended in ushering to the world pernicious pages, which tend to vitiate the taste and corrupt the heart."[6] And novels are repeatedly a cause of corruption in Rowson's tales. In *Mentoria* (1791), for example, "The History of Dorcas" has at its core the revelation that she had been allowed in her youth to read freely in novels: "these books served only to soften my mind and encrease my passion, so that by never attempting to repel it in its first approach, it in time gained an entire ascendancy over my heart, formed a part of my existence, twined round the chords of my life, and can be extinguished only by the hand of death."[7] In "Women as They Are" (1804), another tragedy is born of the same source:

> Poor LINDAMIRA, deep in novels read,
> When married, keeps the path she taught to tread.
> And while the novel's page she's eager turning,
> The pot boils over, and the meat is burning;
> And while she is weeping o'er ideal woes,
> Her poor neglected little infant goes
> With uncomb'd hair, torn frock, and naked toes.
> Her husband disappointed, quits his home,
> At clubs to loiter, or with bucks to roam;
> While LINDAMIRA still the tale pursues,
> And in each heroine, her own sorrow views.[8]

These cautionary tales about the dangers of uninhibited novel reading were relatively conventional. In early American literary studies, we have been taught to presume that those who decried the dangers of novel were invariably speaking from a position of class and gender privilege, worrying over the ways in which the novel threatened stable class and gender roles by encouraging readers to imagine themselves outside of their proper station. When novelists themselves decried imaginative fiction, often advertising their own productions as tales "founded on fact," as Rowson did in *Charlotte Temple*, we are to understand that they are "co-opting" the critique, subverting the system from within. So prevalent has this reading become that today we hardly hesitate over critiques of the novel such as those Rowson herself raised repeatedly, dismissing them as a sign of the savvy of the writer or, if the critic is less forgiving, of her cowardice.

And yet the critique of the early novel is ultimately not so easily dismissed in its entirety as latter-day Puritanism, cynical marketing, or subversive ventriloquism. Although moralistic concerns of a more simplistic and predictable form existed, many of those criticizing the novel in the early years of the nineteenth century were focused on serious concerns about the dangers novels posed to readers in terms of agency, reason, and self-knowledge. Far from worrying about the potential for novels giving readers too much agency, many critics of the novel worried about the potential for authorial *tyranny*. Another repeated concern focused on the anxiety that novel readers would lose all interest in things as they are, in the mixed world of everyday life, and would become either delusional or depressed as a result. As Dorcasina, the heroine of Tabitha Gilman Tenney's *Female Quixotism* (1801), writes at the end of her long humiliating career as a novel junkie, "I now find that I have passed my life in a dream, or rather a delirium; and have grown grey in chasing a shadow, which has always been fleeing from me, in pursuit of imaginary happiness, which, in this life, can never be realized."[9] As she advises her correspondent, instead of novels one should present children with life "as it really is, . . . chequered with good and evil."[10]

The critique of the novel especially found favor in the pages of early American magazines, a fact that initially seems confusing considering that many of these magazines published fiction and regularly reviewed novels. However, periodicals had good reason to foment suspicion of the novel, precisely because the critique favored the formal properties of the magazine. If the novel was prone to authorial tyranny over the imagination of the reader, the periodical offered multiple texts and authors, overseen by a judicious editor. If the novel presented, in the frequently cited admonition of Goldsmith, a "delusive" vision of a "happiness which never existed," the periodical was devoted to the mixture of pleasure and pains, novelty and mundanity that was life "as it really is."[11] And if the primary risk of novels was in their indiscriminate consumption, then, as Patricia Okker has demonstrated, "with an editor's guidance could people read novels safely."[12] After all, few argued that the novel was *itself* inherently corrupting; instead, the dangers of the form lay in the profound difficulties for young or uneducated readers in determining *what* to read, which books would "elevate" and which "inflame" the mind. The problem with novels, these critics argued, was that nine out of ten were more productive of evil than good; as the *Mirror of Taste* put it in 1811, "to the deep novel reader, this world and its uses 'seem weary, flat, stale and unprofitable.'"[13] The only solution, then, is "to mark out those novels, as they come from the press, which appear least noxious, and most conducive to such advantages, as can be derived from that species of composition."[14]

In 1803, in the *Boston Weekly Magazine's* serial essay "The Gossip," we find an editorial on the dangers of novel reading. After telling in previous installments the story of an inveterate reader of novels whose education left her woefully unprepared for the challenges real life had to offer, the Gossip pauses to reflect at length on the dangers of indiscriminate novel reading. The critique here is a familiar one, as is the solution: the Gossip calls for a "literary Censor" (precisely the role the *Weekly Magazine* set out for itself) to help readers make decisions as to which novels are worth reading and which will "serve only to confuse and weaken" the understanding.[15] To prove that not *all* novels vitiate the understanding, the Gossip offers some important exceptions, including the novels of Fanny Burney, Sophia Lee, and Frances Brooke, then offers somewhat more muted approval for some novels by Rowson:[16] "There are some Novels also from the pen of a lady, whom I know not how to term with propriety either European or American, (Mrs. *Rowson*,) which might be read with advantage, especially by females; but even her works are not without their dangerous tendency, and perhaps of all her numerous productions, there are not more than three which could by an impartial Censor be recommended. *Reuben and Rachel*, an historical romance is the best; *Charlotte*, and the *Inquisitor*, have a considerable degree of merit."[17] What makes this essay particularly striking is not the nature of the critique of the novel or the call for a "literary Censor," but the fact that it was likely written by Rowson herself.

We cannot be certain how much of a role Rowson actually played in the *Boston Weekly Magazine* and in the production of the long-running Gossip series in particular. Nineteenth-century biographers and contemporaries routinely credited Rowson as a contributing editor to the *Weekly Magazine* and as the primary author of "The Gossip." For example, her 1824 obituary in the *Boston Gazette* lists her as "the conductor, at one time, of the 'Boston Weekly Magazine,' in which she wrote many valuable essays on various

moral and interesting subjects."[18] Samuel L. Knapp's "Memoir," attached to
the posthumously published *Charlotte's Daughter* (1828), similarly credits
her with having "conducted the Boston Weekly Magazine, and contributed
largely to the success of that popular periodical, by her ability as an editor
and writer."[19] The first book-length biography of Rowson in 1870 describes
at some length her periodical work, including her work as "editor" for
the *Weekly Magazine*, and as contributor of "a series of light and graceful
papers, after the manner of the *Spectator*, . . . called the Gossip."[20]

Rowson's twentieth-century biographers, on the other hand, have largely
ignored or diminished her periodical work. In 1986 Cathy Davidson does
identify her in passing as a contributing editor to the *Boston Weekly Magazine*, but that same year Patricia L. Parker's critical biography of Rowson
went to some length to challenge the supposition that Rowson had served in
any extensive capacity at the periodical. Among the reasons for her doubts
are a later claim by the magazine's publishers that *they* were the primary
editors of the journal; the conceit that the serialization of Rowson's novel
Sincerity was anonymously submitted to the magazine as an ordinary contribution; and the unlikelihood that anyone as overcommitted as Rowson
(managing as she was a successful and demanding boarding school and an
unsuccessful and demanding husband) would consider taking on anonymous
and largely profitless periodical work at the same time. Ten years earlier,
Dorothy Weil laid the groundwork for challenging Rowson's contributions
as the Gossip, arguing that it was extremely unlikely that any author would
write so dismissively of their own productions as the Gossip does in discussing the novels of "Mrs. Rowson."[21] In more recent biographical treat-
ments of Rowson's career, there is almost no mention of any contribution
to periodicals to be found whatsoever. The fact of her periodical career,
once celebrated by her contemporaries, has become a critical gray area, a
minefield of issues inherent to the early American magazine and anathema
to the critical biographer.

Although I confess myself inclined to trust the judgment of Rowson's
contemporaries, especially that of Knapp—a periodical editor (*Boston
Monthly Magazine* from 1825 to 1826), literary biographer, and a devoted
collector of periodical works—my goal in raising these issues is not to seek
out a definitive answer to what is ultimately an unanswerable question
when working with early American periodicals.[22] As we have seen, the
magazines of the eighteenth and early nineteenth centuries were largely
anonymous, collaborative, cacophonous affairs. They were a place where
authors like Rowson and Brown came to escape; they offered neither fame
(most were anonymous) nor profits (most were financial disasters), and

thus to the eyes of modern literary historians they often appear frustrating, even perverse, spaces.

In these terms, the case Weil and Parker make against Rowson's periodical career is instructive. They raise very good points, not just against Rowson's editorial work at the *Weekly Magazine* or her authorship of the Gossip series, but also against the early magazine as an alternative site of literary culture. For example, let us take Parker's point that the magazine's publishers, Thomas Dean and Samuel Gilbert, claimed they were responsible for the magazine's contents. There runs throughout early magazine publishing in the United States something of a tension between publishers and contributing editors, especially those who provided the content for ongoing serial essays like "The Gossip." We see a productive version of this tension, for example, in "The Gleaner." While Isaiah Thomas certainly played a large role in organizing and soliciting content for the magazine, in many ways he served as something closer to manager of a joint stock company of contributing editors. Prominent among these was Judith Sargent Murray. While from the perspective of Thomas, Murray remained a "contributor," "The Gleaner" itself functioned as a kind of magazine-within-the-magazine, soliciting letters, contributions, and editorial decisions independent of the larger periodical. And of course, the Gleaner is just one such "subeditor" within the co-op that is the *Massachusetts Magazine*. It is on similar terms that Rowson served at the *Boston Weekly Magazine* a decade later: as editor of "The Gossip" and of related contributions, along with her collaborator and fellow contributor, none other than Murray herself. In most early magazines, while the publishers (in this case, Dean and Gilbert) might understand themselves as "editors," the ground-level editorial work was happening within the columns and series that made up the magazine. But this is cold comfort to the literary historian, searching for clear authorial fingerprints. (The likelihood that "The Gossip" was a collaborative enterprise, involving Rowson, Murray, and others, only makes the whole project messier still.)

Weil's and Parker's other concerns can also be addressed, but still not in ways that are likely to be entirely satisfying. That Rowson in "The Gossip" treats her earlier books fairly dismissively (even ranking the miscellaneous production *The Inquisitor* alongside *Charlotte Temple*) seems less surprising when placed alongside Brown's expressed desire, at almost the exact same time, to be disconnected from *all* of his own earlier works. Just as Brown was undergoing a radical sea change in his literary career, Susanna Rowson was herself reorienting her own career away from the novel and the stage and toward her new career in education and in periodicals.

Part of the problem for our contemporary readings of early magazines lies in the fact that almost all of these early magazines were financial failures, and therefore the work of contributors smacks of dilettantism, a hobby taken up after more "serious" work as novelists was largely behind them.[23] Why did the two most important writers of the early republic end their careers working primarily in periodicals? The usual story told is that they left the novel because it was unprofitable, but compared to magazine work, novel-writing—even in those days of rampant piracy—was a veritable gold mine. In the long run, of course, we know that the novel "triumphed." By the 1820s novels were sufficiently profitable that James Fenimore Cooper could make a very good living writing them. And for the literary critical profession that emerged in the decades to follow, the novel provided the necessary footing on which to build a literary history of great books and authors, ultimately traced back to a point of "origins" in the 1780s and 90s. The early novel is so blessed largely because of the work of literary scholars themselves, but there is little evidence that many of our pioneering "novelists" of the period shared this vision. Brown's dedication to the novel form lasted only four years (and since most scholars too easily dismiss his final two novels of 1801, only three years of novel writing are at the heart of his oeuvre); his dedication to the periodical form, however, extended over the full range of his career and dominated his last decade of work. Hannah Webster Foster, author of *The Coquette*, is the author of precisely one novel, her other major work, *The Boarding School*, being something else entirely: a collection of anecdotes, lessons, pedagogical meditations, and letters between the alumni of a board school—something, that is, like *Mentoria* (which it closely resembles), more magazine than novel. William Hill Brown, the author of the "first American novel," devoted much of his energy following the publication of *The Power of Sympathy* to periodical writing, including "The Reformer" series for Isaiah Thomas's *Massachusetts Magazine* and "The Yankee" series for the *Columbian Centinel*. These are today the most widely taught and reprinted writers of the early republican period, and yet only their novels remain available in accessible editions.

In the early years of the new century, for all of these pioneers of the novel, the anonymous, collaborative periodical was where these writers devoted much of their energies. Following her work at the *Weekly Magazine*, Rowson served as contributor to the magazine's successor and then, toward the very end of her life, as a contributor (largely of poetry) to the *New-England Galaxy*. And while she, unlike Brown, never entirely abandoned the novel, it is interesting to note that the only nineteenth-century novel published in her lifetime was *Sarah; or, the Exemplary Wife*, a novel that was originally serialized anonymously as *Sincerity* in the *Boston Weekly Magazine* in 1803–4.

Sincerity is an odd novel in many respects among Rowson's work. In addition to being her only serialized novel, it is also entirely epistolary, a structure Rowson had used sparingly in her earlier books, primarily in the largely unsuccessful *Trials of the Human Heart*. It is interesting that Rowson turns to the epistolary form in 1803 at the same time that she was overseeing "The Gossip" series in the *Boston Weekly*, a series that was comprised in substantial measure of letters (real and fictional) from readers, as was the convention at the time. It is an unconventional novel in other regards as well, most strikingly because it begins where most novels of the period *end*, with marriage: "the die is cast—I am a wife."[24] Indeed, *Sincerity* stands as something of a willful refusal of the conventions of the novel, telling the story of an unhappy marriage and of the costs of maintaining that marriage against all obstacles and despite myriad cruelties—and the many reasons why a seemingly strong and intelligent woman continues to do so. The novel rejects sentimentality, but it also eschews the didacticism of *Charlotte Temple*, denying us the alternately comforting and chastising schoolmaster/narrator through its choice of an epistolary format. Instead, we have here the torturous and ultimately tragic history of a bad marriage in a "novel" written not, as are most of Rowson's earlier novels, "for the perusal of the young and thoughtless of the fair sex," but for the more mature reader of the early magazine.

Who these readers were is evidenced, at least in part, by the numerous letters to "The Gossip." One such letter was printed the week after the Gossip's diatribe against novels—a reminder that the creation of such space for readerly interaction was one essential feature that differentiated the magazine from the novel. The letter is from "A Sorrowful Brother," who writes to express his deep concerns about his sister's unhappy marriage to a morose and dissolute man. "How it will terminate or end," he laments, "God only knows."[25] The next four installments of the column are devoted to meditations on the subject of unhappy marriages, especially in cases such as that which the "Sorrowful Brother" describes, between a loving and devoted wife and a violent and dissipated husband. As the Gossip insists, "Women, from their retired situations, from their education and habits, have not the opportunity of investigating characters, and forming opinions on men and manners, with that discriminating accuracy, which the opposite sex enjoy; they should therefore be extremely cautious how they choose their partners, and suffer not a pleasing exterior to blind them to the errors, of either head or heart."[26] But once the tragic poor choice is made, the Gossip warns, "there is no hope of being extricated, but by death."[27]

The tragedy of unhappy marriages is decidedly not the stuff of novels at the time. As one of the correspondents in *Sincerity* wryly notes, "Don't you know when a heroine is married, the Novel always ends—there is nothing worth relating in the every day incidents of a family circle."[28] By the time Anne, our primary epistolary narrator throughout the story to follow, writes this, she has already spent many letters recounting the sad story of Sarah, a "novel" that *began*, not ended, with marriage. A couple of installments later, Anne is dead, depriving Sarah of her primary support in her hardships. As the Gossip had predicted, for Sarah, the story of her unhappy marriage to a vile husband can end only one way: "by death." The Gossip's extended meditations on "the subject of matrimonial unhappiness" appeared in January–February 1803, just a couple of months before the serialization of *Sincerity* began in the pages of the same periodical. As the Gossip declared, the subject "has awakened every feeling of my soul . . . I have now twenty stories apropos to the subject, which I could tell, but I have just heard some news which I am on tenter hooks till I promulgate, so I cannot stay to write another syllable at present."[29] In the winking style of the early magazine, such a gesture to the "stories" inspired by the subject and the "news" that must be circulated are clearly designed to indicate to the active reader (and annotations and commentary in surviving copies show how attentive these readers were) that the Gossip and the author of *Sincerity*—a novel about an unhappy marriage that explicitly extends upon the theme suggested by the "Sorrowful Brother"—were one and the same.[30]

Another meaningful link between the two is provided in the name of Sarah's unfortunate choice of husband. In the first installment of *Sincerity*, Rowson had experimented with the name "Darnby," but by the second she settled had on "Darnley." A couple of months later, in "The Gossip," Rowson spelled out the significance of the name in discussing her meditations on Mary, Queen of Scots, during a visit to Edinburgh, a city Rowson knew well:

> One evening as I was returning from my usual ramble, musing on the beauty, sensibility, and weakness of Mary; lamenting that folly and precipitancy, which led her to unite herself with a man so little capable of appreciating her merit as lord Darnley was; for it ever appeared to me, had she been married to a man of discernment, tender, delicate, yet of unshaken resolution . . . Mary would, under the guidance of such a man, have transmitted her name to posterity as a pattern and honour to her sex. . . . It was Mary's fate, to meet a man of this disposition in her second husband: her youthful fancy had been caught by his

graceful exterior; but their minds did not assimilate. Mary's soul was capacious, and eagerly sought knowledge; Darnley's was narrow, and content to dwell in ignorance.[31]

Thus we are told that Sarah's ill-matched husband received his name from Queen Mary's ill-matched second husband, Lord Darnley (and Sarah herself might have been named after the queen had not Rowson published *Mary, or, A Test of Honour* in 1789). And what follows from the Gossip's meditation on Mary's unhappy marriage is yet another story of matrimonial unhappiness. Indeed, even as *Sincerity*'s story unfolds toward its final, inevitable tragic ending, "The Gossip" continues to be punctuated by stories of unhappy unions, a repeated rending of the veil from the lies told by novels about the inevitably happy ending of matrimony.[32]

Sincerity (or *Sarah*) has rightly interested Rowson scholars for its bleak portrait of a marriage that clearly resembled her own in many ways, and for its detailed explanation of the forces that kept a smart and resourceful woman in such matrimonial bonds long after any pretense of love had been dispelled. But placed back in its original periodical context and in dialogue with "The Gossip" and the active correspondence the *Weekly Magazine* circulated, we can also see that for Rowson the anti-novel of "matrimonial unhappiness" was in many ways borne from other adult readers' stories of what happened after "the Novel . . . ends," stories that resonated with her own and that, once shared, provided at least the promise that they were not alone. When Sarah begins her story by declaring "I am a wife," her novel is, as Anne later says, already over. But the "every day incidents of a family circle" are just beginning, and nothing in Sarah's earlier uninhibited novel reading prepared her for what lay ahead. As Anne declares in her first letter about Sarah's story, "do not expect any romantic scenes, flaming lovers, or cruel false friends." Instead, she continues, "what I have to relate, are incidents, perhaps, frequently to be met with in the common life."[33]

As the text works toward its conclusion, the format, initially told primarily in letters from Anne to a friend, often enclosing letters from Sarah, becomes more varied, including a wider range of correspondents and texts. For several installments we get direct transcriptions from Sarah's journal, followed by notes from an "Editor" (explicitly not Anne, as she dies well before the conclusion of the tale) offering an "abstract" of "suppressed" documents, the letters from Sarah to her adopted brother, from Rev. Hayley to the brother, and finally an editorial note that struggles to come up with a moral to what is ultimately a yearlong serialization about an unhappy marriage that ends in the long-suffering heroine's death. "From this account of our Heroine's sufferings," the editor writes, "let no one say, where then is the reward of virtue, if such a woman is not happy?"[34] Such questions of rewards and punishments are the stuff of "novels," which, despite her labeling of *Sarah* as such, Rowson clearly does not intend it to be. Instead, the "novel" ends by dissolving itself back into the magazine, the larger periodical form with its own enveloping collection of letters, anecdotes, and everyday observations.[35]

Part of the frustration of working with early American magazines lies in precisely such dissolves: the anonymity of our author's voice as one among many, writing (as Rowson described her periodical career in the preface to *Sarah* in 1813) "in snatches of time, and under the pressure of much care and business."[36] We are inclined to see the repeated turn of the first generation of American novelists to the magazine as apostasies, martyrdoms, or personal tragedies. That Brown might have *chosen* anonymous periodical editing over the novel almost never occurs to scholars, except as a sign of a failure of will or a flagging of creative energy. That Rowson might have *chosen* to devote herself to non-novelistic writing is almost unimaginable to her contemporary biographers, who often read her turn away from the novel form after *Reuben and Rachel* (1798) as a sign of the financial pressures she struggled with due to her constitutionally insolvent husband. A common narrative of Rowson's career looks strikingly similar to that used to describe the case of Brown: After a period of progressive republicanism and proto-feminism, Rowson retreats into increasingly diminished claims for the role of women, a retreat that is coincident with her withdrawal from the public stage and from full-time novel writing. Thus, Eve Kornfeld finds in *Sincerity* an example of Rowson "resign[ing] her ideal American woman to a sort of martyrdom."[37] Here "Passive domestic virtue overshadows active choice in Rowson's new ideal woman."

Rowson clearly did not envision *Sincerity* as a retreat but as a culmination of a career of meditating about the limitations of the novel, as the bleak but moving preface to the book edition of 1813 makes clear. Repeating the concerns about novels raised in her earlier "Gossip" column, Rowson writes, that while "every sublunary good, are to be found abundantly in every novel, but alas! where shall we find them in real life? Such examples . . . instead of stimulating the young or inexperienced mind to emulate the virtues represented, misleads it by fallacious hopes and expectations which can never be realized."[38] This, the last novel published in her lifetime, is in many ways an explicit response to her own long-standing reservations about the novel, reservations articulated throughout the early American magazine at the time.

Toward the end of Rowson's life, the *New-England Galaxy*, where she was a regular poetry contributor, published a brief account of the direction of her career after the early fame *Charlotte Temple* brought her: "With powers to make herself distinguished, she has been content to be useful. If she has lost a portion of the world of fame which was within her reach, it has not been by reclining in idleness, or running after golden apples; but in tarrying to cultivate the delicate flowers and savory herbs in the garden of youthful intellect; in teaching that the highest knowledge is goodness and the purest fame is virtue."[39] For contemporary critics, any attempt to describe Rowson's turn away from her earlier phenomenal celebrity to a relatively anonymous life as an educator and periodical editor and contributor is likely to appear, at best, forced and, at worst, as laden with the backhanded patriarchal "compliments" with which women writers have long been burdened ("usefulness" and "virtue" as opposed to public "fame"). But given her known involvement in the magazine, it is entirely possible that Rowson herself wrote this essay for the *Galaxy*, in which case the account of her ambitions and the choices of her late career must be read in a different light. And even if it was written by one of the editors, it was most certainly written with and for her approval.

The fame offered by the early novel was not the fame some of its earliest practitioners sought. It is only by taking seriously the doubts about the rising novel offered by its most important pioneers and by rediscovering the anonymous and cacophonous pleasures of the early American magazine into which so many of those pioneers immersed themselves later in their career that we can finally make sense of the big question that for so many continues to make Rowson's involvement in the *Weekly Magazine* and other periodicals so implausible. Why would a woman charged with one hundred students at her school and mounting familial and professional responsibilities take on duties at a magazine that was surely, like all those that came before, doomed to failure? And why would a woman, by this time associated with the novel and without question the most famous American novelist of her day, have taken on anonymous work for a weekly magazine? The answer to these and related questions lies in following Rowson beyond *Charlotte Temple* at last, such that the early experiments with periodical forms from *Inquisitor* and *Mentoria* and her later nineteenth-century periodical career might allow us more fully to understand not only the full range of her remarkable career but also the full range of possibilities beyond the "great American novel" through which Rowson and other literary pioneers of the early Republic sought to imagine a literary culture for the new nation.

II

In 1809, Charles Brockden Brown began "The Scribbler," his last published essay series for Dennie's *Port-Folio*. In six installments between January and August of that year (six months before he succumbed to tuberculosis and ongoing complications from the yellow fever he contracted more than a decade earlier), Brown presented his "Scribbler," in many ways an explicit bookend to "The Rhapsodist" series he had published in the *Columbian Magazine* precisely twenty years earlier. Beginning with a meditation on the intense fondness of all authors for the products of their own pens, "The Scribbler" is ultimately a meditation on the liberating egolessness of embracing one's role as a "scribbler" as opposed to an "author." No doubt thinking back to the periodical start of his own career, Brown writes:

> When he commences his career, and before he is enlightened by experience, he may possibly imagine that every reader will find as many charms in his performance as he has found; that his paper will be taken up by all with the same eagerness and laid down with the same reluctance as he experiences. This error will, however, have had a very short reign. He will see his essay taken up with an air of immoveable vacancy, and the leaves turned over carelessly, or with impatience. The stranger will run his eye through this page, dip into a single paragraph of another, catch up a single sentence from a third, and then, laying it aside, return to ordinary business or foreign conversation, with as much tranquillity as if the essay had never been indited.[40]

In response to the impossibility of ever making another read (and love) your own words as you read (and love) them, the author has but two choices: to give up writing or to give up being an author and embrace instead the role of scribbler.

"Scribbler" is a term found everywhere in the early American magazine, often used, as in "The History of Philander Flashaway; or the Misfortunes of a Scribbler" (1791), as a playful (or self-deprecating) description for one who becomes obsessed with the idea of "literary fame," especially for one who would have done better to stick to his proper occupation.[41] In Brown's case, the most immediate source of the term would have been the series published under this title ("The Scribbler") in the *New-York Magazine* when he was a young man in the city, deeply enmeshed with the Friendly Club and just then plotting his own career as an author. The *New-York Magazine*'s Scribbler had presented himself as an artisan who has become obsessed with the idea of achieving literary fame through periodical publication, but far from proving a danger or an embarrassment, this Scribbler's ambitions, far beyond his station, are quickly transformed, as if by the spirit of the periodical form itself, into a public good. The *New-York Magazine*'s Scribbler goes on to write about charity, gratitude, the follies of youth, and the importance of industry. The mania for scribbling can thus lead to the transformation of the humble artisan into one of the leading moralists of his community, as in the case of the *New-York Magazine*'s Scribbler, or it can lead to disaster, as in the case of poor, deluded Philander Flashaway. The magazine promises to recognize and elevate the former, albeit anonymously, and to exclude or ridicule the latter.

Brown's 1809 "Scribbler" was an occasion for him to think more deeply about his lifelong interest in the relationship between writer and reader. As he writes in his second installment, "Between those who trifle with books and those who trifle with the pen there, is, indeed, an intimate connection: some laborious or frivolous readers are generally extremely prone to commit the fruits of their studies to paper."[42] And it is the periodical that especially has encouraged this intimate connection between reader and writer. The question Brown mulls over at the end of his life, however, is one of *value*: If we can never translate directly our own passion for our writing save in inspiring our readers to become writers themselves, what is the point? What can be agreed upon? He starts (and restarts) to frame the question at the end of his essay: "By what means every scribbler of volumes that are never read, and every dreamer over musty and antiquated tomes, can conjure up perseverance and zeal in a composition or pursuit which, to every observer, that has not come within the influence of the same spell, and which, even to himself before the date of his own enchantment, appeared stale, tedious, and unprofitable as the *Beldame's twice told tale*[?]" But the irony, of course, is that Brown cannot answer even this question in a way that would be universally meaningful for his readers: "my reader, I doubt not, will be best pleased to have it left to his own ingenuity."

The inherent paradox at the heart of the idealized periodical space was on Brown's mind from the beginning of his career with the Rhapsodist through the end of his periodical career in the Scribbler. In a form where the truest sign of the value of writing is in its ability to inspire others to become writers, how can literary judgments be made or profits be realized? The periodical demanded that authors surrender the fantasy that one could convey thoughts, feelings, and arguments intact from writer to reader. No longer "a prisoner chained to the triumphal car of an author of great celebrity," the reader can find pleasure in the writing of others only insofar as it becomes grist for his own mill as author. Thus all questions of literary or intellectual value become ultimately solipsistic ones—in which a reader will only be pleased if the answer is "left to his own ingenuity."

Interestingly, Brown used "The Scribbler" as the title for an anonymous essay series one other time, although the exact date of its composition is not known. Among the many fragments of unpublished writing included in Dunlap's biography in 1816 was an unfinished pieced called "The Scribbler." This Scribbler presents himself as a poor young man struggling mightily with his conflicting desire for anonymity and his need for publicity—and especially, as his sister Jenny reminds him, the need for financial compensation for his work. In Dunlap's edition, the text ends abruptly after a brief debate between Jenny and the Scribbler as to whether he should interrupt his work to accompany her on a walk, to which he finally agrees.

Given this summary, it is not surprising that this fragment has excited no critical attention in Brown scholarship. It also has a decidedly unfinished feel, as if transitions are lacking which would explain how we get, for instance, from a discussion of how "I could . . . beg from door to door" to, in the next sentence, "Why truly, sister, I have no objection," a statement that turns out to refer to the aforementioned walk. Yet, in 1822, the Philadelphia *Cabinet* published a version of this "Scribbler" that was very different from the one found in Dunlap's biography.[43] *This* "Scribbler" is divided into numbered installments, as in a periodical series, and these section breaks make sense of the missing transitions in Dunlap's text. And in this text the matter is reordered, such that the debate about the walk precedes the anxieties about the state of his finances and the fate of his sister. Most importantly *this* "Scribbler" has a conclusion—in which just as the Scribbler seems ready to sink beneath his misfortunes, a stranger, who had read his essays in the magazine, appears at the garret door and offers a job and security for him and his sister. And the ending is by far the most interesting part of the text, as the Scribbler pronounces himself no longer a slave to the pen and to the demands of his readers, only to consign himself over as secretary for a gentleman. Given the pleasures and self-discoveries the Scribbler had found in his periodical writing, the reader is forced to question whether the Scribbler and reader are indeed so happily relieved from his "petty lucubrations."

It is likely that the posthumous "Scribbler" was in fact an earlier stab at the series Brown published in the *Port-Folio*. As in the *Port-Folio*, here we see serious meditation on the price of anonymity and the business of writing. While other periodical writers and editors would often wax rhapsodic about the utopian ideal of the periodical—its anonymity and its volunteerism— Brown does not hesitate to remind the reader that both come at real cost for the author. (In all probability the longer version found its way to press via Brown's family, eager to capitalize on the late author's rising reputation and on the new practice of paying for contributions to periodicals in the 1820s.)

Yet, even as Brown was expressing these concerns in his final periodical series, he was working on his periodical masterpiece, the *American
Register*. To modern readers, the *Register* is a daunting affair, and Brown
himself recognized the degree to which it was "a work entirely new in this
country." In laying out his methods, Brown highlights the role of the editor
as "compiler," forced to sift through mountains of material, much of it too
new and charged for proper reflection, and to arrange it so as to encourage
individual readers to take up the task of continuing the editorial process in
the weeks, months, and years ahead. Here Brown is in many ways putting
into editorial practice the theoretical concerns articulated in the essay he
had published the previous year, "Remarks on Reading," which called on
readers to embrace the "laborious task of forming ideas" instead of the "the
facile pleasures" of merely reflexive response to texts. The *Register*, Brown's
last great work, serves as the site in which he most fully experiments with
his ideals for writer, reader, and the editorial function.

The journal's structure changes over the course of its seven volumes, but it
remains fundamentally consistent in its principles. The opening long section
is dominated by the "Annals of Europe and America," a continuous narrative
account of recent events, divided into chapters and essentially presented as a
cohesive narrative. The long sections and appendixes that follow, however,
serve as vital counterpoint to the novelistic structure of the "Annals." Here
are compiled the documents, reading lists, and scrapbook entries that Brown
compulsively maintained at this time, the material that Brown the editor
works through in order for Brown the author to construct the narrative
that is the "Annals." But the status of this material is *not* that of academic
footnote—it is not marshaled as supporting evidence for the arguments of
the "Annals"; instead it serves as raw material for counternarratives the
reader is encouraged to construct of the events that are transpiring around
him. Surrendering from the start narrative authority over the events he will
describe, Brown invites (and facilitates) a collaborative and even contradictory narrative on the part of his readers.

Indeed, in setting up the methodology that will govern his "Annals," Brown
sounds very much like his own earlier hero, Edgar Huntly, caught up in the
midst of events impossible to narrate without sacrificing either accuracy or
coherence. In these terms Brown's turn away from the novel form is not a
turn away from the theoretical issues and literary concerns raised by his
novels themselves; throughout the "Annals," problems of narrative authority,
evidence and skepticism, crime and punishment, and the fraught relationship between psychology and politics remain central to his meditations.
Throughout the often disarmingly neutral narration of the "Annals" are

threaded complex disquisitions on the inseparability of past and present, on the intricate interdependencies of the Atlantic world, and a subtle but ineluctable call for a radically new form of writing.

Here global history is conceived as a kind of serial novel, and each volume concludes with the cliffhanger's anticipation of events yet to be written, yet to be lived. Indeed, Brown uses the techniques of the novelist throughout the "Annals," setting up nations as complex characters invested with particular psychologies, fears, and ambitions, and cohabiting in an interdependent realist space. While it would be tempting to focus on these elements of the "Annals" to argue for Brown's continued, if repressed, novelistic designs, to do so would be to miss the point. Instead, we need to take seriously the folding in on one another of a series of modes and narrative discourses assumed to be fundamentally opposed. Here the novelistic becomes merely *one* way of narrating and making sense of the swirl of events, but by no means the right one or the only one. That it does bring something vital to the discussion might be seen in the privileged position this mode occupies in the "Annals"; that it does not serve to end the discussion is seen in the novelistic resolution that both subject and literary ambition militate against. Thus the supplementary documents must not be understood as subordinate to the novelized account but as the raw materials—the unedited footage—that stands always ready to dissolve the foundational text, to turn the "Annals" themselves into supplement or raw material for a new narrative.

It is in the Constitution itself that Brown finds his model for this understanding of the living text already subjected to the revisions that will transform its fundamental identity: "The federal constitution resemble[s] the human in this: that provision was made only for maintaining the body in health and existence for a limited time, and since the individual must perish, a peculiar organization was annexed to it, by which it is enabled to produce a creature like itself, in an endless succession."[44] These changes are by design so gradual and evolutionary as to be almost invisible as they unfold, creating the enabling illusion that the body that confronts us in one generation is continuous, identical with that of the last. But such is not the case, Brown reminds us in the *Register*, and even the first two decades have witnessed changes to the Constitution that have profoundly transformed the character, psychology, and motivations of the national body: "The history of the changes it has already undergone . . . is a fit task for a philosophical hand, but would require qualities hardly possible to be united in the same workman. He should so far mingle in the tumults and intrigues of parties as to be intimately acquainted with their plans and movements, and yet be perfectly exempt from all their sinister biases and blinding passions."[45]

While Brown modestly refuses to ascribe this rare combination to himself, this is precisely the ambition laid out throughout for the *Register* itself.

Throughout the *Register*, Brown also calls into question the individual and national agendas that inform the different accounts from which he works to assemble his narrative. As he writes, "Those who . . . examine and compare different accounts of the same military transactions, perceive the insuperable difficulty of gaining exact information on the subject." There is for Brown no impartial witness—merely a web of partial accounts, and no clear formula for how to distill an accurate narrative: "We cannot judge of the degree in which one narrator deviates from the truth on one side [simply] by noticing the deviations of an adverse witness on the other"; "We are generally unable to penetrate into the motives from which the political conduct of nations or their rulers follow." In the face of the impossibility of objective truth, the historian can only write a provisional history, one that remains always open, serially and textually, to interventions of time and distance, new evidence and perspectives, new insights and ambitions. Like the Constitution, history is a body that must perish but must also reproduce itself so as to maintain the illusions of continuities, of identity, necessary for us to tell the stories, however provisional, that keep us anchored *in* identity, individual and national.

Indeed this relationship between the character of individuals and nations is a recurring theme throughout Brown's late writing: "The last national confederacy is, even now, only twenty years old. Political constitutions sometimes sink and expire, like human beings, with age; and, like human beings, they are frail and tottering in their infancy; . . . As national interest is the sole foundation of . . . Government, and as this interest, . . . necessarily varies in a nation which doubles its numbers and its peopled territory in a single generation, there are perpetual changes in the points from which we draw our political arguments. The constitution which is best adapted to our situation to-day becomes unsuited to our new situation to-morrow."[46] As a preface to an account of Aaron Burr's schemes out west, which along with the mounting tensions with Britain dominate much of the first volumes of the *Register*, this is a surprising text.

And throughout the history that follows, despite Brown's deep personal condemnation of Burr's character and actions, he refuses here to pass definitive judgment on the conspiracy or its origins, even going so far as to call into question the documentary evidence provided by the government: "With regard to the general probability of these charges, the grounds of our judgment . . . are too complex and various to allow of uniform or universal conclusions. . . . Amidst this labyrinth, it is incumbent on a pen studious of impartiality to proceed without caution; but the due caution, on occasions like the present, leads to no certainty, and is obliged to content itself with leaving the reader to decide on his own conclusions of the credibility of witnesses, and the probability of events."[47]

Nonetheless, the impossibility of moral absolutes and objective realities, impossibilities that the *Register* insists on at every turn, do not lead Brown to the retreat from history that Dowling sees in the late career of Brown's friend, Joseph Dennie. Instead, the responsibility to sift through multiple perspectives, to strive toward the impossible ideal of becoming the "impartial observer" in the face of world events, requires a more creative and energetic engagement with history, politics, *and* literature. The "larger view" that Brown seeks to enable is one that is not found by stepping outside or standing at a remove from gossip, political ambition, and the grasping demands of daily life. Instead it is found by a *full* immersion within the countervailing tides and texts of daily events—an immersion that Brown both models in the *Register* and also facilitates by collecting and arranging the raw matter that will define the next installment, the next wave, in the ongoing serial narrative that is the nation's history.

Nor does Brown in the "Annals" eschew editorial comment. For instance, one piece of evidence before him, he insists, "suggests many obvious remarks to an impartial reader," which he proceeds to lay out. But as this same document is subsequently included in the supporting materials to the "Annals," the reader is invited to engage in her own interpretations, to construct her own narrative of the events. Narrating the tumultuous diplomatic and political maneuvers of the Leopard–Chesapeake affair in 1807—events that brought the nation perilously close to war—Brown gains a new perspective afforded him not by time or distance—luxuries that he repeatedly acknowledges are not at his disposal—but by the complexity of his archive and the multiple (local, partisan) perspectives that it contains.

The focus here has been on the "Annals," but they cannot be separated from the other departments in the *Register*, where the same overriding principles prevail. For example, the literary criticism in the *Register* focuses on "classing and enumerating the various publications" rather than "entering into . . . particular estimate of their merits, or any analytical detail of their contents," allowing a better appreciation of their "relative" as opposed to "absolute" value. As Brown argues, "no [reader] . . . will be satisfied with the sentence of another. This sentence, indeed, considering the materials which must necessarily compose a professed critic, can hardly ever conform to the standard of abstract justice. . . . Each man reads what his own judgments, right or wrong, disposes him to approve, and what his own curiosity, formed and guided by accidents peculiar to himself, and generally, in some respects, different from that of all other men, renders interesting and important in his own eyes."[48] And here Brown offers radical intervention into the literary debates of his period, challenging the fundamental premise of the judgment against American literature's lack of "originality," highlighting instead the important contribution of America in terms of the "enormous quantity of original *publication*"—in which printer and editors contribute the invaluable energies that allow literature to be both disseminated and animated.

In 1821, over a decade after Brown's death and the same year that Cooper begins the career that would secure the novel's place at the center of the literary culture of the young nation, the Philadelphia lawyer and linguist Peter Du Ponceau wrote, "The merit of the writings of the late Charles B. Brown of our city, I mean of his novels, has begun to be discovered in England; I wish it had been first discovered here; but the value of his excellent American Annual Register from 1806 to 1809 . . . has not yet been noticed any where; I hope some of our literary critics will take that work in hand to make it known as Addison did the Paradise Lost. It is by no means an every day work."[49] By the 1820s, it has become clear that it will be with the novel and not the magazine that the nation's cultural ambitions inhere, and it is in these terms that the British are willing belatedly to recognize genius on the shores of their former colony. But what is surprising to a modern reader is Du Ponceau's desire to see Brown's legacy restored by "our" critics on the basis of his work as magazine editor. And to even the most sympathetic reader of the early magazine, the *Register* is a surprising text to single out for such efforts. Of all Brown's late periodical experiments, the *Register* is the most anonymous, the most devoid of what we recognize as imaginative energies. Largely a repository of state and public documents, it is the text in which Brown's fantasies, as expressed in his introduction the *Literary Magazine*, are best realized: The author of novels is entirely submerged in the editorial function and nothing can be "traced" to his pen. Du Ponceau lived to see the celebrated editors and magazines of his youth lost forever in the rising fame of the novel, and Brown's magazine never did find its Addison.

But in that very conceit, we might pause to consider what it would mean for a periodical work to receive such critical attention, to be canonized, as the *Spectator* had done for Milton a century earlier. If Addison worked to rescue Milton's epic poem from the Aristotelian standards that could not recognize its value, by developing a new notion of the canon and of literary taste, Du Ponceau at this moment earnestly wishes for someone to do the same for Brown and the magazine that was his final legacy.

Although certainly nobody's Addison or Boswell, Paul Allen and William Dunlap, Brown's first biographers, did seek to tell a very different story of Brown's late career than the one that emerged in the next generation. Both Allen and Dunlap, for all the profound differences in their vision of Brown, shared a deep sense of the importance of the periodical work Brown was engaged in at the end of his career. And both put the novel-writing career in a different perspective than would subsequent critics and biographers. In explaining the family's reasons for revising the one volume Allen did in fact write (to the frustration of his second biographer, Dunlap, who was bound by this fact) and set before he left Philadelphia, Charles Bennett has suggested that it was in part the overly critical nature of Allen's biography that disturbed the Brown family, especially as this criticism is directed at the few novels Allen even bothers to acknowledge. But if this were so, then surely the family would have been equally disappointed by Dunlap's biography, which identifies faults in several of his major novels. Allen and Dunlap offer vastly different visions of Brown. For Allen, who got to know him late in his career when Allen was assistant editor under Joseph Dennie at the *Port-Folio*, Brown is an obsessively disciplined, workaholic genius. The novels for Allen are not of particular interest, as he makes clear by dismissing them largely as being in an "unfinished state," as "evidences of what he *might* have done, not of what he has accomplished."

But while the novels fare better at the hands of Dunlap, the young novelist fares far worse. Where Allen found in Brown's youthful career much to admire and identify with, Dunlap, who knew the younger Brown intimately and who, though only a few years older, had long set himself up in the relation of chastising older brother, is much harder on the young novelist's character. Where Allen sympathetically describes Brown's turn from law to literature, Dunlap uses the occasion to deride the "freedom almost amounting to licentiousness with which Charles roved unguided in pursuit of knowledge" and sees the loss of the discipline and order the legal profession would have provided as what led "Charles" to the dangerous "romancing vein" that colors all of his productions for the next decade.[50] While Dunlap spends a great deal of time on the novels, he finds all of them marred by faults that are the result of the wandering rhapsodic temperament Dunlap identified in his subject and pointed to over and again as his greatest fault.

From the critical tradition and the literary nationalism that has grown up around the novel in the past two centuries, it is hard not to read into Dunlap's disparagement of the young novelist signs of the Puritanical culture against which Brown struggled in vain. As the story has traditionally been told, these are the forces by which the romantic Brown ultimately met his martyrdom. But it is important to note that, unlike most modern biographies, Dunlap's story does *not* conclude with the romantic artist turning his back on either his gifts or his society. Instead, the Brown of Dunlap's final pages is a changed man, a change that is emblematized for Dunlap by the *American Register*. Indeed, after pages of affectionate fault-finding and disappointed expectations with regards to "Charles," it is here that Dunlap becomes the eulogist one would have expected him to be from the start (note, he is not "Charles" now):

> The death of Mr. Brown alone prevented the universal Circulation of a work so extensively useful, and conducted with such brilliant talents and profound knowledge. That felicity of style at which Mr. Brown had so long aimed . . . ; that thorough knowledge of history, ancient and modern; that intimate acquaintance with geography . . . ; and his general habits of study and investigation qualified him for the historical part of such an undertaking beyond most men. . . .
>
> From the regions of poetry and romance; from visionary schemes of Utopian systems of government and manners, Mr. Brown . . . became a sober recorder of things as they are; but he never dismissed from his heart the sincere desire of ameliorating the condition of mankind, or admitted into his political views of speculations that inveterate bitterness . . . which so generally characterizes our political writers. As Mr. Brown's motives were pure, so his views of political men, measures and events, were unclouded.

Thus for all the differences in vision and critical temperament between Brown's first two biographers, both ultimately privilege the career that follows from that which has dominated critical attention in the past century. It is hard for us to imagine, perhaps, what it would mean to be a critic (let alone an Addison) of the *American Register*, to wonder what kind of literary culture and what model of literary career these men had in mind. But what we must first begin to accept is that this was a model that was not unique to Dunlap, Dennie, Allen, Brown, and Du Ponceau, even if it is unrecognizable to us today.

The earliest biographical assessments of his work after his death described a Brown vastly different from the one we have come to know. Writing in the *Port-Folio* in 1811, "A. R." (likely Richard Allen) describes Brown as "a writer who had all his talents at all times so perfectly under self command," a man of incredible discipline and modesty.[51] "The early style of Brown's writings," this memorialist writes, "was characterized by its diffusiveness, the ordinary fault of men of letters," but "the frequent exercise of the pen, and the pruning of its luxurience overcame this defect."[52] But it is not the novels on which the tribute's laurels hang, but the writing that followed in the last decade of his life. "He never himself," the writer insists, "regarded his novels in a serious light; he considered them as the sportive effusions of his juvenile pen." "But Brown's peculiar and characteristic merits are founded on a much broader base," one ultimately best displayed in his periodical work. There, "almost every science has received the tribute of his pen, and the same characteristic novelty is attendant on whatever he wrote." An obituary written by a "friend" five years earlier for *Poulson's American Daily Advertiser* describes the departed as "Editor of the Semi-annual Register" and as author of "several other productions of genius and merit."[53] Not one novel is mentioned by name.

For the most part, aside from his devoted friends and admirers, including Dunlap, Allen, Du Ponceau, and Dennie, Brown's passing did not receive great attention in the press—and neither did the publication of Dunlap's biography in 1816. However by the 1820s, Brown was beginning to gain attention from the place where literary-minded Americans most desperately sought approval. In 1821, the London *New Monthly Magazine* published "On the Writings of Charles Brown, the American Novelist."[54] The overview made no mention of Brown's periodical career, and it began what would quickly become the familiar story: of genius neglected and forsaken in his own time, awaiting a more enlightened time (and country) to appreciate his true merit. Three years later, in *Blackwood's Edinburgh Magazine*, Brown is again treated at length and presented as a perhaps the best novelist America had ever produced, which the author intends as a decidedly backhanded compliment. Portraying him as an imitative writer with "no poetry; no pathos; no wit," *Blackwood's* nonetheless holds him up as an example of America's ingratitude and neglect of the arts: he "lived miserably poor; died, as he lived, miserably poor; and went into his grave with a broken heart."[55] That none of this is true matters little to the author of the essay; this is the figure of the romantic novelist as himself a protagonist *in* a novel: "his pale, sallow, strange complexion; straight black hair—'black as death;' the melancholy, broken-hearted look of his eyes; his altogether extraordinary face—if seen once, was never to be forgotten. He would be met, week after week—month after month—before he died, walking to and fro, in some unfrequented street of his native town, for hours and hours together—generally at a very early time in the morning—lost in thought, and looking like a ship-wrecked man. Nobody knew him—nobody cared for him—(till *we* took up his cause)."[56]

Correctly ascribing the essay to the American novelist John Neal, the *Port-Folio* tears into all of Neal's central claims, focusing the bulk of its attention on "what is said of *Charles B. Brown*; a man whom we knew and loved."[57] But what especially outrages the *Port-Folio* is the account of Brown as "*literally starving* in this 'Athens of America,'" who went "down to the grave with a broken heart" after his "heart-rending" career of misery and neglect. As the author of the *Port-Folio* refutation writes: "We have spent many hours in the house here intended to be designated. . . . Instead of being in embarrassed, as this libel represents, Mr. Brown was always able to keep a hospitable and liberal table; he had wealthy brothers, and when the sisters of his wife lost their father, he adopted them as his own. Does this look like starving, and going down 'to the grave with a broken heart?' . . . Although several years younger than Mr. Brown, the writer of this was on the most intimate terms with him; and therefore can contradict this statement with perfect confidence."[58]

In point of fact, however, Neal's tale of Brown's artistic martyrdom was winning out over the story offered by the *Port-Folio* and Dunlap even as this debate was staged. The man the *Port-Folio* would preserve for posterity—the editor and periodical writer whose home "formed as cheerful a circle as ever excited the aspiration of a bachelor"—was giving way to the story of Brown as the neglected, romantic martyr to the novel, a man who wandered alone, like one of his characters, in a haze of abstractions and poured his soul into works his society was too materialistic and puerile to understand. By the 1820s, those who would look for an American literary culture turned to the novel, and not the magazine culture of Dennie and Brown, as its foundation. What is at stake in the battle between the *Port-Folio* and Neal in 1824 is a battle for more than Brown's legacy—it is a battle for the literary culture. But it is a battle that even the *Port-Folio*, never one to accept unpleasant realities, must have recognized had already been lost. The energy they pour into defending the legacy of Brown is at least in part surrogate for the energy they would devote to the defense of their late editor, Joseph Dennie, had anyone bothered to assail *his* memory. Looking about for monuments of the two fallen giants of their youth, the *Port-Folio*'s writers of the 1820s can find only paltry monuments to Brown, focusing primarily on a vision of Brown as novelist that bears no resemblance to the man they knew.

But at least Brown had written novels and thus merited the attention of the next generation, looking about for a genealogy for the efforts of Cooper to write the national romance. In reviewing Cooper's *The Spy*, W. H. Gardiner in the *North American Review* identifies Brown as Cooper's predecessor in the virgin land he is clearing for himself, while at the same time denying Brown's status as a "true" American novelist; instead, Brown is made to appear an opium-addled romanticist, whose visions and demons could be made to haunt any land and any time. Turning, a short time earlier in the essay, to look at the monument Cooper has carved, Gardiner writes, "It is astonishing what changes are effected in manners, customs, names and outward appearances; in the course of a single human generation."[59] It is with a very similar look back that Cooper will open his next novel, *The Pioneers*, considering the distance traveled in the single generation that separates his generation from that of his own father. But in *The Spy*, Cooper has Brown on his mind, and it is Brown he must both summon and put in his place, by ridiculing *Edgar Huntly*; and in 1823, in *The Pilot*, Cooper can declare the distance that separates him from his predecessor clearly: "we manifestly reject the prodigious advantage of being thought a genius, by perhaps foolishly refusing the mighty aid of incomprehensibility to establish such a character." Brown by 1823 has been reduced to the half-cracked romancer of Philadelphia, whose deranged genius coupled with the miserable qualifications of his culturally impoverished audience led to his lonely death, sometime around the turn of the century. His career and life were, along with the magazine culture on which Brown, Dennie, and others had hoped to found a different kind of literary culture, largely forgotten.

In erasing the literary history of the American magazine, we necessarily end up with a literary history with some strange gaps and holes—a canon that flows fairly effortlessly up until the rise of the American novel at the end of the eighteenth century and then skips ahead two decades to the historical romances of Cooper, Sedgwick, and Child in the 1820s. The fact that the pioneers of the early American novel—Brown and Rowson—both had long and largely anonymous periodical careers is effaced in favor of a story of martyrdom or neglect.

The magazine as it had been defined and defended was changing rapidly after 1810, and by 1825, with the demise of the *Port-Folio*, it would be displaced almost entirely by a new model—one increasingly focused on specialization and niche markets on one hand and on literary celebrity on the other. This is the period of trade magazines (the *American Journal of Pharmacy*, the *American Journal of Education*); religious periodicals; ladies magazines (most influentially, *Godey's Ladies Book*); political magazines (the *American Whig Review*); and regional magazines, such as the *New-England Magazine*, the *Southern Literary Messenger*, and the *Western Monthly*. The latter, under its original name, the *Illinois Monthly Magazine*, referred to this period as the "golden age of periodicals" (a term Frank Luther Mott would later use for the subsequent period following 1850), marveling at the explosion of new periodicals after 1825: "Sects and parties, benevolent society, and ingenious individuals, all have their periodicals. Science and literature, religion and law, agriculture and the arts, resort to this mode of enlightening the public mind. Every man, and every party, that seeks to establish a new theory, or to break down an old one, commences operations . . . by founding a *magazine*."[60] But as the author continues, there is reason to cast a longing look back to the "good old fashioned magazines, that we used to read in our youth; within whose well furnished pages, the reader, whatever might be his taste, was sure to find something agreeable."[61] In the magazines of the previous age, "Every one who was blessed with the love of scribbling might then indulge that laudable propensity. . . . The editor of such a work was like a hospitable man, whose door is open to visiters of every degree; while the same functionary in our day, resembles him whose table is spread for a few select guests." Thus in privileging exclusivity and "elegance," the modern magazine has sacrificed the democratic "good cheer and good humor"—the textual commons—of the periodicals of the previous generation.

While the author of the essay on "Periodicals" in the *Illinois Monthly Magazine* sees the change as entirely due to the sheer number of magazines exploding into print in the 1820s and 30s, the changes in periodical culture are not attributable to competition and specialization alone. This was also the period of the earliest successful national monthlies, especially *Graham's Magazine*, which was among the first to begin regularly paying for contributions in order to attract and publicize some of the leading writers of the day. Bryant, Longfellow, and Cooper were remunerated handsomely for their contributions to *Graham's*—contributions, it must also be added, that were not anonymous. By the 1840s, the magazine was a very different space—one where readers came to be dazzled by literary celebrity and rarely, increasingly rarely, invited to participate as "scribblers" themselves.

In the years leading up to Mott's "golden age," the magazines of the early nineteenth century had been vainly defending the rewards of anonymity and the benefits of collaboration as opposed to the romantic ideal of the solitary genius. As the "Contemplator" put it in 1803, even the *Spectator* itself depends on the anonymous and collaborative nature of its production: "Had the far-famed SPECTATOR been written by one hand, even tho' that were a STEEL or an ADDISON, it would never have been so much admired as it justly is."[62] Similarly, these last magazines of the early national period defend the merits of the *fragment* and *variety* over the ideal of the cohesive book and the unity of effect that will come to be privileged later in the century; for example, the *Port-Folio* regularly featured a column dedicated to the beauty of "variety." They decry the mounting obsession with *originality* in favor of a literary culture of borrowings, collage, allusion, and pastiche. Over and again, the periodical essayists of the early years of the nineteenth century declaimed "originality of thought" and continued to call on their readers to join them as correspondents, providing in their response the "originality" that no author could produce alone. And even as a rising tide of suspicion began to be voiced in the newspapers and in politics about the dangers of the culture of anonymity that had been central to the America's transformations from colony to nation, the magazine continued to defend the mutual contract inherent in anonymous periodical publication that bound the author to defend himself by words alone and the reader to judge the writer by the same criterion.

This is the literary history to which Irving's anonymous and serially published *Sketch Book* (despite its phenomenal popularity in its own time, itself increasingly relegated to the backburner of our critical enterprises) serves as a final movement. And this is the literary history that Cooper and those who followed him in the epic search for the great American novel would turn their backs on, seemingly forever. In attaching the largely miscellaneous, anonymous, referential American "novel" of the eighteenth century to the periodical culture that continued into the first two decades of the next, I could rightly be accused of doing little more than resetting the starting line of American literary history to where it was before all of the important work in excavating and reattaching this literary history to the nineteenth century. But that would be so only if we insist that the *only* literary history worth studying is one that centers on the rise and triumph of the novel. In point of fact, the novel might well be nearing the end of a relatively short career at the center of literary culture; and in the emerging postnovelistic literary culture we see the return of an increasingly miscellaneous, anonymous, fragmented, collaborative, and decidedly non-novelistic writing. I am not arguing (at least not here, not quite) that the digital literary culture of the twenty-first century is intimately bound to the periodical culture of the late eighteenth and early nineteenth century. But we might well have more to learn from our neglected literary past as we make sense of our as-yet uncharted literary present than we do from our endless return to the familiar places. The answers lie in the gaps our long-running stories have so usefully exposed for us.

III

In 1802, a periodical essay series was introduced in the New York *Morning Chronicle* under the pseudonym "Jonathan Oldstyle." The choice of pseudonym is a nod to Dennie's "Oliver Oldschool" and the *Port-Folio*, which had launched to much fanfare the previous year. But there is a difference, and a meaningful one, between both "Oliver" and "Jonathan," and "old *school*" and "old *style*." Dennie's "Oliver" was an homage to his idol, Oliver Goldsmith. "Jonathan" had humbler origins as a generic name for an average American, as in Royall Tyler's play *The Contrast* (1787), where Jonathan serves as the comic sidekick to Colonel Manly. And while Dennie's "Oldschool" links him to a past "moral, political, and literary creed," "Oldstyle" suggests a more superficial and casual engagement with the past, and especially with its fashions. Indeed, the first contributions of Oldstyle focuses on fashion and style, not on morals or politics: "Now, our youths no longer aim at the character of *pretty gentlemen*: their greatest ambition is to be called lazy dogs—careless fellows—&c. &c. Dressed up in the mammoth style, our buck saunters into the ball-room in a surtout, hat under arm, cane in hand; strolls round with the most vacant air; stops abruptly before such lady as he may choose to honor with his attention; entertains her with the common *slang* of the day, collected from the conversation of hostlers, footmen, porters, &c until his string of smart sayings is run out, and then lounges off."[63]

This "odd old fellow" who introduces his observations to the *Chronicle* in 1802 is in fact a nineteen-year-old Washington Irving, contributing anonymously to his brother's newspaper, much as the teenaged Ben Franklin had done in *his* brother's *Courant* eighty years earlier. The *Chronicle* was no *Courant*, however; instead it was a fairly typical newspaper of the period, sponsored by political machinery (in this case, Burrite Republicans) and serving primarily political and mercantile interests, and with little in the way of witty and original literary content in the four-page daily. Unlike his brother Peter, the young Irving tended toward a moderate federalism, but he respected the importance of his family's connections to the Burrites. His early entry into the world of partisan newspaper writing is a deliberate attempt to stake out a neutral space, to express an allegiance both to the federalism of Dennie and to the democratic appeal of the Burrites, without speaking in the partisan voice so typical of political discourse during these tumultuous years. In creating "Jonathan Oldstyle," Irving channeled the periodical persona of another age—Franklin's Silence Dogood or Addison and Steele's Mr. Spectator—allowing him to find his own voice in the center of the political and commercial whirlwind of early-nineteenth-century New York City.[64] Irving clearly enjoyed walking the tightrope the name "Jonathan Oldstyle" implied, and during the short run of his first periodical series, his elderly persona alternated between ridiculing the manners of the present age and allowing his persona's crusty nostalgia to be itself the butt of the joke. By the third installment, Irving has backed away from topics even as seemingly safe as marriage and focuses the majority of his energy for the rest of his short run on the theater, itself a dominant topic in the *Tatler* and *Spectator* essays from the previous century.

Even as he was writing his Oldstyle essays, New York politics was taking a turn for the worse with the rapidly declining political prospects of Burr, and Peter Irving set up a second paper, the *Corrector*, more explicitly dedicated to defending his sponsor's reputation. Running only a few issues in 1804, this newspaper gave Irving a chance to try his talents at writing political polemic and biting satire directed against the enemies of his brother's political allies. Irving was extremely good at it, as it turned out, but there was clearly little pleasure in it for the young writer, still struggling to find his place in his family's world of law, politics, and mercantilism. Following the folding of the *Corrector* (which published its last issue on the day of Burr's defeat in the gubernatorial election), Irving left on his first trip for Europe to further his education and to repair his fragile health.

Writing home to his brothers Peter and William (the latter of whom had sponsored his trip abroad), Irving seems to have truly come into his own as a writer as he shared his journals, his stories, and his observations of all he encountered. And when he returned to New York in 1806, he was ready for a very different kind of writing career than that which had stretched before him two years earlier. Increasingly he immersed himself in the company of a society of friends known as the "Nine Worthies" or the "Lads of Kilkenny," including his brothers and James Kirke Paulding, with whom he had collaborated at the *Chronicle* and the *Corrector*. Eschewing political debate for the pleasures of wit, theater, intellectual camaraderie, and bachelor play, the club became the crucible out of which Irving's great periodical project was born: *Salmagundi; Or, the Whim-Whams and Opinions of Launcelot Langstaff, Esq. & Others*—a collaboration between Irving, his brother William, and Paulding.

Salmagundi marks an important moment in the history of the periodical culture I have been tracing, simultaneously its culmination and its end. For the three chief contributors to the pages, especially Irving and Paulding (evidence suggests that William primarily contributed some of the poetry), the pleasures of the project were clearly those long vested in the periodical form: "clubbing" in print, reconnecting to the wit and culture of an earlier age, and engaging with readers in a decidedly interactive way. And indeed, given their newspaper backgrounds, the collaborators proved very good at engaging an audience, using the local papers to publicize and create a buzz around their fugitive periodical and even stir up controversy and rivalries with contemporary periodicals. Borrowing from Goldsmith's *Citizen of the*

World, they introduced one of the series' most popular features in the letters from Mustafa—like Goldsmith's Lien Chi, a visitor from abroad—whose outsider perspective allows him to see truths that the natives cannot bring into focus. Like many of the early American magazines, they offered a mix of contemporary events, criticism, serial stories, and editorial commentary. If anything, *Salmagundi* reads often like a loving if occasionally satirical homage to the magazine form of their youth.

But this was also a periodical that announced openly its refusal of the conventions and contracts that had long governed the form. First, the authors begin by pointedly refusing "to give an account of ourselves," "first, because it is nobody's business; secondly, because if it was, we do not hold ourselves bound to attend to any body's business but our own."[65] And indeed, no space is opened up in the twenty numbers of the periodical for new contributors or readers, aside from some engagement with rival editors and publications. When readers begin sending in their contributions, they are summarily rejected—despite the fact that "they do great credit to the writers, and would doubtless be both pleasing and instructing to the public" (111). A few issues later, their "sage correspondents" (167) are treated more harshly: "We wish to heaven these good people would attend to their own affairs, if they have any to attend to, and let us alone. It is one of the most provoking things in the world that we cannot tickle the public a little, merely for our own private amusement, but we must be crossed and jostled by these meddling incendiaries" (168). Further, when, in looking back on the first volume, Langstaff is insistent that they have never imagined that writing the magazine has been of *any* benefit to the authors: "We seriously assure our readers that we were fully possessed of all the wisdom and morality it contains at the moment we commenced writing," he insists. "It is the world which has grown wiser—not us" (246).

This is as far from the interactive space imagined by the early American magazine as can be imagined. The reader, insofar as he is acknowledged at all, is kept at a decided distance. The world of *Salmagundi* is the world of the club, and all the contributors are friends and relations of the bachelor society. Most of the stories are by and/or about members of their odd bachelor society, and few if any rewards are described that do not ultimately find their origin within that hermetically sealed world. Readers are there to purchase the magazine for their own edification and pleasure, and they are reminded several times in the first number that the authors "write for no other earthly purpose but to please ourselves" (52). Readers are there to be the butt of jokes on the part of the editors, as they "laugh up their sleeves" at the overheard attempts to identify the authors of the production or at a particularly feeble submission or observation.

Unlike Addison and Steele, who a century earlier congratulated themselves on the improvements in the manners and tastes of their readers, in August 1807, Langstaff can take no such comfort. While his and his colleagues' "sole endeavour has been to raise the world to our own level—and make it as wise as we, its disinterested benefactors" (246), in the end they are forced to accept that "the people of New-York are nearly as much given to backsliding and ill-nature as ever" (247). Here in *Salmagundi*, authors and readers, editors and contributors, remain irrevocably separated—even antagonistic.

Of course, it must not be missed that the antagonism—and indeed much of the prose—is playful, humorous. In *Salmagundi*, Irving and Paulding have created arguably the first American parody magazine, a progenitor for *Mad Magazine* a century and a half later, in which the conventions and expectations of the traditional magazine are either exaggerated or turned on their heads. And much of the interactive pleasures of the magazine explicitly lay in the parody (particularly in guessing who was being satirized in the various anecdotes offered) and in the playful newspaper wars and hoaxing that was always a component of the magazine's reception. Irving would carry these games forward in the publicity for his first book, *A History of New York*, in 1809, when he published a series of classified ads about the mysterious disappearance of Knickerbocker, a man "not entirely in his right mind," and the discovery of the manuscript that turns out to be the *History*. Irving scripted all parts in this drama, including the testimonials from men such as "Ludwick von Bynkerfeldt," who vouches for the existence of Knickerbocker and "seeing the original M.S. in the hands of Knickerbocker himself, a short time previous to that gentleman's mysterious and melancholy disappearance."[66] The newspapers took up the game and the ads were reprinted widely, providing precisely the publicity Irving hoped for to launch what became his first important success as an author.

Even the book that would make Irving an international celebrity, *The Sketch Book*, engaged with the periodical form, published in America in seven installments, and launched with a "Prospectus" as if it were in fact a magazine. "The following writings are published on experiment," Irving wrote, "should they please, they may be followed by others."[67] As with *Salmagundi*, Irving promises no "regular plan, nor regular periods of publication." And as with his earlier collaborative project, he promises to write according to only his own "thoughts and feelings." In this way we see how Irving's career emerges very much out of early American periodical culture, but it is always from the start different from that which was theorized and practiced in previous generations. Irving was in many ways charting a path to carry forward the periodical energies and ideals of the previous generation into the new popular media forms of the nineteenth century, including the penny press and the story paper that would emerge in the 1830s and 40s.

If the editors of *Salmagundi* haughtily disposed of their predecessors' modesty and openness to the collaborations of their readers, by *The Sketch Book* in 1819 Irving no longer had a club or collaborators—nor did he assume the role of editor or elderly bachelor. The companions of his youth, as Michael Warner has described, had left him for marriage, the "Lads of Kilkenny" increasingly becoming a virtual, epistolary affair, and his own bachelor state increasingly became the exception and not the rule.[68] In *The Sketch Book*, our protagonist is a young traveler again, unmoored from his homeland and disconnected from the land of his ancestors. Here Irving trades in the editorial function of Langstaff or Knickerbocker for the role of "sketch" artist, and it is a significant trade. As Amanpal Garcha has demonstrated, the sketch allowed for the development and marketing of a distinct authorial style in the emerging literary marketplace of the nineteenth century: "Sketches offered authors an opportunity for the kind of ideological and aesthetic 'position-takings' that Pierre Bourdieu has postulated as essential to survival in the modern literary field, in the sense that, through sketches, authors staked their claim *both* to the development of temporally static forms of fiction . . . *and* to individualized styles, which would ensure that they presented distinctively written products in the marketplace."[69] If the editorial function of the periodical culture of the eighteenth century privileged an egoless, style-less ideal, the sketch was always from the start about individual *style*—and about the sketch *artist*. Both periodical and "sketch book" shared a formal interest in the fragment and the sketch, but they worked them toward very different ends.

And yet *The Sketch Book* remains deeply connected to the periodical form. It is a miscellany, like the periodical a combination of various forms and genres (fiction, fragments, travel writing, biography, history, folklore), even by different "authors"—whether Geoffrey Crayon or the mysterious Dietrich Knickerbocker, to whom is credited the book's most famous stories, "Rip Van Winkle" and "The Legend of Sleepy Hollow." In crediting "Rip" and "Sleepy Hollow" to Knickerbocker, Irving is winking at the problems of arriving at the kind of "original" authorship increasingly valued by the literary marketplace of the 1820s. Both of these stories are based on German folktales familiar to readers both in Europe and America.[70] Irving goes as far as any other writer in the nineteenth century to bring to the book the formal properties of the periodical, even as he uses those properties in the service of a very different project.

Indeed, in "The Art of Book Making," Irving seems to go out of his way to make the distinction between books and periodicals almost invisible, when he "discovers" upon a visit to the British Museum that books are manufactured by raiding "obsolete literature" (809). Studying one particularly energetic "author," Crayon observes, "He made more stir and shew of business than any of the others; dipping into various books, fluttering over the leaves of manuscripts, taking a morsel out of one, a morsel out of another, line upon line, precept upon precept, here a little and there a little. The contents of his book seemed to be as heterogeneous as those of the witches' cauldron in Macbeth" (810). Here it is books that are made of pieces and fragments, assembled randomly from the works of the past. The lie, of course, is that these "authors" pretend the works *are* their own, that the pieces do come together and make a coherent whole—and they offer the reader no way to see through the illusion to the sources and the stitches that hold them together. In proper periodical fashion, at this moment Crayon drifts into a reverie, in which the "old authors" descend from their portraits on the library walls and begin attacking the patrons as "thieves," stripping the would-be authors of all that is not properly theirs until they are left quite ridiculously exposed.

The Addisonian reverie, in fact, makes two appearances in *The Sketch Book*, both times in connection with the making of books and authors. In "The Mutability of Literature," Crayon finds himself pondering the pointlessness of bookmaking while visiting the volumes entombed at Westminster Abbey. Again, Crayon is overtaken by a vision, this time of one of the dusty old volumes complaining volubly about the neglect of the books of the past and the stupidity of cloistering them in a library where none can use them: "I was written for all the world, not for the bookworms of an abbey," the book protests. "I was intended to circulate from hand to hand" (857). Of course, as Crayon counters, had the old volume circulated as he wished, it would have long since ceased to exist—either because of being worn to dust from being passed "hand to hand" or because of the essential "mutability" of the English language that makes, inevitably, all productions of the past "so fleeting" (859): "I consider this mutability of language a wise precaution of Providence for the benefit of the world at large, and of authors in particular. . . . Language gradually varies, and with it fade away the writings of authors who have flourished their allotted time; otherwise the creative powers of genius would overstock the world, and the mind would be completely bewildered in the endless mazes of literature" (860). This mutability is now more pressing than ever, Crayon continues, as technological advances in publishing "have made everyone a writer, and enabled every mind to pour itself into print, and diffuse itself over the whole intellectual world" (861). This nightmare vision of a world drowning in literature ("I tremble for posterity") is ameliorated only by the realization that the vast majority of all print is ephemeral, soon to "fade away" or, as in "The Art of Book Making," destined to be composted and recycled for new manufacture.

Both of these visions—straight out of Addison or any of his countless American periodical descendants—underscore books as ephemeral things and modern authors as essentially compilers. Both, that is, argue for the ways in which the book need not be understood as so very different from the periodical. But even as he writes this, Irving knows all the ways in which it is, indeed, different—ways epitomized by the vengeful authors descending from their portraits or the talking book living forever, frozen in the amber past of its initial publication. Publishing his *Sketch Book* and continuing to proliferate the pseudonyms under which he wrote did indeed maintain the genealogical connections with the periodical culture of Irving's youth. But the transatlantic serial publication, brilliantly and meticulously managed from London, was also about securing copyright and his rights (and laurels) *as* an author. Unlike the Gleaner, the Scribbler, or even Launcelot Langstaff, everyone would know Geoffrey Crayon's name.

What Happened Next

If the magazine of the early republic allowed for the imagination of a virtual salon, of the ongoing, serial conversations of Jürgen Habermas's ideal public sphere, several factors in the early decades of the nineteenth century contributed to make the early American magazine and its model of periodical citizenship seem increasingly antiquated. If the tumultuous birth of the nation was the most tremendous force shaping the first generations of the early republic, by the antebellum period, and especially after the Crash of 1837, the dramatically changing urban landscape was the engine transforming everyday life for millions of Americans. It is thus not surprising that the magazine imagined by this country's first century of editors as offering a model for the literary and political foundations of the new nation increasingly became reimagined after 1810 as a refuge *from* the realities of nation-building—the "retreat from history into the sanctuary of literary or aesthetic consciousness."[1] The virtual salon was no longer the place in which the editor could organize the best and brightest the nation had to offer to do the vital work of steering the ship of state, as early republican periodical editors and serial authors from Webster to Dennie had imagined. It was now a space apart from the fray. One sees this change most clearly in the understated—indeed, when compared to their predecessors, incredibly diminished—terms by which new magazines announced themselves in the 1820s. Samuel L. Knapp, for example, claims in defense of his new *Boston Monthly Magazine* (1825) only that "we are a reading people, and must have a large supply of periodical literature for the demands of the market."[2] The following year, the *Album and Ladies' Weekly Gazette* cites its "entire new type, with new and appropriate embellishments" and its collection of "many of the most esteemed [foreign] literary and scientific journals" to recommend it to the public's attention.[3] And yet, we must not mistake this subdued tone for fatalism or despair. In fact, the diminished rhetorical claims for the magazine are voiced at a time when magazines are, for the first time, becoming profitable. The *Boston Monthly Magazine* and the *Album and Ladies' Weekly Gazette* have reason to be much more optimistic about their prospects than were their ancestors of the 1780s and 90s.

This is not to say that there were no meaningful continuities between the early American magazine and the "golden age" periodical of the nineteenth century. Like the pioneering editors and authors of the early republic, many popular magazines in the nineteenth century would promote an interactive space through the serialization of sensational fiction, inviting readers to participate in the process of guessing at how the heroine would extricate herself from the cliffhanger, in imagining an intimate relationship with the authors themselves, or in at least ceremonially sharing with the editor the work of passing judgment on the relative merits of the different authors and stories. This was especially true for the midcentury story papers such as the *New York Ledger*, edited by Robert Bonner.

But the differences were ultimately more meaningful than the continuities. Unlike the early American magazine, which explicitly invited readers to themselves become authors, Bonner—much like the more openly elite editors of the antebellum monthlies against which he liked to position himself—explicitly does *not* invite his readers to join his stable of professional and highly paid authors. This fact erupts occasionally in the pages of the *Ledger*, as when Fanny Fern from time to time ridicules readers who plead with her to share her limelight: "I will not undertake to tell, lest I should not be believed, how many letters I receive a month from 'literary aspirants,' who lack the first essentials of preparation for the employment they desire."[4] Here, Fern calls out for especial ridicule one young aspirant who is "tired of sewing for a living, and wants to write," who asks Fern "to remember that *I* once struggled myself." Indeed, Fern's success story (culminating in the well-publicized terms of her contract with Bonner) was central to her celebrity. But equally central, as her response to her correspondent suggests, was the notion that this story was not one open to imitation. Nowhere in the pages of the *Ledger* do Fern or Bonner invite readers to become authors or suggest in any way that the boundaries between the two are permeable. Readers are invited to write in, to ask for autographs or advice. They are encouraged to engage actively with the serial nature of the narratives, discussing the work and speculating over its conclusion. They are even asked to see themselves as something like shareholders in the enterprise of the *Ledger* itself, as their opinion of the various features of the periodical are measured carefully and publicly by Bonner in terms of rising or falling subscription numbers. But between the reader and

Bonner's "eminent contributors" lies all the magical and impossible distance and difference of celebrity itself.

In this way, even an explicitly popular periodical such as the *Ledger*, while it set itself up as a very different enterprise from the highbrow magazine of the period, mirrors the transformations of the magazine after the early republic. The *Atlantic Monthly* makes the change especially clear. On one hand, Oliver Wendell Holmes's "The Autocrat at the Breakfast Table" (followed by "The Professor" and "The Poet at the Breakfast Table") secured the magazine's and the author's celebrity through performing the conversational intimacy of an actual breakfast table discourse, just as Fern secured her celebrity through the invitation to her readers to see her as an intimate, a friend. But like Fern in the *Ledger*, Holmes maintains his distance; his breakfast table is ultimately a space that insists on his authority (whether as autocrat, professor, or poet). As Holmes would put it in "The Poet at the Breakfast Table" in 1872, "I am going to take it for granted now and henceforth . . . that I have secured one good, faithful, loving reader, who never finds fault, who never gets sleepy over my pages, whom no critic can bully out of a liking for me, and to whom I am always safe in addressing myself."[5] This "one elect" reader is for Holmes the ideal recipient of the love letter, what Hawthorne called the "one heart and mind of perfect sympathy." But it is a reader who never finds fault, never finds anything to resist or correct—who never, in short, needs to write back.

Other aspects of the monthly magazines of the nineteenth century demonstrate this seismic shift in the model of citizenship at the heart of the periodical. A few years after taking over as editor of the *Atlantic Monthly*, for example, William Dean Howells instituted a new department in the magazine called "The Contributor's Club" devoted largely to literary gossip and debate among the contributors to the magazine. The reader was invited to listen in on the club's proceedings, but most definitely not to be a member himself. At *Harper's*, the "Editor's Drawer" department opened up in 1851 and, by year's end, was joined by "The Editor's Table" and "The Editor's Easy-Chair"—the furnishings of the editor's office increasingly dominating the space of the magazine alongside the celebrity contributors. In 1871 *Lippincott's Magazine of Popular Literature and Science* began a long-running feature entitled "Our Monthly Gossip"; unlike Rowson's "The Gossip" at the beginning of the century, the rumors here were almost invariably focused on authors, politicians, and other public figures—a forerunner of what we might today call "celebrity gossip."

These magazines are the lineal ancestors of today's periodical culture, now in its final stages before undergoing a transformation whose final outcome is still not clearly manifest. While modern magazines resemble in terms of several formal features the magazine of the early republic, they emerge much more immediately from the genetic stew of the antebellum literary marketplace, which by the 1850s had at its center the novel, the author, and the publishing house. The reader in this marketplace was a consumer, the privileged voter of modern capitalism who expressed her will through her purchasing power and allowed her representatives to act (and create) on her behalf.

Not that the model of the early American magazine was one premised on direct democracy or a precapitalist system of barter and exchange. After all, the vast majority of the editors and authors who worked to create an early American periodical culture were themselves staunch federalists, and some of them (Franklin, Thomas) were among the most successful capitalists of their age. And yet within the pages of the early American magazine, these men and women experimented with a form that was clearly designed to encourage a model of literary citizenship very different from that which would ultimately triumph. It was one premised on the notion that through proper arrangement multiple voices might be experienced not as cacophonous but as productive of further conversation and of the entrance into the field of new voices. It was premised on the belief that seemingly unrelated topics and agendas might be judiciously placed side by side so as to produce new fields of inquiry and new correspondences previously unimagined. It was one that refused the binaries of political parties, of American vs. British, of original vs. imitative, and of author vs. reader. It was, in short, premised on a profound confidence—bordering at times on utopianism—that the literary commons imagined by the early American magazine might provide the machinery for a new model of collaborative citizenship. As Joseph Perkins, writing as the "Essayist," put it in the *Massachusetts Magazine* in 1796: "It is . . . the duty, as well as the privilege of all those persons of leisure and ability, who feel interested in retrieving, maintaining, and exalting the dignity of the American character, to lend a helping hand to an undertaking so laudable, laborious, and important."[6]

Of course, the citizenship imagined here, as Perkins (himself a recent graduate of Harvard) put it, was imagined to extend only to "persons of leisure and ability." For this reason, the decline of the ideal of periodical citizenship of the early republic and the rise of mass readership and popular culture must be understood as intimately related. The duties and privileges of periodical citizenship as defined by Thomas, Murray, and Brown were duties and privileges not yet imagined to extend to those who possessed neither leisure nor innate talent. That the early magazine readers possessed "leisure" was presumed by their decision to pick up the magazine in the first place. Whether they possessed ability was the duty and privilege of the editor (or serial essayist) to ascertain, inviting those who were so endowed to participate as authors themselves. With the expansion of literacy and mass audiences, the intimate homogeneity of the early magazine republic necessarily broke down.

But the early magazine failed for far more mundane reasons as well. Like the internet today, which depends inordinately on amateur contributions and a shared investment in a literary commons in which the distinction between author and reader is necessarily permeable, often even invisible, the magazine culture of the early republic struggled to find a business model that would sustain the experiment to the point where its ideals could be realized. For the first generation that would invest so much time and money in the project, time and money inevitably ran out. For those who followed, there was increasingly little to recommend it. And, as the imagined literary audience of the young nation began to expand exponentially in terms of numbers and geography, the intimate republic of letters upon which it was premised began to seem archaic or naive.

Yet, here we are again. The intimate and mobile communities of the internet resemble in many respects the ideals of the early American magazine. Otherwise sensible men and women like Benjamin Franklin, Noah Webster, and Judith Sargent Murray expended considerable time and expense in writing, publishing, and distributing periodicals from which little remuneration could reasonably be expected. That the same energies and ideals that motivated them are still attractive more than two centuries later can be seen in the number of otherwise sensible men and women today who publish or contribute to blogs, wikis, and other online publications. Indeed, the growing numbers of people who willingly write for free, with no more prospect of fame and riches than their eighteenth-century ancestors writing for the *Massachusetts Magazine*, is one of the aspects of the digital revolution most surprising to commentators and troubling to the established print media.

In celebrating the collapse of the literary marketplace that came into place in the nineteenth century, new media enthusiasts like to insist that content naturally wants to be free.[7] But such pronouncements miss the genealogy of what they are describing, a genealogy that has everything to do with the virtual communities of the early American magazine. Content does not *have* desire, but readers do—and the desire to write back, to interact, to pick up the pen and become authors themselves is clearly one that has remained intact in the two centuries since the early magazine culture faded into the background of our literary culture and marketplace dynamics. And as the recent acquisition of the blog site Huffington Post by AOL demonstrates, corporations also have desires—or one desire, which is to make money. In the twenty-first century as in the nineteenth, as this new media becomes for the first time profitable, there is every reason to expect to see a transformation in the culture of the "blogosphere" similar to that which brought to a close the culture of the early American magazine. Even as I write this conclusion, in the wake of its acquisition by AOL for $315 million in 2011, calls are circulating from the Newspaper Guild and other organizations for a boycott of the Huffington Post by former contributors. As Cherie Turner, one of the former writers, explained, "Certainly, we all have written for free for the great exposure the Huffington Post can give us, but what's the cost? Those of us on strike feel it undermines the value of our profession and is unethical, especially in light of great profits by those at the top. We are only asking for a fair share of what we are helping to create."[8]

As both a historian of the early magazine and a writer who has himself contributed unpaid posts to the *Huffington Post* and other online publications over the past several years, it is hard not to see a version of history repeating itself. I say this keeping in mind the overwhelming differences between early American magazine culture and the global new media culture of the twenty-first century—differences in media ecology and economy, in political realities and global politics, and, perhaps most pertinent to the men and women who have been the focus of this book, the unregulated cacophony of the blogosphere. Each and every one of those who devoted their energies to the early American magazine would undoubtedly look on the current state of this new virtual printing press with unmitigated horror. But each and every one of them, I am quite certain, would have set out immediately to organize a corner of the internet that could be shaped by the editorial function, a space apart organized by the editor's hands as early magazine editors from Cave on sought to organize the cacophony of their own day and age. And as in their day, so too in our own, are contributors summoned from their more profitable labors to write back, to become serial essayists (or bloggers), and to engage with their own readers (or commenters) as editors themselves.

And so, in 2012, we have every reason to imagine that the history of the new media "magazine" will look very much like the history of the early American magazine, ultimately transformed by a growing population and number of presses (the number of new internet nodes continues to rise at a logarithmic rate each year) and most urgently by the profit motive's inevitably triumph over those other motives so much harder to characterize and defend (especially in the wake of multimillion dollar mergers and acquisitions). The story of the early national period is often characterized as the shift from republican virtue to liberal self-interest, a narrative that might well seem to be corroborated by the story of the rise and fall of the early American magazine. And yet, in the rise (and even in the likely fall) of early internet culture, we see evidence that this history is not a one-way street. Instead we might recognize the ways in which new media, not yet organized and disciplined by the marketplace, unleash opportunities for the expression of different impulses and communities that allow for the reimagination, however briefly, of a true republic of letters. In the rise and fall of the early American magazine, therefore, we might see reasons to continue to seek out new media forms that will remind us that liberal self-interest and corporate desire do not erase the pleasures to be found in the anonymous, profitless, and even irrational contributions to the reimagining of a very different public sphere. Even now this twenty-first-century version of the story remains far from fully plotted, and its resolution at least partly depends on the lessons we learn from those who set out to create a periodical citizenship two centuries ago.

NOTES

INTRODUCTION

1. [Charles Brockden Brown], "Portrait of an Emigrant. Extracted from a Letter," *Monthly Magazine, and American Review* 1 (June 1799): 161.

2. Brown, "Portrait of an Emigrant," 162.

3. Brown, "Portrait of an Emigrant," 164.

4. For a discussion of fantasies in the Federalist imagination of the day as they circulated around Haiti, France, American Jacobins, and African Americans, see William Stinchome, *The XYZ Affair* (Westport, Conn.: Greenwood Press, 1980).

5. I described these in greater detail in Jared Gardner, *Master Plots: Race and the Founding of an American Literature, 1787–1845* (Baltimore: Johns Hopkins University Press, 1998).

6. For a reading of the novel as a Federalist text playing off the racialist anxieties of the day, see Gardner, *Master Plots*, chap. 3. Even in *Huntly*, Brown articulates ambivalence about the resolution he offers. Indeed, we might register in Edgar Huntly's misguided hopes for the deranged Irish immigrant Clithero (hopes maintained against all evidence and the warnings of his father-figure, Sarsefield) the author's own ambivalence about the "villain" he must exorcise from his fictional landscape. For example, Paul Downes ("Sleep-Walking Out of the Revolution: Brown's *Edgar Huntly*," *Eighteenth-Century Studies* 29 [1996]: 413–31) compellingly reads sleep-walking as symptomatic of the ambivalence of the novel and its critique of the ways in which the dichotomous political vision of the day leaves the citizen inevitably misplaced.

7. A strikingly similar "fragment," which seems to read as a companion piece to the "Portrait," is found in *Monthly Magazine* a year later. In "The Household. A Fragment," the correspondent tells the tale of another unconventional family of "emigrants," of diverse social and national backgrounds, all brought together under the patronage and guidance of the correspondent. As she concludes, "Such is my family. All females, you perceive. I want no man about me. In that respect, I would

have my house be a convent, as I be the mistress of it. Here I can reign without scruple" (3 [1800]: 86).

8. The *Monthly Magazine* (as well as Brown's later magazines) featured critiques of newspaper reading that implicitly privilege the unique space of the literary periodical. For example, in "On American Literature," "Candidus" attributes the failure of the nation to produce a literary culture to the utilitarian and factionalist nature of American citizenship, conditions to which the newspaper contributes spectacularly. The essay concludes by celebrating the literary review as the only means by which Americans can finally know "the exact amount of our wealth" (*Monthly Magazine* 1 [August 1799]: 342). A year later, Brown published "Thoughts on American Newspapers," which similarly decries the fact that Americans read primarily newspapers, which pander to factionalist division and mercantile self-interest, and concludes by celebrating the "Editor" for "introducing the teacher of virtue, and the preceptor in useful arts, to the counters, desks and teatables of every rank and profession in society" (*Monthly Magazine* 3 [October 1800]: 263–64). And the last issue of the *Monthly Magazine* contains the seemingly despondent claim that "in reality, [newspapers] are the only popular and legitimate offspring of American activity and genius" (3 [December 1800]: 475–76).

9. This sketch has been attributed to Brown since Harry R. Warfel's biography of 1949. For a detailed account of the evidence supporting this attribution, see Alfred Weber, "Bibliographical and Critical Notes," in Charles Brockden Brown, *Somnambulism and Other Stories*, ed. Alfred Weber (Frankfurt am Main: Peter Lang, 1987), 255–57.

10. This is in part to build upon the important correction Michael Warner offers to the critical tradition of reading all early novels subversively and "ironically," "assimilat[ing] the novel to a liberal aesthetic of authorial craft," in which the author "rises in artistic status as his aims are seen to be more indirect, artful, and privately anchored" (*The Letters of the Republic: Publication and the Public Sphere in Eighteenth-Century America* [Cambridge, Mass.: Harvard University Press, 1990], 153). As Warner reminds us, for Brown and other writers of the earliest novels in the United States, what is at stake is ways of defining the novel as a legitimate form of *republican* national discourse.

11. Jay Fliegelman, *Declaring Independence: Jefferson, Natural Language, and the Culture of Performance* (Palo Alto, Calif.: Stanford University Press, 1993), 3.

12. The important exception here is Sydney J. Krause's reevaluation of these works in terms of reading them as a test of Godwin's political philosophy in *Political Justice*, a test that Godwin finally fails (see "*Clara Howard* and *Jane Talbot*: Godwin on Trial," in *Critical Essays on Charles Brockden Brown*, ed. Bernard Rosenthal [Boston: G. K. Hall, 1981], 184–211). Krause's reading has provided the foundation for all subsequent reconsideration of Brown's last novels, including my own. Donald A. Ringe, whose own assessment of these novels was similarly transformed by Krause's essay, offers an excellent overview of the critical reception of these novels in his "Historical Essay," in Charles Brockden Brown, *Clara Howard; In a Series of*

Letters with Jane Talbot, a Novel (Kent, Ohio: Kent State University Press, 1986), 452–71. All citations to *Clara Howard* and *Jane Talbot* will be to this edition, cited parenthetically in the text.

13. Harry R. Warfel writes in 1949, "By withdrawing from the areas of terror, he became merely another purveyor of romantic narrative" (*Charles Brockden Brown: American Gothic Novelist* [Gainesville: University of Florida Press, 1949], 193). Indeed almost all biographers have told a version of this same retreat, in which Brown at the end of his career "bowed to popular demand" (223) in his last novels and periodical work. David Lee Clark, for example, identifies at the end of Brown's career a "defection from his former faith in creative writing" (*Charles Brockden Brown: Pioneer Voice of America* [1952; New York: AMS Press, 1966], 242); Norman S. Grabo writes, "When he turned his back on the multistoried world of man's inner guilts and chaos, Brown in effect repudiated his art" (*The Coincidental Art of Charles Brockden Brown* [Chapel Hill: University of North Carolina Press, 1981], 142–43); Alan Axelrod sees the last novels as "wholehearted affirmations of bourgeois American morality" and promises that we need "barely glance at them in order to trace the arc of Brown's late career" (*Charles Brockden Brown: An American Tale* [Austin: University of Texas Press, 1983], 172–73); and Steven Watts, in the most important recent book-length study of Brown, reads Brown's nineteenth-century career similarly: "Brown began a withdrawal from the literary scene. He took one more half-hearted stab at fiction writing two domestic novels that seemed deliberately aimed at a popular audience. As this literary endeavor failed, he bitterly rejected fiction altogether" (*The Romance of Real Life: Charles Brockden Brown and the Origins of American Culture* [Baltimore: Johns Hopkins University Press, 1994], 132). By producing novels and other writings in his last decade that are unrecognizable to the trajectory of literary history as we have come to write it, Brown's radical shift of gears in 1801 has been more easily read as a failure and retreat.

14. [Charles Brockden Brown], "Editors' Address to the Public," *Literary Magazine and American Register* 1 (1803): 4.

15. Warfel sees the *Literary Magazine* as another moment in which "Brown bowed to popular demand" and cites the prospectus as evidence of Brown's renunciation of fiction (Brown, 222, 223). Watts reads this declaration in precisely these terms: "The abandonment of the novel for journalistic enterprises came at heavy personal cost. Brown evidenced extreme bitterness about his failed literary career and attempted to dismiss it altogether. In a public confession of 1803, he denigrated his earlier writings." Watts sees this "confession" as symptomatic of "self-hatred" (*Romance of Real Life*, 144).

16. Brown, "Editors' Address," 3. For a related but somewhat different account of the address and its contexts in Brown's career see Michael Cody, *Charles Brockden Brown and the Literary Magazine: Cultural Journalism in the Early American Republic* (Jefferson, N.C.: McFarland, 2004), chap. 1.

17. Brown, "Editors' Address," 4.

18. In his pioneering essay on the political work of *Wieland* in 1962, Ziff dem-

onstrates how Brown is not only one of the first great practitioners of the novel in America but also its first great critic: "*Wieland* is a monument to the often mentioned and little appreciated historical importance of . . . an author who saw the vicious effects of a *genre* he had set out to work in, and who artistically converted that *genre* into a telling criticism of itself" (Larzer Ziff, "A Reading of *Wieland*," *PMLA* 77 [March 1962]: 53). By demonstrating the failure of Pleyel to read the world beyond the conventional terms of sentimental narrative, "Brown achieves one of the greatest condemnations of that tradition in the history of the American novel" (53).

19. William C. Dowling, *Literary Federalism in the Age of Jefferson* (Columbia: University of South Carolina Press, 1999). As Dowling's study of Joseph Dennie's *Port-Folio* describes in detail, for the literary federalists of the period, literature became a tool by which to strip from Jefferson's party "its assumed mask of republicanism" in order to expose the individual desires and ambitions (in direct opposition to republican virtue federalists sought to defend) that it worked to promote (16). For Dennie and his fellow literary federalists, the magazine became the privileged space in which to reimagine a republican community of virtue and refinement, what Dowling calls a "retreat from history" (27). What separates Brown from his more staunchly Federalist colleague is that Brown, instead of turning from history and the present condition of his age, critiques all narrative forms that work to diminish the potential of the present.

20. In *Master Plots* I far too quickly dismissed these last novels as "models of obsequiousness and circumspection" (78).

21. Hannah Webster Foster, *The Coquette*, ed. Cathy N. Davidson (New York: Oxford University Press, 1986), 22. Subsequent references will be to this edition, cited parenthetically in the text.

22. Davidson reads the novel as an attempt to expose the hypocrisies of republican gender politics in its story of a Franklinian self-made woman denied the freedoms the new nation worked to secure to its (male) citizens (*Revolution and the Word: The Rise of the Novel in America* [New York: Oxford University Press, 1986], 140–50). Almost all subsequent criticism of Foster since has been deeply influenced by this reading of the novel. Carroll Smith-Rosenberg, for example, works to expand the foundation of the critique by reading the subversive tone of the novel as directed toward questions of class and new capitalist ideology in addition to gender (Domesticating 'Virtue': Coquettes and Revolutionaries in Young America," in *Literature and the Body: Essays on Populations and Persons*, ed. Elaine Scarry [Baltimore: Johns Hopkins University, 1988], 160–84); Claire C. Pettingill reads the novel's understanding of "sisterhood" as providing a corresponding complex drama to the overly determined conventions of the seduction plot ("Sisterhood in a Separate Sphere: Female Friendship in Hannah Webster Foster's *The Coquette* and *The Boarding School*," *Early American Literature* 27 [1992]: 185–203); and Sharon M. Harris takes further the subversive reading pioneered by Davidson by reading the novel as an overtly *radical* political text that works to "imagine alternative lifestyles for women" ("Hannah Webster Foster's *The Coquette*: Critiquing Franklin's America,"

Redefining the Political Novel: American Women Writers, 1797–1901 [Knoxville: University of Tennessee Press, 1995], 2).

23. Julia Stern, *The Plight of Feeling: Sympathy and Dissent in the Early American Novel* (Chicago: University of Chicago Press, 1997), 112. While I read especially the role of Lucy in different terms, my sense of the multiple voicings of the novel and its complex political work is indebted to Stern's work on Foster. As Stern writes, "the politics of her novel do not unfold in dualistic fashion but, instead, are intricately knotted. By employing manichean methods of historical analysis in their readings, . . . [s]cholars have located the significance of the novel as an artifact of the early national period in a manner that reprises the rigidly factional language and thought of the 1790s" (73–74).

24. Cathy N. Davidson, Introduction, *The Coquette*, ix–x.

25. In similar terms, Stern argues that the novel refuses to choose sides and serve as "a piece of ideological propaganda in the factional wars of the 1790s"; "instead," she suggests, "it localizes the losses that such divisions produce in its depiction of the spectacular disappearance of a transgressive female voice" (75). Stern rightly insists that we read this novel outside of our dominant critical impulses and work to articulate its "political double vision" (74). What Stern identifies as *Eliza's* "polylinguality" (89)—her ability to speak the multiple and seemingly conflicting ideological positions of both the conduct book minister and the radical agitator—needs to be extended to the novel as a whole. For while Eliza's turn to dominant linguistic modes at strategic moments in her own narrative productions is profitably read in terms of a dialogic resistance to the monologic discourse of her society in the terms that Stern offers, the larger multivocality of the novel begs a different set of terms, one that ultimately seeks to define not an oppositional politics but a new mode of literary politics that refuses such choices altogether.

26. *The Works of John Adams*, 10 vols. (Boston: C. C. Little, J. Brown, 1850–56): 9:216.

27. Here we might think of another genealogical connection between Foster and Dickinson, in terms of what Sharon Cameron has identified as the radical refusal of choice in Dickinson's own editorial practices. See *Choosing Not Choosing: Dickinson's Fascicles* (Chicago: University of Chicago Press, 1992).

28. Charles Brockden Brown, *Alcuin: A Dialogue with Memoirs of Stephen Calvert* (Kent, Ohio: Kent State University Press, 1987), 7.

29. See Stern, *Plight of Feeling*, 113–26. See also Jeffrey H. Richards, "The Politics of Seduction: Theater, Sexuality, and National Virtue in the Novels of Hannah Foster," in *Exceptional Spaces: Essays in Performance and History*, ed. Della Pollock (Chapel Hill: University of North Carolina Press, 1998), 238–57.

30. That one of the few female equestrian performers of the period was to be found at Lailson's Circus, where the subject of Brown's "Portrait of an Emigrant" is employed, leads to the delightful fantasy of Lucy watching the "Emigrant" perform her circus act.

31. Quoted in Stern, *Plight of Feeling*, 128, 129.

32. As Charles Coleman Sellers writes of this episode, "Peale would ever after cherish the lesson he saw in this happy event: the harmony of Nature leads to harmony among men"; and Peale commemorated the event by portraying the chiefs in wax portraits (*Mr. Peale's Museum: Charles Willson Peale and the First Popular Museum of Natural Science and Art* [New York: W. W. Norton, 1980], 92). For an overview of Peale's museum career, see also Sidney Hart and David C. Ward, "The Waning of the Enlightenment Ideal: Charles Willson Peale's Philadelphia Museum, 1790–1820," *Journal of the Early Republic* 8 (1988): 388–418.

33. For the importance of the *American Museum* and the *Massachusetts Magazine, or Monthly Museum*, see Frank Luther Mott, *A History of American Magazines, 1741–1850* (New York: D. Appleton, 1930), 100–103, 108–11. Other early magazines that incorporate "museum" into their title are *Columbian Museum, or, Universal Asylum* (New York, 1793), *South Carolina Weekly Museum* (Charleston, 1797–98), *Literary Museum, or, Monthly Magazine* (Westchester, Pa., 1797), *Connecticut Magazine, and Gentleman's and Lady's Monthly Museum* (Bridgeport, 1801), *Lady's and Gentleman's Weekly Museum, and Philadelphia Reporter* (1818), and *Rural Magazine and Farmer's Monthly Museum* (Hartford, Conn., 1819).

34. For a useful overview of the history of the early American itinerant museum, see Andrea Stulman Dennett, *Weird and Wonderful: The Dime Museum in America* (New York: New York University Press, 1997), chap. 1. On Bowen, Dennett writes, "Daniel Bowen, one of the first Americans to manage a waxworks display, exhibited his figures from 1790 to 1810 at the Columbian Museum and American Coffee House in Boston, the American Museum of Waxworks in Philadelphia, and in New York. . . . As itinerant amusements, waxworks were booked into town halls and lecture rooms" (108).

35. Brown, "Editors' Address," 5.

36. Brown, *Alcuin*, 54.

37. William Dunlap, *The Life of Charles Brockden Brown*, 2 vols. (Philadelphia: James P. Parke, 1815), 2:100.

38. Supporting this assertion is the fact that the British edition of *Clara Howard* was published under the title *Philip Stanley* (a renaming of the central male character, Edward Hartley, probably to distance the protagonist from the recently published *Edgar Huntly*). What this change signifies is that the British publisher could as easily understand the novel as being about Hartley as about Clara Howard.

39. "On the Cause of the Popularity of Novels," *Literary Magazine* 7 (June 1807): 410. The essay is an unattributed reprint from the *Edinburgh Review* (January 1799): 33–36.

40. Bruce Burgett, in one of the only serious studies of *Clara Howard* in recent years, offers a fascinating reading of the masochistic dynamic of this relation, reading it as both symptomatic and constitutive of a shift from the republican ideal of genderless sentimental citizenship in the eighteenth century to the gendered model of citizenship that is codified in the nineteenth (see "Masochism and Male Sentimen-

talism: Charles Brockden Brown's *Clara Howard*," *Arizona Quarterly* 52 [1996]: 1–25).

41. Dowling, *Literary Federalism*, 40.

42. As Ziff describes Brown's career, "The society constituted by Brown's novels is one in which the difference between appearance and reality is uncertain. . . . Representing and misrepresenting were dangerously alike and the individual's capacity to become other than what he had been was not clearly distinguishable from his capacity to deceive" (Larzer Ziff, *Writing in the New Nation: Prose, Print, and Politics in the Early United States* [New Haven, Conn.: Yale University Press, 1991], 82).

43. "Remarks on Reading," *Literary Magazine* 5 (March 1806): 163-68. Signed "N." Until quite recently, this essay has been attributed to Brown by most scholars, including myself. My thanks to Philip Barnard for his bibliographic detective work in correctly attributing this essay to Isaac Disraeli, one of Brown's favorite sources in the *Literary Magazine*. Brown adds one final original paragraph to Isaac Disraeli's essay "On Reading," *Miscellanies* (London: Cadell and Davies, 1796), 189–207.

44. "Remarks on Reading," 165.

45. "Remarks on Reading," 167.

46. Grabo, *Coincidental Art*, 137.

47. See "Historical Characters Are False Representations of Nature," *Literary Magazine* 5 (February 1806): 32–36. Like "Remarks on Reading," this essay is an unattributed reprinting from Isaac Disraeli's *Miscellanies*.

48. Brown wonderfully plays on this tyranny in an advertisement for the continuation of the serialized "Stephen Calvert" in the *Monthly Magazine* of 1800. A correspondent tells of being interrupted while attending "some very urgent business" by a friend who introduces him to Calvert with the promise that he "should be sufficiently entertained with the adventures of the man" ("Note on Stephen Calvert," *Monthly Magazine* 2 [March 1800]: 172). The reluctant correspondent soon finds himself drawn into the narrative; as he reasons, "the dullest story, if we can once be persuaded to begin it, will have charms enough to induce us to continue. Our sympathy is wonderfully prone to make the cause of others our own. Whether the story-teller be Richardson, or Mother-Bunch, Shakespeare, or Esop, let us once have but fairly entered on the tale, and the inertest curiosity will not fail to exclaim at every interruption, '*what next?*'" As if to draw this point home, Calvert, as soon as he realizes that his audience is fully invested in his narrative, abruptly breaks it off "in the very heart of an interesting dialogue" and "whipped out of the house." The distraught correspondent demands continuation of the narrative, promising subservience to the story and the storyteller until the tale comes to its end (173).

49. "Remarks on Reading," 167.

50. "Account of the Philadelphia Museum," *Literary Magazine* 2 (November 1804): 576, 579.

51. Brown, "Editor's Address," 5.

52. Preface, *American Review, and Literary Journal* 1 (1801): iv.

53. See Courtney Weikle-Mills, "Learn to Love Your Book: The Child Reader and Affectionate Citizenship," for an examination of the relationship between Fielding and Foster's texts (*Early American Literature* 43 [2008]: 35–60).

54. Hannah Webster Foster, *The Boarding School; or, Lessons of a Preceptress to her Pupils: Consisting of Information, Instruction, and Advice, Calculated to Improve the Manners, and Form the Character of Young Ladies* (Boston: I. Thomas & E. Andrews, 1798), 18.

55. Foster, *The Boarding School*, 24.

56. "Lines, Sent to a Lady, Addicted to Reading Novels," *Weekly Visitor* 1 (June 9, 1810): 80.

57. In the case of the story of "Ophelia," readers were more immediately familiar with it from newspapers, which had been salaciously telling the real-life tragic tale of Fanny Apthorp, on whom "Ophelia" is based, during the course of the previous year. The letters of "Miss F——T——A——" were reprinted, and the scandal—in which Fanny became pregnant during an affair with her brother-in-law, Perez Morton, and subequentialy committed suicide—was moralized on in newspapers from New Hampshire to Pennsylvania. See, for example, the *Herald of Freedom*, September 15, 1788.

58. William Hill Brown, *The Power of Sympathy: or, The triumph of Nature* (Isaiah Thomas, 1789), 48.

59. Brown, *The Power of Sympathy*, 58.

60. Foster, *The Boarding School* 26.

CHAPTER 1. AMERICAN SPECTATORS, TATLERS, AND GUARDIANS

1. "A Reverie," *Pennsylvania Magazine* 1 (April 1776): 186.

2. Donald F. Bond, ed., *Spectator*, 5 vols. (Oxford: Clarendon Press, 1965), 1:14. All subsequent citations will be to this edition.

3. "A Reverie," *Pennsylvania Magazine*, 186.

4. *The Guardian* (London: J. Tonson, 1714), 141.

5. *Guardian*, 139.

6. [Thomas Paine], "To the Publisher of the Pennsylvania Magazine," *Pennsylvania Magazine* 1 (January 1775): 12.

7. "To the Publisher of the Pennsylvania Magazine," *Pennsylvania Magazine*, 10.

8. "To the Publisher of the Pennsylvania Magazine," *Pennsylvania Magazine*, 10.

9. [Francis Hopkinson], "An Extraordinary Dream," *Pennsylvania Magazine* 1 (1775): 19.

10. [Thomas Paine], *Common Sense* (Philadelphia: R. Bell, 1776), 30.

11. David Paul Nord, "A Republican Literature: Magazine Reading and Readers in Late-Eighteenth-Century New York," in *Reading in America: Literature and Social History*, ed. Cathy N. Davidson (Baltimore: Johns Hopkins University Press, 1989), 131.

12. [Francis Hopkinson], "An Extraordinary Dream," 15.

13. "A Reverie," *Pennsylvania Magazine*, 189.

14. Phillis Wheatley, ["To His Excellency, Gen. Washington"], *Pennsylvania Magazine* 2 (April 1776): 193.

15. [John Witherspoon], "Dialogue on Civil Liberty," *Pennsylvania Magazine* 2 (April 1776): 167. For an incredibly useful study of Wheatley's negotiation of the revolutionary deployment of the rhetoric of "slavery," see Eric Slauter, "Neoclassical Culture in a Society with Slaves: Race and Rights in the Age of Wheatley," *Early American Studies* (Spring 2004): 81–122.

16. Ruth H. Bloch, *Visionary Republic: Millennial Themes in American Thought, 1756–1800* (Cambridge: Cambridge University Press, 1988), chap. 3.

17. Frank Luther Mott, *A History of American Magazines*, 5 vols. (New York: D. Appelton, 1938), 1:19.

18. See Meredith L. McGill, *American Literature and the Culture of Reprinting, 1834–1853* (Philadelphia: University of Pennsylvania Press, 2003); David A. Brewer, *The Afterlife of Character, 1726–1825* (Philadelphia: University of Pennsylvania Press, 2005).

19. Roger L'Estrange, *Citt and Bumpkin in a Dialogue over a Pot of Ale Concerning Matters of Religion and Government* (1680), 32.

20. Mary Astell, *An Essay in Defence of the Female Sex in which are Inserted the Characters of a Pedant, a Squire, a Beau, a Vertuoso, a Poetaster, a City-critick, &c.* (1696), 87.

21. Astell, *An Essay in Defence of the Female Sex*, 88–89.

22. *Spectator*, no. 10, 1:45.

23. Donald F. Bond, ed., *The Tatler*, 3 vols. (Oxford: Clarendon Press, 1987), 2:444. All further citations to *The Tatler* will be to this edition.

24. *Spectator*, no. 49, 1:210.

25. "The Scribbler—No. VI," *New-York Magazine, or Literary Repository* 2 (March 1791): 154.

26. *Spectator*, 1:5.

27. *Spectator*, no. 49, 1:211.

28. Edward Ward, *The London-Spy Compleat, in Eighteen Parts*, 2 vols. [London, 1709], 1:392; *The Extortioners and Stock-jobbers, Detected. Or, an Infallible Receipt for the Circulation of Money* (London: E. Whitlock, 1696), 1.

29. *Spectator*, 1:292, 294.

30. *Spectator*, 3:379.

31. Ibid., 3:380.

32. See, for example, Ward's *The London-Spy* (1698–1700), which described the coffeehouse as something out of Bosch, a purgatory "where the Black-Guard of Quality were playing their Unlucky Tricks, and Damning each other in their Masters Dialect" (*London-Spy*, 1:201); or the anonymous *Character of a Coffee-House*, which painted a still more unflattering portrait: "A *Coffee-House* is a *Phanatique Theatre*, a *Hot-House* to flux in for a *clapt understanding*, a *Sympathetical* Cure for

the *Gonorrhea* of the Tongue, or a *refin'd Baudy-House*, where *Illegitimate Reports* are got in close *Adultery* between *Lying lips* and *Itching Ears*" (*The Character of a Coffee-House, with the Symptomes of a Town-Wit* [London, 1673], 6.

33. J. Thomas Scharf and Thompson Westcott, *History of Philadelphia, 1609–1884*, 3 vols. (Philadelphia: L. H. Everts, 1884), 2:855.

34. Edwin Wolf et al., *Quarter of a Millennium: The Library Company of Philadelphia, 1731–1981* (Philadelphia: Library Company of Philadelphia, 1981), 179.

35. David S. Shields, *Civil Tongues and Polite Letters in British America* (Chapel Hill: University of North Carolina Press, 1997), chap. 3.

36. Advertisement, *Boston News-Letter*, April 26, 1714, 2.

37. Advertisement, *Boston News-Letter*, March 12, 1716, 2.

38. The most comprehensive study of tavern culture in colonial America is Sharon V. Salinger, *Taverns and Drinking in Early America* (Baltimore: Johns Hopkins University Press, 2002).

39. For a discussion of the twinned development of the coffeehouse and the periodical in England, see Jürgen Habermas, *The Structural Transformation of the Public Sphere: An Inquiry into a Category of Bourgeois Society* (Cambridge, Mass.: MIT Press, 1989), chap. 2. On the American relation to coffeehouse culture, see Shields, *Civil Tongues*, chap. 3.

40. Erin Mackie, ed., *The Commerce of Everyday Life: Selections from the Tatler and the Spectator* (Boston: Bedford, 1998), 152.

41. "A Letter to a Gentleman with Regard to English Poetry," *The Museum: Or, the Literary and Historical Register* 3 (1747): 482.

42. [Oliver Goldsmith], *An History of England, in a Series of Letters from a Nobleman to his Son* (London, 1769), 2:139.

43. Samuel Johnson, *The Lives of the Poets of Great Britain and Ireland* (Dublin, 1793–1802), 1:292.

44. Johnson, *Lives of the Poets*, 1:323, 324.

45. *New-England Courant*, August 7, 1721. For a discussion of the role of the *Courant* in the inoculation controversy, see Carla Mulford, "Pox and 'Hell-fire': Boston's Smallpox Controversy, the New Science, and Early Modern Liberalism," in *Periodical Literature in Eighteenth Century America*, ed. Mark Kamrath and Sharon M. Harris, 7–27 (Knoxville: University of Tennessee Press, 2005).

46. *New-England Courant*, April 9, 1722. By way of comparison, the April 2 issue of the *News-Letter* is dominated almost entirely by a summary of news from Europe.

47. Benjamin Franklin, *Writings* (New York: Library of America, 1987), 1320.

48. *Spectator*, no. 124, 1:507.

49. George F. Horner, "Franklin's *Dogood Papers* Re-examined," *Studies in Philology* 37 (1940): 501.

50. *Tatler*, 3:350.

51. *New-England Courant*, March 26, 1722.

52. *Spectator*, no. 1, 1:1.

53. *Tatler*, 1:36–37.

54. *Tatler*, 1:337.

55. *Tatler*, 3:358.

56. "Idea of the English School" (1751) in Franklin, *Writings*, 349, 352, 353.

57. *Spectator*, no. 115, 1:474. On Adams's frustration with both the silence and the fame of Franklin and Jefferson, see Larzer Ziff, *Writing in the New Nation: Prose, Print, and Politics in the Early United States* (New Haven, Conn.: Yale University Press, 1991), 101, 109.

58. *Gentleman's Magazine* 7 (February 1737): 95.

59. "Annals of a Modern Traveller," *Gentleman's Magazine* (February 1737): 111.

60. Gordon S. Wood, *The Americanization of Benjamin Franklin* (New York: Penguin Press, 2004), 46.

61. Quoted in Carl Lennart Carlson, *The First Magazine; A History of the Gentleman's Magazine* (Providence, R.I.: Brown University Press, 1938), 81.

62. Franklin, *Writings*, 1331.

63. Samuel Johnson, Preface, *Gentleman's Magazine* 10 (1740): v.

64. "Roman Newspapers," *Literary Magazine* 4 (1805): 330–34.

65. Alexander Spotswood to Benjamin Franklin, October 12, 1739, in Benjamin Franklin, *The Papers of Benjamin Franklin*, ed. Leonard Woods Labaree, William Bradford Willcox, and Barbara Oberg, 38 vols. (New Haven, Conn.: Yale University Press, 1959), 2:235.

66. Ibid., 2:236.

67. See Walter Isaacson, *Benjamin Franklin: An American Life* (New York: Simon & Schuster, 2003), 115–16.

68. See John Webbe, "The Detection," in Franklin, *The Papers of Benjamin Franklin*, 2:265–69. For an account sympathetic to Bradford of the conflict over the magazines, see Anna Janney De Armond, *Andrew Bradford, Colonial Journalist* (Newark: University of Delaware Press, 1949), 223–39.

69. "The Plan of an Intended Magazine," *Weekly Mercury*, October 30, 1740.

70. *Pennsylvania Gazette*, November 13, 1740.

71. For an excellent account of Franklin and Mecom's relationship, see David Waldstreicher, *Runaway America: Benjamin Franklin, Slavery, and the American Revolution* (New York: Hill and Wang, 2004), 127–34.

72. This was actually Rogers and Fowle's second attempt at a magazine, the first being the *Boston Weekly Magazine* earlier in 1743, which lasted only three issues.

73. "The Quintessence of Books—A Great Book is a Great Evil," *New-England Magazine* 1 (1758): 14, 15, 16, 17.

74. "The Design &c.," *New-England Magazine* 1 (1758): 7, 10.

75. *To the Publick of Connecticut* (New Haven: Benjamin Mecom, 1765).

76. "The Design, &c.," *New-England Magazine* 1 (1758): 8.

77. Benjamin Mecom, Dedication, *New-England Magazine* 1 (1758): title page.

78. *Worcester Magazine* 1 (April 1786): 46–47.

CHAPTER 2. THE AMERICAN MAGAZINE
IN THE EARLY NATIONAL PERIOD

1. Frank Luther Mott, *A History of American Magazines*, 5 vols. (Cambridge, Mass.: Harvard University Press, 1957), 1:13.

2. Benjamin Rush, *Letters of Benjamin Rush*, ed. L. H. Butterfield, 2 vols. (Princeton: Princeton University Press, 1951), 1:450.

3. [Noah Webster], Introduction, *American Magazine* 1 (1787): 3.

4. Noah Webster, *An Examination into the Leading Principles of the Federal Constitution Proposed by the Late Convention Held at Philadelphia* (Philadelphia: Prichard & Hall, 1787), 47.

5. Ibid., 49.

6. Harlow G. Unger, *Noah Webster: The Life and Times of an American Patriot* (New York: John Wiley & Sons, 1998), 139.

7. Webster, Introduction, 3.

8. Ibid., 4.

9. The earliest printing of the sketch I have found in U.S. papers is in the July 15, 1785, issue of the *State Gazette of South-Carolina*.

10. [Noah Webster], Acknowledgements, *American Magazine* 1 (1788): 130.

11. Giles Hickory [Noah Webster], *American Magazine* 1 (December 1787): 13.

12. Webster, Introduction, 3.

13. Judith Sargent Murray, "The Gleaner. No. V," *Massachusetts Magazine* 4 (1792): 421.

14. Ibid., 420–21.

15. For Rush's suggestion, see Rush, *Letters of Benjamin Rush*, 450. Franklin's suggestion is cited in Richard M. Rollins, *The Long Journey of Noah Webster* (Philadelphia: University of Pennsylvania Press, 1980), 154, n. 1.

16. David Ramsay, *The History of the American Revolution*, 2 vols. (Philadelphia: R. Aitken & Son, 1789), 1:65, 2:319.

17. Quoted in Jeffrey L. Pasley, *"The Tyranny of Printers": Newspaper Politics in the Early American Republic* (Charlottesville: University Press of Virginia, 2001), 34.

18. Alexander Hamilton, James Madison, and John Jay, *The Federalist Papers* (New York: Penguin, 1987), 93.

19. "Miscellanies," *New-Haven Gazette* 2 (1787): 9; "Against the Newspaper Slanderers," *American Museum* 2 (1787): 98.

20. "Directions to Conduct a Newspaper Dispute, According to the Most Approved Method Now in Practice," *American Museum* 3 (January 1788): 52.

21. Giles Hickory [Noah Webster], "On Government," *American Magazine* 1 (March 1788): 205.

22. Giles Hickory [Noah Webster], *American Magazine* 1 (December 1787): 13.

23. Giles Hickory [Noah Webster], "Government," *American Magazine* 1 (February 1788): 139.

24. Webster defended his magazine against its imagined critics in almost identical

terms to those he used to defend the proposed constitution. As he argued toward the end of *An Examination*, the voter must not discard the whole of the constitution "because *he* thinks some part of it defective or exceptionable" (Webster, *An Examination*, 51). And similarly he pleads in his introduction to the *American Magazine* that "*Small faults*" should "never condemn a work that is substantially good" (Webster, Introduction, 4).

25. Noah Webster, *Letters of Noah Webster*, ed. Harry R. Warfel (New York: Library Publishers, 1953), 74–75.

26. Webster, *Letters of Noah Webster*, 75.

27. For an invaluable study of voluntary societies in New York, see Bryan Waterman, *Republic of Intellect: The Friendly Club of New York City and the Making of American Literature* (Baltimore: Johns Hopkins University Press, 2007).

28. In truth, Belknap had little faith in magazines and did not think highly of the *American Magazine*. As Mott notes, Belknap's "idea of a good magazine was a repository of state papers" (Mott, 106–7).

29. Webster, *Letters of Noah Webster*, 76.

30. Rush to Webster, February 13, 1788, Rush, *Letters of Benjamin Rush*, 1:450; Gary Coll, "Noah Webster, Journalist: 1783–1803," in *Newsletters to Newspapers: Eighteenth-Century Journalism*, ed. Donovan H. Bond and W. Reynolds McLeod (Morgantown: School of Journalism, West Virginia University, 1977), 309. For a valuable account of Webster's plans for the magazine's expansion and the responses of his correspondents, see Thomas H. Brown, "Friends and Foes: Noah Webster's Involvement in Personal Politics in Eighteenth-Century American Periodical Publishing," *Library Chronicle* 45, no. 1–2 (1981): 104–14.

31. Hazard to Belknap, March 5, 1788, in "Correspondence between Jeremy Belknap and Ebenezer Hazard: Part II," *Collections of the Massachusetts Historical Society* 3, 5th series (1877): 23.

32. The magazine was truly a "one-man enterprise," with Webster handling almost every aspect of the production, including chief correspondent, business, contracts, distribution, and advertising. Ronald Lora and William Henry Longton, *The Conservative Press in Eighteenth- and Nineteenth-Century America* (Westport, Conn.: Greenwood Press, 1999), 85.

33. Diary entry for November 8, 1788, in Noah Webster, *The Autobiographies of Noah Webster: From the Letters and Essays, Memoir, and Diary*, ed. Richard M. Rollins (Columbia: University of South Carolina Press, 1989), 260.

34. Webster, *Letters of Noah Webster*, 82.

35. Noah Webster, "The Editor's Address to the Public," *American Minerva*, December 9, 1793.

36. Quoted in Coll, "Noah Webster, Journalist: 1783–1803," 311.

37. Webster, *Letters of Noah Webster*, 76.

38. "Belknap Papers," *Collections of the Massachusetts Historical Society* 4, 6th series (1891): 331.

39. Spotswood was also relying on Belknap to help him secure reliable agents in Massachusetts. Facing growing competition in Philadelphia and then in New York with the launching of Webster's *American Magazine*, Spotswood hoped to recoup losses with reprints and bound volumes, as well as additional subscriptions. Magazines, like newspapers, traveled the post free at this time, so the incentive for a publisher to secure widespread subscriptions was not mitigated by postal costs. But securing those subscriptions proved very challenging, requiring the employment of agents whose commissions ate considerably into the publisher's razor-slim margins and whose reliability was often in serious question. Belknap was invaluable to Spotswood in helping him find trustworthy agents, but he could do little to improve the energy to which the New England agent was devoting to the task. Spotswood instructed Belknap to offer a still greater abatement on the costs if it would "induce Mr. Larkin to extend the sale in the New England States." "Exertions must be made to ensure even a tolerable portion of success, and I am determined nothing in my power shall be wanting." Ibid, 392.

40. Preface, *Columbian Magazine* 1 (1786): i.

41. Mathew Carey, *Philosophy of Common Sense: Containing Practical Rules for the Promotion of Domestic Happiness* (Lee & Blanchard, 1838), 153.

42. The topic of the Algerian corsairs—whose capture of American seamen in the 1780s provided the new nation with its first sensational hostage crisis and with ready fantasies of pirate nations eager to invade American shores, which would be deployed to great effect during the constitutional debates—was an ongoing obsession of the magazine; its Intelligence section, a regular feature of the magazine, almost always included some word of the state of hostage negotiations and political intrigues in North Africa. This obsession with Algerian corsairs filtered easily into what was the magazine's dominant staple in its earliest original fiction, the "oriental" or "eastern tale," which was a regular feature throughout its existence.

43. "The Shipwreck. A Fragment," *Columbian Magazine* 1 (September 1786): 7.

44. "Thoughts on the Present Situation of the Federal Government of the United States of America," *Columbian Magazine* 1 (December 1786): 174.

45. "To the Editor of the Columbian Magazine," *Columbian Magazine* 1 (1786): 182, 183.

46. For a useful account of the "policy" regarding fiction and the novel, see William J. Free, *The Columbian Magazine and American Literary Nationalism* (The Hague: Mouton, 1968), 60–64.

47. "Amelia" was reprinted several times in other magazines, most immediately in Isaiah Thomas's *Massachusetts Magazine*. The story of Amelia clearly served as a source for the novel Thomas would publish that same year, *The Power of Sympathy*. "Amelia" would be reprinted three more times in American magazines in the following decade, including in the *New-York Magazine* in 1795.

48. [Charles Brockden Brown], "The Rhapsodist, No. I," *Columbian Magazine* 3 (August 1789): 466.

49. "The Rhapsodist, No. I," 467.

50. [Charles Brockden Brown], "The Rhapsodist, No. III," *Columbian Magazine* 3 (October 1789): 598.

51. "The Rhapsodist, No. I," 465.

52. [Charles Brockden Brown], "The Rhapsodist, No. IV," *Columbian Magazine* 3 (November 1789): 663.

53. William Dunlap, *The Life of Charles Brockden Brown*, 2 vols. (Philadelphia: James P. Parke, 1815), 1:17.

54. "The Retailer, No. II," *Columbian Magazine* 2 (March 1788): 150.

55. "The Retailer, No. III," *Columbian Magazine* 2 (April 1788): 203.

56. One of the collaborators on "The Retailer" might be the poet Charles Crawford, a regular contributor to the *Columbian Magazine* and a vocal member of Philadelphia's fledgling abolitionist movement. See Free, *Columbian Magazine*, 99. I am not entirely confident in this attribution, since it is based in part on a misreading of the initials at the end of one letter.

57. "The Retailer, No. XIII," *Columbian Magazine* (November 1789): 646.

58. "Autobiography," Isaiah Thomas papers, Box 1, Folder 2, American Antiquarian Society.

59. Isaiah Thomas, *The History of Printing in America* (1810; New York: Weathervane Books, 1970), 142.

60. "Utility of Well Regulated Magazines," *Massachusetts Magazine* 1 (January 1789): 8.

61. Ebenezer Andrews to Isaiah Thomas, 3 November 1792, Isaiah Thomas Papers, box 2, folder 3, American Antiquarian Society.

62. Ebenezer Andrews to Isaiah Thomas, 3 November 1792, Isaiah Thomas Papers, box 2, folder 3, American Antiquarian Society.

63. Andrews to Thomas, 7 August 1791, Isaiah Thomas Papers, box 2, folder 3, American Antiquarian Society.

64. Andrews to Thomas, 18 April 1793, Isaiah Thomas Papers, box 1, folder 9, American Antiquarian Society.

65. An indication of the financial concerns facing Thomas and Andrews is found in a letter from Andrews, April 19, 1793, in which Andrews writes, "Am very sorry you are so harassed for money, and I think I know how to pity you, having been in the same predicament for some time past—Hope soon, however, to see better days" (Isaiah Thomas Papers, box 2, folder 4, American Antiquarian Society).

66. In fact, shortly after Andrews's attempts in late 1792 to get rid of the magazine the first time, he suddenly changes his tone regarding the subject in terms that suggest that his initial proposals to Thomas met with little encouragement. In January 1793 he comes up with a plan by which the operation of the magazine might be changed without having to actually give it up: If they could convince Thaddeus Mason Harris to take over the editorship of the magazine, he suggests, then they could focus on what it was that was truly their business, printing.

67. Mathew Carey, "Autobiography of Mathew Carey. Letter III," *New-England Magazine* 6 (1834): 65.

68. Carey, "Autobiography," 66.

69. Further, as post office law made clear, even at these prices post riders were not required to carry magazines "where from the size of the mail and the manner of carrying it there would be inconvenience" (*Post Office Law* [Washington, 1800], 31). Andrews frequently expresses his frustration with the problems such policies presented for consistent distribution, "I am amazingly disappointed that the Mags did not go on [the stage]," Andrews complains. "They told me they did not think they could carry them, but I requested if they could not take the whole to carry a part, and they promised me they would" (Andrews to Thomas, 12 January 1791).

70. "To the Public," *Royal American Magazine* 1 (1774): inside cover of June issue.

71. "*Originality*, as far as the infancy of their work rendered it possible, has been their aim," Preface, *Massachusetts Magazine* 1 (1789): iii. Despite frequent apologies regarding their failures in this regard, there is evidence that the *Massachusetts Magazine* did at least as well as its chief rivals in terms of securing original contributions.

72. [Judith Sargent Murray], "The Gleaner. No. I," *Massachusetts Magazine* 4 (1792): 97.

73. [Joseph Dennie, ed.], *The Spirit of the Farmer's Museum, and Lay Preacher's Gazette* (Walpole, N.H.: Thomas & Thomas, 1801), 215.

74. [Judith Sargent Murray], "To the Editors of the Massachusetts Magazine. The Repository. No. I," *Massachusetts Magazine* 4 (1792): 568.

75. "The Trifler," *Columbian Magazine* 1 (1786): 164–65.

76. Thomas and Andrews, "Proposal for Continuing the Publication of the Massachusetts Magazine," February 1793, 4 (tipped in at the end of the February 1793 issue of the *Massachusetts Magazine*).

77. "To the Publick," *Massachusetts Magazine* 5 (1793): 3.

78. "Preface," *Boston Magazine* 1 (1783–84): ii.

79. Thomas papers, folder 7, letter from Mathew Carey February 19, 1789.

80. Thomas papers, folder 7, October 20, 1789.

81. Thomas papers, folder 8, Thomas to William Young, November 22, 1790.

82. Richard D. Brown, *Knowledge Is Power: The Diffusion of Information in Early America, 1700–1865* (New York: Oxford University Press, 1991), 247; Sandra Gustafson, *Eloquence Is Power: Oratory and Performance in Early America* (Chapel Hill: University of North Carolina Press, 2000), 150.

83. Trish Loughran, *The Republic in Print: Print Culture in the Age of U.S. Nation Building, 1770–1870* (New York: Columbia University Press, 2007).

84. Isaiah Thomas to Thomas & Thomas, 25 March 1808, oversize mss. box, folder 1.

85. Thomas, *History of Printing*, 1:10.

CHAPTER 3. THE AMERICAN MAGAZINE
IN THE EARLY NATIONAL PERIOD

1. Bryan Waterman, *Republic of Intellect: The Friendly Club of New York City and the Making of American Literature* (Baltimore: Johns Hopkins University Press, 2007), 27.

2. David Paul Nord, "A Republican Literature: Magazine Reading and Readers in Late-Eighteenth-Century New York," in *Reading in America: Literature and Social History*, ed. Cathy N. Davidson (New York: Oxford University Press, 1989), 119.

3. Mathew Carey Papers, American Antiquarian Society.

4. Mathew Carey, "Autobiography of Mathew Carey. Letter III," *New-England Magazine* 6 (1834):" 65–66.

5. Preface, *American Museum* 4 (July 1788): v.

6. Preface, *Massachusetts Magazine* 1 (1789): iii.

7. "On the Utility of Well Regulated Magazines," *Massachusetts Magazine* 1 (January 1789): 8.

8. "The Reformer. No. 1: On Scandal and the Wickedness of Newspapers," *Massachusetts Magazine* 1 (February 1789): 79.

9. D. L., "To the Editor of the COLUMBIAN MAGAZINE," *Columbian Magazine* (May 1789): 314.

10. The "Friend to the Ladies" earned a more biting reply from another anonymous correspondent who accuses the "Friend" of plagiarism; assuming the author of "New Simile" to have been Swift, the correspondent writes: "The simile, its true, has humour, / Yet can't be claim'd by each presumer— / Is not the offspring of your brain; / But—Swift is dead, and can't complain." ("To the person who styles himself 'The Ladies Friend,'" *Columbian Magazine* [1789]: 313).

11. On the death of Murray's firstborn son, see Sheila L. Skemp, *First Lady of Letters: Judith Sargent Murray and the Struggle for Female Independence* (Philadelphia: University of Pennsylvania Press, 2009), 177–86. Skemp's biography is the most complete and authoritative account of Murray's life.

12. "Lines, Occasioned by the Death of an Infant," *Massachusetts Magazine* 2 (January 1790): 57.

13. Constantia [Sarah Wentworth Morton], "To the Editors of the *Massachusetts Magazine*," *Massachusetts Magazine* 1 (1789): 449.

14. For a full account of the scandal and its relationship to *The Power of Sympathy*, see Cathy N. Davidson, *Revolution and the Word: The Rise of the Novel in America* (New York: Oxford University Press, 1986), chap. 5.

15. A farce, likely by Brown as well, published early in 1789 on the scandal, called attention to Perez Morton's attempts to "suppress the publication, and that immediately" of a "Novel, that will brand him a villain centuries to come." *Occurences of the Times. Or, The Transactions of Four Days* (Boston: Benjamin Russell, 1789), 11.

16. Euphelia, "To Constantia," *Massachusetts Magazine* (October 1789): 654.

17. Euphelia, "To Harmony," *Massachusetts Magazine* 1 (December 1789): 790.

18. "The Consolation.—An Ode. Humbly Inscribed to Constantia," *Massachusetts Magazine* 2 (February 1790): 117.

19. "To the Favorites of the Muses," *Massachusetts Magazine* 2 (January 1790), inside cover.

20. Constantia, "Lines to Philenia," *Massachusetts Magazine* 2 (April 1790): 249.

21. "Explanation of the Frontispiece," *Massachusetts Magazine* 3 (1791): iv.

22. I have not been able to ascertain the identity of "Lavinia."

23. "The Gleaner. No. 1," *Massachusetts Magazine* 4 (February 1792): 96.

24. "The Gleaner. No. 1," 96.

25. "The Friend. No. 1," *New Hampshire Journal, or the Farmer's Weekly Museum*, June 30, 1795.

26. *Massachusetts Magazine* 3 (November 1791), inside cover.

27. *Massachusetts Magazine* 4 (February 1792), inside cover.

28. Jennifer J. Baker, *Securing the Commonwealth: Debt, Speculation, and Writing in the Making of Early America* (Baltimore: Johns Hopkins University Press, 2005), 137; Marion Rust, *Prodigal Daughters: Susanna Rowson's Early American Women* (Chapel Hill: University of North Carolina Press, 2008), 98; Davidson, *Revolution and the Word*, 208.

29. Sharon M. Harris, Introduction, *Selected Writings of Judith Sargent Murray* (New York: Oxford University Press, 1995), xxx.

30. "The Gleaner. No. III," *Massachusetts Magazine* 4 (April 1792): 244.

31. "The Gleaner. No. V," *Massachusetts Magazine* 4 (July 1792): 418.

32. "The Gleaner. No. III," 248.

33. "The Gleaner. No. VI," *Massachusetts Magazine* 4 (Agust 1792): 477.

34. "The Gleaner. No. VI," 480.

35. "The Gleaner. No. VII," *Massachusetts Magazine* 4 (September 1792): 549.

36. "The Gleaner. No. VII," 550.

37. "The Gleaner. No. VII," 551.

38. "The Gleaner. No. VIII," *Massachusetts Magazine* 4 (November 1792): 675.

39. "The Gleaner. No. XII," *Massachusetts Magazine* 5 (March 1793): 137.

40. "The Gleaner. No. XII," 138.

41. "The Gleaner. No. XII (cont.)," *Massachusetts Magazine* 5 (April 1793): 211.

42. "The Gleaner. No. XIII," *Massachusetts Magazine* 5 (May 1793): 265.

43. "The Gleaner. No. XVI," *Massachusetts Magazine* 5 (September 1793): 395–96.

44. November 6, 1791, in *The Letters of Joseph Dennie, 1768–1812*, ed. Laura Green Pedder (Orono, Me.: University Press, 1936), 93.

45. January 1794, in *Letters of Joseph Dennie*, 138.

46. January 1794, in *Letters of Joseph Dennie*, 136.

47. April 24, 1795, in *Letters of Joseph Dennie*, 145.

48. October 2, 1795, in *Letters of Joseph Dennie*, 151.

49. April 26, 1797, in *Letters of Joseph Dennie*, 157.

50. April 26, 1797, in *Letters of Joseph Dennie*, 159.

51. May 20, 1800, in *Letters of Joseph Dennie*, 181.

52. May 20, 1800, in *Letters of Joseph Dennie*, 182.

53. William C. Dowling, *Literary Federalism in the Age of Jefferson* (Columbia: University of South Carolina Press, 1999), 45.

54. "The Farrago," *Tablet*, June 23, 1795, 21.

55. "To The Publick," *New Hampshire Journal: Or, The Farmer's Weekly Museum*, April 11, 1793.

56. Catherine Kaplan, "'He Summons Genius . . . to His Aid': Letters, Partisanship, and the Making of the Farmer's Weekly Museum, 1795–1800," *Journal of the Early Republic* 23 (2003): 553–54.

57. Kaplan, "'He Summons Genius,'" 559.

58. *The Lay Preacher; or Short Sermons, for Idle Readers* (Walpole, N.H: David Carlisle Jr., 1796), 51.

59. [Joseph Dennie], "The Lay Preacher," *Port-Folio* 1 (January 18, 1806): 18.

60. "Domestic Occurrences," *Port-Folio* 1 (June 27, 1801): 207.

61. [Joseph Dennie], *Prospectus of a New Weekly Paper, Submitted to Men of Affluence, Men of Liberality, and Men of Letters* (Philadelphia, 1801), 1.

62. [Dennie], *Prospectus*, 2.

63. July 15, 1809, in *Letters of Joseph Dennie*, 198.

64. July 15, 1809, in *Letters of Joseph Dennie*, 198.

CHAPTER 4. THE EARLY AMERICAN MAGAZINE IN THE NINETEENTH CENTURY

1. Susanna Rowson, *The Inquisitor; or, The Invisible Rambler* (1788; Philadelphia: William Gibbons, 1793), 1:52.

2. Susanna Rowson, *Mentoria; or the Young Lady's Friend* (1791; Philadelphia: Samuel Harrison Smith, 1794): 1:75.

3. Rowson, *Mentoria*, 2:116.

4. It is extremely unlikely that this was the first publication of these stories, as the *Polite Repository* focused on publishing "a selection . . . from the best modern publications."

5. See "The Midnight Hour. From Mrs. Rowson's 'Inquisitor,'" *Weekly Museum* 12 (March 22, 1800): 2. This selection was reprinted several times in newspapers and magazines around the country. Other popular excerpts were "The Lounger" and "The Methodist," both from *The Inquisitor*.

6. Rowson, *The Inquisitor*, 155.

7. Rowson, *Mentoria*, 90.

8. Susanna Rowson, *Miscellaneous Poems* (Boston: Gilbert & Dean, 1804), 112.

9. Tabitha Gilman Tenney, *Female Quixotism* (Oxford: Oxford University Press, 1992), 323.

10. Tenney, *Female Quixotism*, 325.

11. Quoted in "On Romance and Novel Reading," *The Gleaner; or, Monthly Magazine* 1 (1809): 453.

12. Patricia Okker, *Social Stories: The Magazine Novel in Nineteenth-Century America* (Charlottesville: University of Virginia, 2003), 36

13. "On Novels and Novel Reading," *Mirror of Taste and Dramatic Censor* 3 (February 1811): 87.

14. "On Novels and Novel Reading," 93.

15. "The Gossip—No. XIII," *Boston Weekly Magazine* 1 (January 22, 1803): 53.

16. Rowson celebrated both Burney and Lee as novelists who would "snatch the British novel from oblivion" in *Trials of the Human Heart* (Philadelphia: Wrigley and Berriman, 1795), 4:74.

17. "The Gossip—No. XIII," 53.

18. Quoted in "Female Literature," *Daily National Intelligencer*, October 6, 1824.

19. Samuel L. Knapp, "Memoir of the Author," in Susanna Rowson, *Charlotte's Daughter Or the Three Orphans* (Boston: J. H. A. Frost, 1828), 10.

20. Elias Nason, *A Memoir of Mrs. Susanna Rowson* (Albany, N.Y.: J. Munsell, 1870), 114, 117.

21. Dorothy Weil, *In Defense of Women: Susanna Rowson, 1762–1824* (University Park: Pennsylvania State University Press: 1976), 171.

22. For example, in 1816 he took out ads in the *Newburyport Herald*: "The Subscriber finds by looking over his Periodical Collection, that several numbers are missing, from different Works, and forgetting to whom he loaned them, would thank the person who may have *any volume* belonging to him to return it" ("Books Missing," *Newburyport Herald*, April 12, 1816, 4).

23. See chapter 1 of Leon Jackson's *The Business of Letters: Authorial Economies in Antebellum America* (Palo Alto, Calif.: Stanford University Press, 2008), for an important critique of the ways in which our overemphasis on an anachronistic notion of literary "professionalism" has led to a significant misapprehension of the contours of American literary history.

24. "Sincerity; A Novel. Letter I," *Boston Weekly Magazine* 1 (June 4, 1803): 132.

25. "The Gossip—No. XIV," *Boston Weekly Magazine* 1 (January 29, 1803): 57.

26. "The Gossip—No. XV," *Boston Weekly Magazine* 1 (February 5, 1803): 61.

27. "The Gossip—No. XIV," 57.

28. "Sincerity—A Novel. Letter XXX," *Boston Weekly Magazine* 2 (April 28, 1804): 108.

29. "The Gossip—No. XV," 61.

30. Other puns offered even more cagey clues for readers inclined to guess after the identity of the Gossip, as was fairly conventional at the time, despite the familiar protest in the first installment of the series that "conjecture as you please, I will not unmask. Whether male or female, young or old . . . are secrets which I shall not unravel." In the third installment, a fictional correspondent, "Vaticinator," writes in a letter threatening to expose the identity of the author if "he" exposes any of the "*Row's*, or *Goe's*, to which you cannot help sometimes be a witness." The wink at "Rows" seems obviously placed for Rowson's closest and most devoted readers, including her students at her academy, whose achievements were regularly reported in the *Weekly Magazine*.

31. "The Gossip—No. XXXVII," *Boston Weekly Magazine* 1 (August 13, 1803): 169.

32. The final story told in "The Gossip" is the tragic story of Lucy Belmont, yet another woman forced to marry the wrong man, with tragic results.

33. "Sincerity—A Novel. Letter II," *Boston Weekly Magazine* 1 (June 11, 1803): 136.

34. "Sincerity—A Novel. Letter XXXIII," *Boston Weekly Magazine* 1 (June 30, 1804): 144.

35. Although "The Gossip" will continue to run occasionally for the next several months, it becomes increasingly infrequent as Rowson pulls back from her commitments to the periodical at the end of 1804.

36. Susanna Rowson, *Sarah, Or, The Exemplary Wife* (Boston: C. Williams, 1813), i.

37. Eve Kornfeld, "Women in Post-Revolutionary American Culture: Susanna Haswell Rowson's American Career, 1795–1824," *Journal of American Culture* 6 (Winter 1983): 59.

38. Rowson, *Sarah*, ii.

39. "Remarks on Novels," *New-England Galaxy* 1 (February 6, 1818): 3.

40. "The Scribbler. No. I," *Port-Folio*, 3rd series 1 (January 1809): 57.

41. "History of Philander Flashaway; or the Misfortunes of a Scribbler," *Universal Asylum and Columbian Magazine* 6 (March 1791): 142–44.

42. "The Scribbler. No. II," *Port-Folio*, 3rd series 1 (February 1809): 162.

43. The *Cabinet* had reprinted the whole of *Wieland* before turning its attention to the previously unpublished "The Scribbler."

44. "Annals of America," *American Register* 5 (1809): 7.

45. "Annals of America," *American Register* 5 (1809): 8.

46. "Annals of America," *American Register* 2 (1808): 81.

47. "Annals of America," *American Register* 2 (1808): 93.

48. "General Catalogue and View of British Publications, for the Year 1806," *American Register* 1 (1807): 154.

49. Peter S. Du Ponceau to Samuel M. Burnside, April 20, 1821, American Antiquarian Society.

50. William Dunlap, *The Life of Charles Brockden Brown*, 2 vols. (Philadelphia: James P. Parke, 1815), 1:14.

51. A. R., "Critique of the Writings of Charles B. Brown," *Port-Folio* 6 (July 1811): 30.

52. A. R., "Critique," 34.

53. *Poulson's American Daily Advertiser*, February 27, 1810.

54. "On the Writings of Charles Brown, the American Novelist," *New Monthly Magazine* 14 (1821): 609–17.

55. "American Writers. No. II," *Blackwood's Edinburgh Magazine* 16 (1824): 421, 422.

56. "American Writers. No. II," 425.

57. "Literary Intelligence," *Port-Folio* 18 (1824): 494.

58. "Literary Intelligence," 495.

59. "The Spy," *North American Review* 15 (1822): 255.

60. "Periodicals," *Illinois Monthly Magazine* (April 1831): 302.

61. "Periodicals," 303.

62. "The Contemplator. No. VIII," *Philadelphia Repository and Weekly Register* 3 (1803): 213.

63. *Morning Chronicle*, November 15, 1802, 3.

64. For a useful account of the political engagements of Irving's family as his career began, see Andrew Burstein, *The Original Knickerbocker: The Life of Washington Irving* (New York: Basic Books, 2007), chapter 1.

65. "Salmagundi No. I," January 24, 1807, in Washington Irving, *History, Tales and Sketches* (New York: Library of America, 1983), 49. Subsequent citations will be given parenthetically in the text.

66. *Federal Republican & Commercial Gazette*, December 14, 1809.

67. *The Sketch Book of Geoffrey Crayon, Gent.*, No. I (New York: C. S. Van Winkler, 1819), iii.

68. Michael Warner, "Irving's Posterity," *ELH* 67 (2000): 773–99.

69. Amanpal Garcha, *From Sketch to Novel: The Development of Victorian Fiction* (Cambridge: Cambridge University Press, 2009), 23.

70. Almost immediately after the publication of *The Sketch Book*, these source materials began to show up in magazines. See, for example, "Peter Klaus. The Legend of the Goatherd.—Rip Van Winkle," *Port-Folio* (August 1822): 144.

Conclusion

1. William C. Dowling, *Literary Federalism in the Age of Jefferson: Joseph Dennie and the Port Folio, 1801–1812* (Columbia: University of South Carolina Press, 1999), xv.

2. Samuel L. Knapp, "Prospectus," *Boston Monthly Magazine*, 1 (1825).

3. "Prospectus," *Album and Ladies' Weekly Gazette* (1826): 2.

4. Fanny Fern, "To Unfledged Writers," *New York Ledger*, January 15, 1870.

5. Oliver Wendell Holmes, "The Poet at the Breakfast-Table. No. II," *Atlantic Monthly* 29 (February 1872): 224.

6. [Joseph Perkins], "The Essayist," *Massachusetts Magazine* 8 (October 1796): 557.

7. See Chris Anderson, *Free: The Future of a Radical Price* (New York: Hyperion, 2009).

8. "Guild Tells HuffPost Writers: 'Don't Work for Free,'" March 16, 2011, http://www.newsguild.org/index.php?ID=10712 (accessed May 24, 2011).

INDEX

JARED GARDNER is an associate professor of English and film studies at Ohio State University and the author of *Master Plots: Race and the Founding of an American Literature, 1787–1845*.

THE HISTORY OF COMMUNICATION

The University of Illinois Press
is a founding member of the
Association of American University Presses.

Composed in 10/13 Sabon LT Std
by Celia Shapland
at the University of Illinois Press
Manufactured by Sheridan Books, Inc.

University of Illinois Press
1325 South Oak Street
Champaign, IL 61820-6903
www.press.uillinois.edu